GW00836182

Let us catch it before the regulators do!

SAR Investigations

The Complete
BSA/AML
Desktop Reference

Howard Steiner
Stephen L. Marini

SAR Investigations
The Complete BSA/AML Desktop Reference

© ImpactAML LLC
All Rights Reserved

Published By
ImpactAML–INX3 Financial Press
Las Vegas, Nevada

Let us catch it before the regulators do!

Other Books by the Authors:

- Enhanced Due Diligence – The Complete BSA/AML Desktop Reference
- BSA Independent Review for Banks – The Complete Audit Workbook
- BSA Independent Review for MSBs – The Complete Audit Workbook

FORWARD

If one pictures the totality of a financial institution's anti-money laundering (AML) compliance practice, the very last output, the piece that is supported by all the other inputs to the process, is the Suspicious Activity Report, or SAR. Regulators view SARs as windows through which they can judge the efficiency of an institution's Bank Secrecy Act (BSA) policies and procedures. From SARs, examiners can readily compare any bank's BSA compliance operation to other financial institutions with the same risk profile or geographic and business product footprint. Such comparisons will naturally lead to assumptions regarding how well a bank's investigations staff is trained, how well the transaction monitoring system is functioning, and generally, how capably a bank's entire AML compliance program meets the broad requirements of the Bank Secrecy Act.

Given the importance of the suspicious activity reporting function, it is somewhat surprising that so many brand name financial institutions have been on the receiving end of severe enforcement actions that describe gross failures across numerous, basic BSA detection and investigative management functions. Perhaps part of the problem is that it took about thirty-five years for the government to publish a unified, truly helpful resource for AML professionals (i.e., the FFIEC BSA/AML Examination Manual). And yet clearly, that is not enough. It is still difficult, even using The Manual, FinCEN's website and other government and NGO resources, to locate information that is presented in a useful way and all in one place.

This book aims to address that problem for a huge, essential part of the AML compliance function, i.e., resolving unusual and suspicious activity alerts. In this book, we have sought to bring together all the available knowledge concerning suspicious activity investigation and reporting from scores of documents and dozens of source agencies, NGOs, etc. While much of the information contained between its covers is available from public non-copyrighted sources (and the authors make no claim of originality), the editing process adds tremendous value by sifting out only the SAR relevant information and avoiding redundancy. The editing additionally reconciles the nuances contained in documentation from numerous organizations whose audiences and agendas may differ for specific topics (for example, regulatory, law enforcement, private sector, etc.). For the suspicious activity analyst, we have hopefully realized the goal of parsing relevant and useful suspicious activity information from all the background noise, and brought substance and clarity where previously there was information overload and noise.

While some information presented has been edited from public sources, much of the book contains originally authored advice and best practices that have been developed for analyzing alerts, conducting investigations, and managing a SAR unit. Best practices are born of experience. My company (ImpactAML LLC) has employed, worked with and worked for some of the most experienced and creative professionals in the AML field, primarily doing remediation work for large financial institutions operating under AML enforcement actions. Many of the methods presented here were developed as a result of the remediation work performed and have subsequently been adopted as standards of AML excellence for much of the financial industry. A particular debt of gratitude is owed by the authors to the Dominion Advisory Group and Mr. David Caruso.

Finally, while a printed book with a good cross linked index can prove to be an invaluable job aid, even better is an electronic version that lives on your PC's desktop and is fully searchable. The eBook version of this book is just such a resource. Desktop availability and the speed of access to a large body of SAR related information will change the way you've conducted investigations in the past. You can get copy by sending an email to support@impactaml.com or by visiting our website.

Happy hunting!

Howard Steiner

Table of Contents

Tables

Section I – Introduction to SAR Investigations & Reporting

Banks must file suspicious activity reports in accordance with the statutory requirements of 12 C.F.R. 563.18 and the guidelines set forth by the Federal Financial Institution Examination Council's (FFIEC).

The core mission of a bank's BSA/AML investigations unit is to evaluate unusual account activities indicative of money laundering and/or terrorist financing and, when appropriate, file Suspicious Activity Reports (SARs) with the Financial Crimes Enforcement Network (FinCEN). Most banks set up dedicated investigations units charged with the responsibility of ensuring that alerts and cases that stem from alerts are processed as expeditiously as possible. Depending upon the circumstances of each matter under investigation, the objective where the final disposition is a SAR filing, is not to exceed 90 days from origination to final disposition. This includes the 30 days allotted for the actual filing of the Suspicious Activity Report once the investigation is complete and the matter has been deemed suspicious.

In order to ensure an effective program, five core principles serve as the foundation of a sound alert disposition and SAR reporting process:

1. **A Defined Process:**
    The process to identify unusual or illicit activities should be well defined, documented, and follow a risk based methodology. Written procedures are an integral part of the process definition and they should identify the responsibilities and lines of communication for all involved in the process.

2. **Sound Decisions:**
    When unusual activities are identified, decisions to either escalate for investigation or dismiss as explainable should be thoroughly documented. For each particular instance, such documentation should clearly articulate the details that lead to the decision. Any decision to escalate an alert for investigation or to file a SAR with FinCEN must be reasonable and predicated by comprehensive review of all available information.

3. **Supportable Decisions:**
    The decisions to dismiss as explainable or report as suspicious must be supported by a comprehensive review or investigation and be clearly reflected in the case's narrative. Physical or electronic case files should be populated with the documents, images and materials that support the decision and would lead another reviewer to a similar conclusion.

4. **Consistent Application:**
    The process must be consistent, from one case to another and from one investigator to another. Management oversight and quality control functions must be uniformly applied. Although investigative decisions are subjective,

the process to arrive at the SAR/No-SAR decision must be consistent and repeatable.

5. **Repeatable and Sustainable:**
   The unusual activity alert reviews, investigations and supporting case files must be accurate, thorough and completed in reasonable time frames. The review and investigations processes must be demonstrably consistent from month-to-month and should be supported and managed by tracking reports.

Suspicious activity reporting forms the cornerstone of the BSA reporting system. It is considered critical to the United States' ability to utilize financial information to combat terrorism, terrorist financing, money laundering, and other financial crimes. Within this system, FinCEN and the federal banking agencies recognize that, as a practical matter, it is not possible for a bank to detect and report all potentially illicit transactions that flow through the bank. Therefore, regulatory agencies emphasize that banks focus on evaluating their policies, procedures, and processes in place to identify and research suspicious activity. Examiners review individual Suspicious Activity Report (SAR) filing decisions to determine the effectiveness of the suspicious activity monitoring and reporting process. Additionally, the regulatory agencies recognize that the quality of SAR data is paramount to the effective implementation of the suspicious activity reporting system.

Section II – Legislation, Regulation & Guidance

Introduction

Legislation, regulation and guidance serve as the driving forces for monitoring customer accounts to detect and report suspicious activity.

Primary Legislation is enacted by the U.S. Congress and serves as the cornerstone of the US anti-money laundering effort. Legislation in the form of the Bank Secrecy Act (e.g., which is a part of the United States Code or USC – a compilation of federal legislation), gives the U.S. Department of the Treasury the mandate to issue *regulations* implementing its provisions.

Regulations specifically place additional legal and administrative requirements on relevant financial businesses and are published in the Code of Federal Regulations (CFR). To ensure consistency with the application of BSA/AML requirements, various regulators issue *guidance*.

Guidance provides official advice and counseling that assists financial institutions with their efforts to comply with the regulations. Guidance additionally provides financial institutions with information that allows them to implement in the most practical manner, internal policies, procedures and controls.

The BSA authorizes the Secretary of the Treasury to require financial institutions to establish AML programs, file certain reports, and keep certain records of transactions. These BSA regulations are issued and enforced by the Financial Crimes Enforcement Network (FinCEN) of the US Treasury which also has the authority to impose monetary penalties for non-compliance.

As part of a strong BSA/AML compliance program, the Federal banking agencies assess banks' policies, procedures, and processes to ensure that banks can sufficiently identify and report suspicious transactions. Regulatory examinations scrutinize banks' ability to provide sufficient detail in their reports as well as banks' adherence to quality guidance. The best investigation process in the world is useless if the results of the investigation are not clearly documented and communicated in a way useful to law enforcement personnel.

The Annunzio-Wylie Anti-Money Laundering Act gave the US Treasury the power to require financial institutions to report suspicious activity via the *Suspicious Activity Report* (SAR). Variations of the SAR were developed to be used by all reporting organizations in the United States, including banks, casinos, money services businesses, and others. A banking organization is required by regulation to file a SAR whenever it detects a known or suspected criminal violation of Federal law, a suspicious transaction related to money laundering activity, or a violation of the BSA. Regulations implementing mandatory suspicious activity reporting for banks and other depository institutions took effect on April 1, 1996.

In November 2003, FinCEN, in consultation with the Federal regulatory authorities, issued a guidance package in three parts designed to assist financial institutions in the preparation of Suspicious Activity Report (SAR) forms and to improve the quality of

3

information provided in SAR narratives. The Narrative section of the SAR form describes all applicable information gathered, analyzed, and documented in the course of an investigation, as well as the reasoning behind the filing decision. Law enforcement agencies rely on this information and analysis to assist in money laundering, terrorist financing, and financial crimes investigations.

In July 2007, the Federal Financial Institutions Examination Council (FFIEC) re-released the Bank Secrecy Act/Anti-Money Laundering Examination Manual (*The Manual*). The Manual was developed in collaboration with the Financial Crimes Enforcement Network (the delegated administrator of the BSA) by:

- o   The Board of Governors of the Federal Reserve System;
- o   The Federal Deposit Insurance Corporation;
- o   The National Credit Union Administration;
- o   The Office of the Comptroller of the Currency; and,
- o   The Office of Thrift Supervision

In addition, through the Conference of State Bank Supervisors, the state banking agencies played a consultative role. Moreover, the Federal banking agencies worked with the Office of Foreign Assets Control (OFAC) to develop sections of the manual pertaining to OFAC compliance. The Manual's release marked an attempt to ensure consistent application and regulation of the Bank Secrecy Act and related anti-money laundering regulations.

While the FFIEC manual represents a valuable collection of anti-money laundering regulatory compliance information, AML professionals must be familiar with a variety of regulatory releases issued by FinCEN pursuant to its authority as the administrator of the Bank Secrecy Act.

Legislative History

- **1970:**

  The money laundering control system of the United States originated in 1970 with enactment of the **Bank Secrecy Act (BSA)** (Title 31, USC Sections 5311–5355). The formal name of the BSA is the *Currency and Foreign Transactions Reporting Act*. The BSA is enforced by the US Treasury Department and is the regulatory centerpiece of the entire U.S. anti-money laundering effort.

  The Bank Secrecy Act was designed to fight drug trafficking, money laundering and other crimes. Congress enacted the BSA to help prevent banks and other financial service providers from being inadvertently used as intermediaries by criminals seeking to hide or transfer money derived from their activities. The BSA, by virtue of its reporting requirements, was intended to supply law enforcement agencies certain reports and/or records that might have a high degree of usefulness in criminal, tax, regulatory investigations or proceedings. Among other items, the BSA created an investigative paper trail by establishing regulatory reporting standards and requirements (e.g., the Currency Transaction Report, more commonly known by its acronym *CTR, which* requires reporting to the IRS transactions over $10,000 in cash in one transaction or two or more related transactions.), and through a later amendment, established record keeping requirements for wire transfers. The BSA gives the Treasury an extremely broad mandate to issue regulations to implement its provisions.

- **1986:**

  Money laundering itself was not a criminal offense until Congress enacted the **Money Laundering Control Act (MLCA)** (PL 99-570) in 1986. With this law, money laundering was finally recognized as being more than an incidental product of other criminal activity. The MLCA, as codified in Title 18, USC, Sections 1956 and 1957, outlaws a wider range of financial transactions than merely the transfer of currency, as found in the BSA. The MLCA is a very powerful law enforcement tool which criminalized money laundering and, in effect, converted the proceeds of a crime into contraband, by criminalizing the use or the expenditure of such funds. It also provides for very substantial criminal and civil penalties for those convicted under the statutes.

  The provisions of the MLCA extend to those who introduce criminal proceeds into laundering channels, as well as bankers and others who *willfully* assist such operations. Willfully assisting a launderer does not need to include open and premeditated collusion on the part of a banker. Instead, government agents and prosecutors assign a *should-have-known* standard in determining if a bank or its employees were willful in their activities. This means that as a bank or a banker, the government expects that one will be trained and experienced enough to detect suspicious activity related to money laundering. If the government determines a bank or a banker willfully turned a blind eye to activity an otherwise reasonable person would have concluded was suspicious, then the bank and the banker may likely to be targets of an investigation and prosecution.

- **1988:**
  Congress passed the **Anti-Drug Abuse Act of 1988** which reinforced and supplemented existing anti-money laundering efforts primarily by increasing the level of penalties and sanctions for money laundering crimes. The law significantly increased penalties and required strict identification and record keeping for cash purchases of certain monetary instruments. In addition, the legislation permitted the U.S. Department of the Treasury to force financial institutions to file additional geographically targeted currency transaction reports. The Secretary of the Treasury can issue an order requiring financial institutions in a specific geographic area to file currency transaction reports for less than the $10,000 threshold.

- **1990:**
  Congress passed the **Crime Control Act of 1990** where Section 2532 of the Act enhanced the Federal banking agencies' enforcement position by giving it powers to work with foreign banking authorities on investigations, examinations, or enforcement actions dealing with possible bank or currency transaction-related violations.

- **1992:**
  In 1992, Congress passed the **Annunzio-Wylie Anti-Money Laundering Act** which gave Treasury the power to require financial institutions to report suspicious activity (Title 31, USC Sec. 5318(g)). Formal reporting of suspicious activity via a standard form began in 1996.

- **1994:**
  The **Money Laundering Suppression Act of 1994** required regulators to develop enhanced examination procedures and to increase examiner training to improve the identification of money laundering schemes in financial institutions.

- **1998:**
  The **Money Laundering and Financial Crimes Strategy Act of 1998** required the Secretary of the Treasury, in consultation with the Attorney General and other relevant agencies, including state and local agencies, to coordinate and implement a national strategy to address money laundering.

- **2001:**
  The **USA PATRIOT Act**, enacted in 2001, significantly changed the BSA. The Act expanded the reach of the BSA internationally and now includes elements designed to aid in intelligence and counter-intelligence activities. In addition to strengthening anti-money laundering statutes, the Act addressed the importance of combating terror financing, (i.e., the diversion of funds to support terrorist activities.) The Act encouraged both foreign and domestic banks as well as other financial institutions to voluntarily share information related to instances of money laundering and terror financing. The Act mandated that financial institutions develop effective anti-money laundering programs and appoint a designated anti-money laundering officer. The

Act prohibits banks from conducting business with foreign shell banks or those banks without a physical presence. It requires banks to perform due-diligence reviews of their correspondent relationships with foreign banks. The Act set forth the minimum requirements for account opening and greatly increased the subpoena authority of the U.S. government.

Regulatory Interpretations and Guidance, Advisories, and Assessments

FinCEN, pursuant to its authority as the administrator of the Bank Secrecy Act, issues a variety of regulatory releases. It is important that BSA officers and investigators understand the finer nuances of the specific release types, as each type may imply varying obligations.

Regulations:

As administrator of the Bank Secrecy Act, the Financial Crimes Enforcement Network issues regulations implementing the Bank Secrecy Act. These regulations are codified in title 31 of the Code of Federal Regulations, part 103 (31 C.F.R. part 103). Related publications include:

- o   Final rules
- o   Interim final rules
- o   Notices of proposed rule makings
- o   Advance notices of proposed rule makings
- o   Corrections

Final rules issued by FinCEN in accordance with the procedures specified in section 553(c) of the Administrative Procedure Act, and interim final rules published in accordance with section 553(b)(B) of the Administrative Procedure Act,[1] (including any subsequent *corrections* to these rules), are *binding obligations on individuals and entities* within the scope of such rules pursuant to FinCEN's authority to issue such rules under the Bank Secrecy Act.

Regulatory Interpretations and Guidance

FinCEN routinely issues interpretations of Bank Secrecy Act regulations as well as guidance to financial institutions on complying with its regulations. Interpretation and guidance fall into one of three categories:

1. **Administrative Rulings**
    FinCEN will issue administrative rulings interpreting the regulations contained in part 103 either unilaterally or in response to specific requests made and submitted to it consistent with the procedures outlined at 31 C.F.R. § 103.81. Administrative rulings *are binding on the requestor. Administrative rulings that are published in the Federal Register shall have persuasive precedential effect and, to that extent, may be relied upon by those similarly situated.* (FinCEN actively seeks to publish all administrative rulings in the Federal Register, in addition to making them available on its web site.)

2. *Interpretive* **Guidance**
    FinCEN routinely issues written interpretive regulatory guidance in various forms, both formal and informal. Examples of the same include:
    - ▪ **Interpretive releases**, including written responses to informal inquiries on the application of 31 C.F.R. part 103 that are not made and submitted to the Financial Crimes Enforcement Network consistent with the procedures outlined at 31 C.F.R. § 103.81

- **Frequently Asked Questions**
- **Staff Commentaries**

Such interpretations of regulations issued pursuant to the Bank Secrecy Act in 31 C.F.R. part 103 *that are published in the Federal Register shall have persuasive precedential effect* and, to that extent, may be relied upon by those financial institutions subject to the specific provision of 31 C.F.R. part 103 being interpreted until such interpretation is superseded, revoked, or amended. *If written guidance is not published in the Federal Register, although not binding, such guidance provides useful insight into FinCEN's view of the application of the Bank Secrecy Act and its implementing regulations* at the time that the guidance is issued.

3. **Statements of Policy**
   These are statements outlining or describing FinCEN's policy with respect to specific issues arising under the Bank Secrecy Act. Although not binding, these statements provide useful insight into FinCEN's view of the application of the Bank Secrecy Act and its implementing regulations at the time the statement is issued.
   a. **Advisories** – Issued to financial institutions for the purpose of enabling them to guard against money laundering or terrorist financing threats and vulnerabilities. Such publications often contain guidance on complying with FinCEN's regulations to address those threats and vulnerabilities.
      i. *If published in the Federal Register*, to the extent such publications interpret regulations issued pursuant to the Bank Secrecy Act in 31 C.F.R. part 103, they shall have persuasive precedential effect and *may be relied upon by those financial institutions* subject to the specific provision of 31 C.F.R. part 103 being interpreted until such interpretation is superseded, revoked, or amended.
      ii. If such publications are *not published in the Federal Register*, although *not binding*, such guidance provides useful insight into FinCEN's view of the application of the Bank Secrecy Act and its implementing regulations at the time that the guidance is issued.

Enforcement and Consent Assessments
FinCEN issues releases involving the assessment of civil money penalties against financial institutions for systemic non-compliance with the Bank Secrecy Act.
   o An enforcement assessment and a consent to such assessment are binding on the subject financial institution.
   o Although an enforcement action applies exclusively to the subject financial institution, *regulatory interpretations contained in such assessments shall have persuasive precedential effect and, to that extent, may be relied upon* by those financial institutions subject to the specific provision of 31 C.F.R.

part 103 being interpreted until such interpretation is superseded, revoked, or amended.

USA PATRIOT Act Section 311

Overview

Section 311 of the PATRIOT Act added 31 USC 5318A to the BSA, which authorizes the Secretary of the Treasury to require domestic financial institutions and domestic financial agencies to take certain special measures against foreign jurisdictions, foreign financial institutions, classes of international transactions, or types of accounts of *primary money laundering concern*. Section 311 provides the Secretary of the Treasury with a range of options that can be adapted to target specific money laundering and terrorist financing concerns. Section 311 is implemented through various orders and regulations that are incorporated into 31 CFR Part 103. As set forth in section 311, certain special measures may be imposed by an order without prior public notice and comment, but such orders must be of limited duration and must be issued together with a Notice of Proposed Rulemaking.

Section 311 establishes a process for the Secretary of the Treasury to follow, and identifies federal agencies to consult before the Secretary of the Treasury may conclude that a jurisdiction, financial institution, class of transactions, or type of account is of primary money laundering concern. The statute also provides similar procedures, including factors and consultation requirements, for selecting the specific special measures to be imposed against a jurisdiction, financial institution, class of transactions, or type of account that is of primary money laundering concern. It is important to note that, while a jurisdiction, financial institution, class of transactions, or type of account may be designated of primary money laundering concern in an order issued together with a Notice of Proposed Rulemaking, special measures of unlimited duration can only be imposed by a final rule issued after notice and an opportunity for comment.

Types of Special Measures

The following five special measures can be imposed, either individually, or in any combination:

1. **Record-keeping and Reporting of Certain Financial Transactions**
   Under the first special measure, banks may be required to maintain or to file reports concerning the aggregate amount of transactions or the specifics of each transaction with respect to a jurisdiction, financial institution, class of transactions, or type of account that is of primary money laundering concern. The statute contains minimum information requirements for these records and reports and permits the Secretary of the Treasury to impose additional information requirements.

2. **Information Relating to Beneficial Ownership**
   Under the second special measure, banks may be required to take reasonable and practicable steps, as determined by the Secretary of the Treasury, to obtain and retain information concerning the beneficial ownership of any account opened or maintained in the United States by a foreign person (other than a foreign entity whose shares are subject to public reporting requirements or are listed and traded on a regulated exchange or trading market), or a representative of such foreign person, that

involves a jurisdiction, financial institution, class of transactions, or type of account that is of primary money laundering concern.

3. **Information Relating to Certain Payable Through Accounts**
    Under the third special measure, banks that open or maintain a payable through account involving a jurisdiction, financial institution, class of transactions, or type of account that is of primary money laundering concern, may be required to: (i) identify each customer (and representative) who is permitted to use the account or whose transactions are routed through the account; and (ii) obtain information about each such customer (and representative) that is substantially comparable to that which a United States depository institution obtains in the ordinary course of business with respect to its customers residing in the United States.

4. **Information Relating to Certain Correspondent Accounts**
    Under the fourth special measure, banks that open or maintain a correspondent account in the United States involving a jurisdiction, financial institution, class of transactions, or type of account that is of primary money laundering concern may be required to: (i) identify each customer (and representative) who is permitted to use the account or whose transactions are routed through the account; and (ii) obtain information about each such customer (and representative) that is substantially comparable to that which a United States depository institution obtains in the ordinary course of business with respect to its customers residing in the United States.

5. **Prohibitions or Conditions on Opening or Maintaining Certain Correspondent or Payable Through Accounts**
    Under the fifth, and strongest, special measure, banks may be prohibited from opening or maintaining any correspondent account or payable through account for, or on behalf of, a foreign financial institution if the account involves a jurisdiction, financial institution, class of transactions, or type of account that is of primary money laundering concern. The imposition of this measure can prohibit U.S. banks from establishing, maintaining, administering or managing a correspondent or payable through account for, or on behalf of, any financial institution from a specific foreign jurisdiction. This measure may also be applied to specific foreign financial institutions and their subsidiaries. The regulations that implement these prohibitions may require banks to review their account records to determine that they maintain no accounts directly for, or on behalf of, such entities. In addition to the direct prohibition, banks may also be:
    - Prohibited from knowingly providing indirect access to the specific entities through its other banking relationships;
    - Required to notify correspondent account holders that they must not provide the specific entity with access to the account maintained at the U.S. bank; and,

- Required to take reasonable steps to identify any indirect use of its accounts by the specific entity.

Special Measures Guidance

Orders and regulations implementing specific special measures taken under section 311 of the PATRIOT Act are not static; they can be issued or rescinded over time as the Secretary of the Treasury determines that a subject jurisdiction, institution, class of transactions, or type of account is no longer of primary money laundering concern. In addition, special measures imposed against one jurisdiction, institution, class of transactions, or type of account may vary from those imposed in other situations.

Investigators should be cognizant of the special measures required to be taken and include the background information of the special measure(s) for consideration in any suspicious activity investigation that may have a geographic or other nexus to the special measures designee.

Special Measures Designees

The Treasury Department has recently (April 10, 2008) identified the following institutions as "primary money laundering concerns," pursuant to Section 311:

- Asia Wealth Bank 4/12/04
- Banco Delta Asia 3/14/07
- Belmetalnergo (Includes Infobank) 9/30/04
- Burma 4/12/04
- Commercial Bank of Syria 3/09/06
  (Includes Syrian Lebanese Commercial Bank)
- Infobank (Includes Belmetalnergo) 8/24/04
- Myanmar Mayflower Bank 4/12/04
- VEF Banka 7/12/06

Section III – Suspicious Activity Indicator Guidance

SAR Filings by Financial Institution

SAR filings generally fall into one or more of twenty-two categories, as defined by FinCEN and the Bank Secrecy Act Advisory Group. The following table details the number of SAR filings by financial institutions in 2007. The trend of suspicious activities reported by financial institutions is heavily skewed towards BSA violations, with almost one half of all SARs filed being identified as such. Typically, *structuring* has been the number one reported suspicious activity by BSA investigations units, with some banks' BSA FIUs experiencing from two thirds to almost 75% of all their SAR filings related to structuring.

Table 1: SAR Filings by Characterization of Suspicious Activity[2]

Rank	Suspicious Activity Type	Filings (Overall)	Percentage (Overall)
1	BSA/Structuring/Money Laundering	1,503,003	48.28%
2	Check Fraud	333,862	10.72%
3	Other	270,152	8.68%
4	Counterfeit Checks	155,141	4.98%
5	Credit Card Fraud	154,506	4.96%
6	Mortgage Loan Fraud	113,071	3.63%
7	Check Kiting	101,107	3.25%
8	Identity Theft [3]	69,325	2.23%
9	False Statement	67,902	2.18%
10	Defalcation / Embezzlement	63,392	2.04%
11	Unknown/Blank	63,069	2.03%
12	Consumer Loan Fraud	53,588	1.72%
13	Misuse of Position / Self Dealing	30,899	Less than 1%
14	Wire Transfer Fraud	29,574	Less than 1%
15	Mysterious Disappearance	26,465	Less than 1%
16	Debit Card Fraud	17,480	Less than 1%
17	Commercial Loan Fraud	16,524	Less than 1%
18	Counterfeit Instrument (Other)	13,542	Less than 1%
19	Computer Intrusion [4]	12,307	Less than 1%
20	Counterfeit Credit / Debit Card	12,177	Less than 1%
21	Terrorist Financing[3]	3,178	Less than 1%
22	Bribery and Gratuity	2,932	Less than 1%

Relationship of Suspect to Financial Institution

This table extends back to 1996. For the full table and all other statistical information, please refer to the latest edition of the SAR Activity Review – By the Numbers.

Table 2: Relationship of Suspect to Financial Institution

Relationship	2001	2002	2003	2004	2005	2006
Accountant	82	159	198	315	532	582
Agent	523	1,078	661	956	1,138	745
Appraiser	372	476	881	2,172	2,531	3,827
Attorney	47	67	74	104	191	179
Borrower	6,151	6,809	8,866	14,410	19,988	32,414
Broker	1,512	1,702	2,450	4,516	7,453	12,497
Customer	142,780	198,177	198,952	273,868	373,439	395,043
Director	190	210	209	209	268	236
Employee	11,693	11,445	12,337	13,165	14,629	16,032
Officer	694	763	730	791	838	997
Shareholder	740	689	758	1,320	1,329	1,848
Other	28,256	36,157	41,016	52,586	77,175	93,790
None Indicated	25,969	33,996	40,193	41,046	55,193	55,884

Suspicious and Unusual Activities Defined

A suspicious activity may be defined as an account, transaction or other activity that gives rise to a belief that a violation of law or regulation may have occurred. This includes activity which is a violation of law or regulation not otherwise required to be reported under the Bank Secrecy and USA PATRIOT Acts.

A transaction might be considered suspicious, and is reportable, if it involves:
- Insider abuse involving any dollar amount.
- Violations of federal law aggregating $5,000 or more where a suspect can be identified.
- Violations of federal law aggregating $25,000 or more regardless of a potential suspect.
- Transactions aggregating $5,000 or more that involve potential money laundering or violations of the Bank Secrecy Act if the bank knows, suspects, or has reason to suspect that the transaction:
  - Involves funds derived from illegal activity or is intended to disguise the source, ownership, or control of funds or assets derived from illegal activity as part of a plan to evade federal law or reporting requirements;
  - Is designed, whether through structuring or other means, to evade Bank Secrecy Act Reporting; or,
  - Serves no apparent legitimate business purpose, and your bank knows of no reasonable explanation for the transaction (e.g., when asked, the customer cannot provide a reasonable explanation).

(**Note:** For reporting purposes, a SAR need not be filed for robberies and burglaries that are reported to local authorities, or (except for savings associations and service corporations) for lost, missing, counterfeit, or stolen securities that are reported pursuant to the requirements of 17 CFR 240.17f-1.)

While the boundary may not be altogether clear, an investigator should be cognizant that not all unusual activity is necessarily suspicious. The key to differentiating the two lies with understanding enough about the customer, the customer's expected activities, and the types of money laundering schemes used by criminals. Generally, a transaction may be deemed unusual if it is inconsistent in amount, origin, destination, or type with a customer's known, legitimate business or personal activities. The unusual quality is *fact based* and may have itself been the trigger for generating an alert.

Suspicion, on the other hand, is both personal and subjective. It has at times been defined by the courts as being "beyond mere speculation and based on some foundation, but falling short of knowledge or belief." Suspicion may be aroused by a:
- Single unusual act because of the time and circumstances in which it occurs; or,
- Series of acts over time –viewed collectively, even though the individual acts viewed by themselves might not.

Definitions and Criminal Statutes

In response to requests for an explanation or definition of the various characterizations of suspicious activity appearing in Item #35 of the depository institution Suspicious Activity Report form (Form TD F 90-22.47), FinCEN, with the assistance of members of the Bank Secrecy Act Advisory Group SAR Feedback Subcommittee, prepared the following tables.

These tables provide a listing of each category of suspicious activity, certain federal criminal statutes associated with the violation, and its explanation or definition. Please note that SAR filers may select more than one type of characterization, if applicable, when completing the Suspicious Activity Report Form.

BSA Structuring – Money Laundering

Characterization of Suspicious Activity – Reportable Condition	Possible Federal Criminal Statute(s)	Explanation/Description
Bank Secrecy Act Structuring/Money Laundering	31 U.S.C. Section 5311 and 31 C.F.R. Part 103 Bank Secrecy Act	1. The transaction involves funds derived from illegal activities or is intended or conducted in order to hide or disguise funds or assets derived from illegal activities (including, without limitation, the ownership, nature, source, location or control of such funds or assets) as part of a plan to violate or evade any law or regulation or to avoid any transaction record keeping and reporting requirement under federal law and reporting requirement under federal law; or, 2. The transaction is designed to evade any regulations promulgated under the Bank Secrecy Act; or, 3. The transaction has no business or apparent lawful purpose or is not the sort in which the particular customer would normally be expected to engage, and the financial institution knows of no reasonable explanation for the transaction after examining the available facts including the background and possible purpose of the transaction.
Bank Secrecy Act Structuring/Money Laundering	31 U.S.C. Section 5324 – Structuring Transactions to Evade Reporting	There are four types of structuring activities that are reportable: 1. To avoid generating any Currency Transaction Report, Form 8300 and supporting records, and to avoid any record keeping connected to monetary instruments; 2. To avoid the identification requirements, e.g. connected with non-bank money transmissions and purchase of monetary instruments; 3. To avoid suspicious detection and conventional monitoring thresholds and filters; 4. To avoid enhanced scrutiny or additional

Characterization of Suspicious Activity – Reportable Condition	Possible Federal Criminal Statute(s)	Explanation/Description
		review frequently triggered by higher transaction amounts and thresholds.
Bank Secrecy Act Structuring/Money Laundering	18 U.S.C. Section 1956 – Laundering of Monetary Instruments 18 USC Section 1957– Engaging in Monetary Transactions in Property Derived From Specified Unlawful Activity	

Bribery and Gratuity

Characterization of Suspicious Activity – Reportable Condition	Possible Federal Criminal Statute(s)	Explanation/Description
Bribery and Gratuity	18 U.S.C. Section 215 – Bank Bribery	Anyone who, in connection with bank business, corruptly gives, offers or promises anything of value to a bank official with the intent to influence or reward that official.

Check Fraud

Characterization of Suspicious Activity – Reportable Condition	Possible Federal Criminal Statute(s)	Explanation/Description
Check Fraud	18 U.S.C. Section 1344 – Bank Fraud	This type of fraud takes on many forms including: altered checks; check kiting; charge-back check fraud; closed account fraud; and variations on check forgeries. Other common check fraud violations noted are the withdrawal of funds against checks with forged endorsements or maker's signatures and counterfeit checks.

Check Kiting

Characterization of Suspicious Activity – Reportable Condition	Possible Federal Criminal Statute(s)	Explanation/Description
Check Kiting	U.S.C. Section 1344 – Bank Fraud 8 U.S.C. Section 656/657– Embezzlement, Theft or Misapplication of Funds	A practice in which an individual with accounts at two or more financial institutions intentionally utilizes the delay in the check clearing process to write checks from one account to deposit into the second account, all the while knowing that the first account does not have collected funds. The subject continues this cycle, moving checks between accounts, to make it appear as if funds are available and using the balance in the accounts for expenditures.

Commercial Loan Fraud

Characterization of Suspicious Activity – Reportable Condition	Possible Federal Criminal Statute(s)	Explanation/Description
Commercial Loan Fraud	U.S.C. Section 1344 – Bank Fraud 18 U.S.C. Section 656/ 657 – Embezzlement, Theft or Misapplication of Funds	Fraudulent loan involving a corporation, commercial enterprise, or other type of business, usually secured by some form of collateral. One example includes banks advancing loan funds to car dealers via floor plan lines of credit secured by the automobiles in inventory. Collateral is later sold, out of trust, and proceeds are not applied to the loan thus creating a loss to the lender.

Computer Intrusion

Characterization of Suspicious Activity – Reportable Condition	Possible Federal Criminal Statute(s)	Explanation/Description
Computer Intrusion	18 U.S.C. Section 1030 – Computer Fraud	A person who gains access to a computer system of a financial institution to: • Remove, steal, procure or otherwise affect funds of the institution or the institution's customers; • Remove, steal, procure or otherwise affect critical information of the institution including customer account information; or, • Damage, disable or otherwise affect critical systems of the institution. Note: Does not mean attempted intrusions of websites or other non-critical information systems of the institution that provide no access to institution or customer financial or other critical information See The SAR Activity Review for additional information on Computer Intrusion at the following hyperlink: http://www.fincen.gov/sarreviewissue3.pdf

Consumer Loan Fraud

Characterization of Suspicious Activity – Reportable Condition	Possible Federal Criminal Statute(s)	Explanation/Description
Consumer Loan Fraud	18 USC Section 1344 – Bank Fraud 18 U.S.C. Section 656 / 657– Embezzlement, Theft or Misapplication of Funds	A loan extended to an individual for personal or household use that is obtained fraudulently. Incidents of consumer loan fraud primarily involve the submission of false or forged statements by loan applicants.

Counterfeit Checks

Characterization of Suspicious Activity – Reportable Condition	Possible Federal Criminal Statute(s)	Explanation/Description
Counterfeit Checks	18 U.S.C. Section 1344 – Bank Fraud	A legitimate check that is altered or forged by hand or through the use of a computer or electronic/digital device that is compromised or scanned into a computer. The payee's name, dollar amount, check serial number, and date are changed though other data (including the authorized signature) remain as they appear on the original check. The counterfeit check is purported to be genuine and negotiated.

Counterfeit Credit / Debit Card

Characterization of Suspicious Activity – Reportable Condition	Possible Federal Criminal Statute(s)	Explanation/Description
Counterfeit Credit / Debit Card	18 U.S.C. Section 1029 – Fraud and Related Activity in Connection With Access Device 18 USC Section 1344 – Bank Fraud	A person who knowingly commits fraud by producing, using, or selling one or more counterfeit credit or debit cards. A counterfeit or fake card is created through technology to emboss stolen or fictitious card numbers, along with hologram and card issuer images, and magnetic stripes on white plastic. The cards are used for fraudulent purchases or sold to other criminals for their use.

Counterfeit Instrument

Characterization of Suspicious Activity – Reportable Condition	Possible Federal Criminal Statute(s)	Explanation/Description
Counterfeit Instrument	18 USC Section 1344 – Bank Fraud	The manufacture, copy, reproduction, or forgery of an instrument with the intent to defraud a financial institution. Instruments could include notes, checks, securities, bonds, certificates and other negotiable financial instruments.

Credit Card Fraud

Characterization of Suspicious Activity – Reportable Condition	Possible Federal Criminal Statute(s)	Explanation/Description
Credit Card Fraud	18 USC Section 1344 – Bank Fraud	The intentional procurement of goods, services or money, without the authorization of the cardholder, credit card member or its agent, by using a stolen, lost, or canceled credit card. May include illegal purchases made in person, via the Internet or telephone, or through cash advances.

Debit Card Fraud

Characterization of Suspicious Activity – Reportable Condition	Possible Federal Criminal Statute(s)	Explanation/Description
Debit Card Fraud	18 USC Section 1344 – Bank Fraud	The unauthorized use of a stolen, lost, or canceled debit card for payment of goods or to acquire services or money. Debit cards are used in place of checks or cash and usually are tied to a checking account. Fraudulent use of the debit card depletes available funds in that account causing a loss to the bank customer or to the bank.

Defalcation / Embezzlement

Characterization of Suspicious Activity – Reportable Condition	Possible Federal Criminal Statute(s)	Explanation/Description
Defalcation / Embezzlement	18 U.S.C. Section 656/657 – Theft, Embezzlement, or misapplication of funds	A person who, for unauthorized personal use, embezzles, abstracts, purloins or willfully misapplies any of the moneys, funds or credits of a bank, branch, agency or organization or holding company or any moneys, funds, assets or, securities entrusted to the custody or care of such bank, branch, agency, organization, or holding company.

False Statement

Characterization of Suspicious Activity – Reportable Condition	Possible Federal Criminal Statute(s)	Explanation/Description
False Statement	18 U.S.C. Section 1001 – False Statements or Entries 18 U.S.C. Section 1005 – False Entries 18 U.S.C. Section 1014 –False Statements on Loan or Credit Application	A person who knowingly and willfully commits one of the following: • Falsifies, conceals or covers up by any trick, scheme or device, a material fact; • Makes any materially false, fictitious or fraudulent statement or representation; or • Makes or uses any false writing or document knowing the same to contain any materially false, fictitious or fraudulent statement or entry. The false statement must occur in a matter within the jurisdiction of a branch of the United States Government; essentially, making a false statement to a government agency when it is carrying out its mission. Section covers oral or written false statements or misrepresentations made knowingly on a loan or credit application to an insured bank (e.g., willful over-valuing of land, property, securities, or other assets or the understatement of liabilities). Such statements or misrepresentations must have been

Characterization of Suspicious Activity – Reportable Condition	Possible Federal Criminal Statute(s)	Explanation/Description
		capable of influencing the bank's credit decision. Actual damage or reliance on such information is not an essential element of the offense. The statute applies to credit renewals, continuations, extensions or deferments and includes willful omissions as well as affirmative false statements. Obsolete information in the original loan application is not covered unless the applicant reaffirms the information in connection with a renewal request. The application will trigger the statute even if the loan is not made.

Identity Theft

Characterization of Suspicious Activity – Reportable Condition	Possible Federal Criminal Statute(s)	Explanation/Description
Identity Theft	18 U.S.C. Section 1028 – Identity Theft	A person who knowingly transfers or uses, without lawful authority, a means of identification of another person with the intent to commit, or to aid or abet, any unlawful activity that constitutes a violation of Federal law, or that constitutes a felony under applicable state or local law. See: http://www.fincen.gov/sarreview2issue4web.pdf to view Issue 2, page 14 of The SAR Activity Review for further details pertaining to identity theft.

Misuse of Position / Self Dealing

Characterization of Suspicious Activity – Reportable Condition	Possible Federal Criminal Statute(s)	Explanation/Description
Misuse of Position / Self Dealing	18 U.S.C. Section 656/657 – Theft, Embezzlement, or Misapplication of Funds 18 U.S.C. Section 644 – Banker Receiving Unauthorized Deposit of Public Money 18 U.S.C. Section 215 – Bank Bribery	A person, who is not an authorized depositary of public moneys, who knowingly receives from any disbursing officer, collector of internal revenue, or other agent of the United States, public money on deposit, or by way of a loan or accommodation, with or without interest, or otherwise than in payment of a debt against the United States, or uses, transfers, converts, appropriates, or applies any portion of the public money for any purpose not prescribed by law.

Mortgage Loan Fraud

Characterization of Suspicious Activity – Reportable Condition	Possible Federal Criminal Statute(s)	Explanation/Description
Mortgage Loan Fraud	18 U.S.C. Section 1344 – Bank Fraud 18 U.S.C. Section 656/657 – Theft, Embezzlement, or Misapplication of Funds	A person who fraudulently obtains a mortgage for property or other asset primarily by the submission of false or forged statements on loan applications.

Mysterious Disappearance

Characterization of Suspicious Activity – Reportable Condition	Possible Federal Criminal Statute(s)	Explanation/Description
Mysterious Disappearance	18 U.S.C. Section 656/657 – Theft, Embezzlement, or Misapplication of funds	Unexplained disappearance of money or other instruments of value, in bearer form, from a financial institution's branch, agency, organization, or holding company.

Other

Characterization of Suspicious Activity – Reportable Condition	Possible Federal Criminal Statute(s)	Explanation/Description
Other		A category used to report suspicious activity that does not fit into any other violations characterization.

Terrorist Financing

Characterization of Suspicious Activity – Reportable Condition	Possible Federal Criminal Statute(s)	Explanation/Description
Terrorist Financing	18 U.S.C. 2339(a) and, 18 U.S.C. 2339(b) – Harboring and Concealing Terrorists	Persons or entities who provide material support or resources to various enumerated terrorist acts, including concealing or disguising the nature, location, source or ownership of the material support or resources. Also, persons or entities providing material support or resources to designated foreign terrorist organizations, or attempting or conspiring to do so. The statute explicitly provides for extra-territorial jurisdiction, meaning it can be applied to actions occurring outside the United States.

Wire Transfer Fraud

Characterization of Suspicious Activity – Reportable Condition	Possible Federal Criminal Statute(s)	Explanation/Description
Wire Transfer Fraud	18 U.S.C. Section 1956 – Laundering of Monetary Instruments 18 U.S.C. Section 1343 – Fraud by Wire, Radio or Television	A person who, intending to defraud or obtain money or property by fraudulent means of false pretenses, representations or promises, transmits an electronic funds transfer.

Money Laundering Defined

What is money Laundering?

Money Laundering is defined as the processing of criminal proceeds in order to disguise their origin, thereby enabling their use without jeopardizing their source. Money laundering is an integral support function common to all profit producing criminal activities. The principal goal of the launderer is to transform illegitimate gain into legitimate investment. The transformation occurs by obscuring the source of the illegal proceeds as well as the nature of the gained wealth. This is done by resorting to transactions which are designed to confuse and confound an investigator. The process of money laundering is typically conducted in three distinct stages:

1. **Placement** – Defined as the process of placing, through deposits, unlawful cash proceeds into financial institutions or the retail economy. Often these proceeds take the form of cash or cash equivalents such as monetary instruments, money orders, and cashiers checks. Criminal proceeds can also take the form of wire transfers and checks.

2. **Layering** – The concealing or disguising the source of ownership of the funds by creating complex layers of financial transactions designed to disguise the audit trail and provide anonymity. Its intent is the disassociation of the illegal monies from their true source.

3. **Integration** – The stage at which money is integrated into legitimate economic and financial systems and is assimilated with other assets, making the money appear to have been lawfully earned or indistinguishable from other legal wealth. Integration is the stage where the profits of crime are put back to use by the criminal, either to fund on-going criminal activity or fund their lifestyle.

The structuring of deposits in order to avoid currency reporting requirements, or churning within accounts (where deposits and withdrawals are made frequently and with no apparent purpose), are indicative of money laundering. Money laundering schemes may also be perpetrated through the use of professional fronts, by creating dummy or off-shore shell corporations with fraudulent accounts, and the use of multiple electronic transfers, deposits or withdrawals. Asset and monetary instrument purchases using bulk cash are other means in which the launderer can change the form of the illegal proceeds. Informal money transfer systems such as the Hawala and Hundi are also utilized by money launderers. Additionally, the exchange of U.S. currency for foreign currencies (Colombian or Mexican Peso) or foreign bank drafts is a common practice among money launderers.

Although money laundering has existed as long as criminals have needed to conceal and convert their illegally acquired profits, the most recent growth of money laundering in the United States is clearly attributed to the proliferation of the international trade in unlawful drugs. Nevertheless, investigators should also be aware that money laundering activities may be related to financial institution frauds, credit card or telecommunication frauds, advance fee frauds and the like.

Legal Definition of Money Laundering (from 18 USC §§ 1956(a))

1. Whoever, knowing that the property involved in a financial transaction[5] represents the proceeds of some form of unlawful activity, conducts or attempts to conduct such a financial transaction which in fact involves the proceeds of specified unlawful activity—(A) (i) with the intent to promote the carrying on of specified unlawful activity; or (ii) with intent to engage in conduct constituting a violation of section 7201 or 7206 of the Internal Revenue Code of 1986; or (B) knowing that the transaction is designed in whole or in part— (i) to conceal or disguise the nature, the location, the source, the ownership, or the control of the proceeds of specified unlawful activity; or (ii) to avoid a transaction reporting requirement under State or Federal law.

2. Whoever transports, transmits, or transfers, or attempts to transport, transmit, or transfer a monetary instrument or funds from a place in the United States to or through a place outside the United States or to a place in the United States from or through a place outside the United States— (A) with the intent to promote the carrying on of specified unlawful activity; or (B) knowing that the monetary instrument or funds involved in the transportation, transmission, or transfer represent the proceeds of some form of unlawful activity and knowing that such transportation, transmission, or transfer is designed in whole or in part— (i) to conceal or disguise the nature, the location, the source, the ownership, or the control of the proceeds of specified unlawful activity; or (ii) to avoid a transaction reporting requirement under State or Federal law.

3. Whoever, with the intent— (A) to promote the carrying on of specified unlawful activity; (B) to conceal or disguise the nature, location, source, ownership, or control of property believed to be the proceeds of specified unlawful activity; or (C) to avoid a transaction reporting requirement under State or Federal law, conducts or attempts to conduct a financial transaction involving property represented to be the proceeds of specified unlawful activity, or property used to conduct or facilitate specified unlawful activity.

Money Laundering Red Flags

The following is a list of red flags for money laundering compiled from multiple sources. Trying to compare an identified activity from a list as long as this is not a very efficient undertaking. The electronic version of this book, however, greatly facilitates searching and matching criteria to this list. (For information on ordering the electronic version, please send an email to support@impactaml.com)

Account / Transactions Activity

o   Consistent cash deposits or withdrawals under the CTR reporting threshold;

o   Deposits/withdrawals frequency among various branches or tellers;

o   Accounts with many small cash deposits and a small number of large withdrawal checks with the balance of the account remaining relatively low and constant;

o   Large balances in non-interest bearing accounts;

o   Accounts with missing tax ID numbers;

o   Multiple customers sharing a common address and/or telephone number;

o   Commercial and consumer accounts with the same address;

o   Deposits or purchases of monetary instruments to/from multiple related accounts conducted by third parties;

o   A customer's corporate account(s) has deposits or withdrawals primarily in cash rather than checks;

o   The customer engages in unusual activity in cash purchases or traveler's checks, money orders, or cashier's checks;

o   A large volume of cashier's checks, money orders, and/or wire transfers are deposited into an account in which the nature of the account holder's business would not appear to justify such activity;

o   A Customer frequently makes large dollar transactions (such as deposits, withdrawals, or purchases of monetary instruments) without an explanation as to how they will be used in the business, or the purchases allegedly are for a business that generally does not deal in large amounts of cash;

o   A business account history that shows little or no regular, periodic activity; the accounts appear to be used primarily as a temporary repository for funds that are transferred abroad. For example, numerous deposits of cash followed by lump-sump wire transfers;

o   A customer's place of business or residence is outside the financial institution's service area;

o   A retail business has dramatically different patterns of cash deposits from similar businesses in the same general location;

o   The currency transaction patterns of a business experience a sudden and inconsistent change from past activities. The amount and frequency of cash deposits are inconsistent with that observed at the customer's place of business or what can be reasonably understood about how a business operates;

o   The business is one that is likely to make frequent deposits of cash, but checks or other debits drawn against the account are inconsistent with the customer's retail business;

○ Businesses that do not normally generate currency make numerous currency transactions (i.e., a sanitation company that makes numerous deposits of cash);

○ Financial transactions involving monetary instruments that are incomplete or contain fictitious payees, remitters, etc., if known;

○ A business owner, such as an owner who has only one store, who makes several deposits the same day using different bank branches;

○ An automatic teller machine or machines are used to make several bank deposits below a specified threshold;

○ Wire transfer activity to/from high risk countries without an apparent business reason or when it is inconsistent with the customer's business or history. Periodic wire transfers from a personal account(s) to accounts within high risk countries;

○ Large incoming wire transfers on behalf of a foreign client with little or no explicit reason;

○ Frequent or large volume or wire transfers to and from offshore banking centers. Large, round dollar deposits, withdrawals or wire transfers;

○ Funds transferred in and out of an account on the same day or within a relatively short period of time;

○ Payments or receipts with no apparent link to legitimate contracts, goods, or services. Transfers routed through multiple foreign or domestic banks. Unexplained, repetitive or unusual patterns of activity;

○ Deposits of funds into several accounts, usually in amounts less than $3,000 which are consolidated subsequently into one master account and transferred, often outside of the country;

○ Instructions to a financial institution to wire transfer funds abroad and to expect an incoming wire transfer of funds (in an equal amount) from other sources;

○ Regular deposits or withdrawals of large amounts of cash, using wire transfers to, from, or through countries that either are known sources of narcotics or whose laws are ineffective in controlling the laundering of money;

○ Many small incoming wire transfers of funds received or deposits made using checks and money orders, with all but a token amount almost immediately being wire transferred to another city or country, in a manner inconsistent with the customer's business or history;

○ Large volume of wire transfers from persons or businesses that do not hold accounts, i.e. the originator of the wire is not a bank;

○ Substantial deposit(s) of numerous $50 and $100 bills;

○ Mailing address outside the U.S.;

○ Frequent exchanges of small dollar denominations for large dollar denominations;

○ Certificate(s) of deposit or other investment vehicle used as loan collateral;

○ A large loan is suddenly paid down with no reasonable explanation of the source of funds. Frequent deposits of large amounts of currency wrapped in currency straps that have been stamped by other banks;

o Frequent deposits of currency wrapped in currency straps or currency wrapped in rubber bands that are disorganized and do not balance when counted. Frequent deposits of old style, musty or extremely dirty bills;

o A customer who purchases cashier's checks, money orders, etc., with large amounts of cash;

o A professional service provider, such as a lawyer, accountant, or broker, who makes substantial deposits of cash into client accounts or in-house company accounts, such as trust accounts and escrow accounts;

o A customer insists on meeting bank personnel at a location other than their place of business;

o Domestic bank accounts opened in the name of a Casa de Cambio (money exchange house), followed by suspicious wire transfers and/or structured deposits (under the threshold) into these accounts;

o Suspicious movements of funds from one bank into another bank and back to the first bank. For example: 1) purchasing cashier's checks from bank A; 2) opening up a checking account at bank B; and 4) wire transferring the funds from the checking account at bank B into an account at bank A;

o Off-shore companies, especially those located in high risk countries, asking for a loan from a domestic U.S. bank, or a loan secured by obligations of off-shore banks;

o Use of loan proceeds in a manner inconsistent with the stated loan purpose.

o Safe deposit box being the only relationship with the bank;

o Customer observed to access safe deposit box prior to or following a cash deposit or withdrawal;

o Loans repaid with cash. A person or business that does not hold an account and that purchases a monetary instrument with large denomination bills;

o A customer who purchases a number of cashier's checks, money orders, or traveler's checks for large amounts under a specified threshold, or without apparent reason;

o Couriers, rather than personal account customers, make the deposits into the account;

o Money orders deposited by mail, which are numbered sequentially or have unusual symbols or stamps on them;

o Use of Personal Investment Companies (PICs) or other "off-shore" entities by U.S. citizens;

o For no apparent reason, the customer has multiple accounts under a single name or multiple names, with a large number of inter-account or third-party transfers.

Account Opening

o A customer exhibits an unusual concern regarding the bank's compliance and government reporting;

o A client is reluctant to reveal information regarding his business activities;

o A client is reluctant to provide identification or business documents or furnishes unusual documentation;

o A customer wants to engage in transactions without any apparent business or investment purpose;

o A customer's initial transactions are inconsistent with his stated business purpose;

o A customer has been the subject of news reports indicating possible criminal or regulatory action or has a questionable background;

o A customer requests that transactions be processed in such a manner as to avoid the firm's normal documentation requirements;

o A customer appears to be acting as an agent for an undisclosed principal, but declines or is reluctant, without legitimate commercial reasons, to provide information or is otherwise evasive regarding that person or entity;

o The customer exhibits a lack of concern regarding risks, commissions, or other transaction costs;

o The information provided by the customer that identifies a legitimate source for funds is false, misleading, or substantially incorrect;

o Upon request, the customer refuses to identify or fails to indicate any legitimate source for his or her funds and other assets;

o The customer appears to be acting as an agent for an undisclosed principal, but declines or is reluctant, without legitimate commercial reasons, to provide information or is otherwise evasive regarding that person or entity;

o The customer has difficulty describing the nature of his or her business or lacks general knowledge of his or her industry.

Automated Clearing House (ACH) Transactions

o Large-value, automated clearing house (ACH) transactions are frequently initiated through third-party service providers (TPSP) by originators that are not bank customers and for which the bank has no or insufficient due diligence;

o TPSPs have a history of violating ACH network rules or generating illegal transactions, or processing manipulated or fraudulent transactions on behalf of their customers;

o Multiple layers of TPSPs that appear to be unnecessarily involved in transactions.

o Unusually high level of transactions initiated over the Internet or by telephone;

o National Automated Clearing House Association (NACHA) information requests indicate potential concerns with the bank's usage of the ACH system.

Avoidance of Reporting or Record Keeping

o A business or new customer asks to be exempted;

o A customer intentionally withholds part of the currency deposit or withdrawal to keep the transaction under the reporting threshold;

o A customer is reluctant to provide the information needed to file the mandatory report, to have the report filed, or to proceed with a transaction after being informed that the report must be filed;

o A customer or group tries to coerce a bank employee into not filing any required record keeping or reporting forms;
o An automatic teller machine or machines (ATM) are used to make several bank deposits below a specified threshold;
o Unusually large deposits of U.S. food stamps (often used as currency in exchange for narcotics);
o A customer is reluctant to furnish identification when purchasing negotiable instruments in recordable amounts;
o The customer requests that a transaction be processed in such a manner to avoid the firm's normal documentation requirements.

Bank to Bank Transactions
o Significant changes in currency shipment patterns between correspondent banks;
o Increase in large amounts of cash without a corresponding increase in the filing of mandatory currency transaction reports;
o Deposits with a Federal Reserve bank or its branches are disproportionate to the previous historical volume or volumes of similarly sized depository;
o Significant turnover in large denomination bills that would appear uncharacteristic given the bank's location;
o Inability to track the true account holder of correspondent or concentration account transactions;
o A large increase in small denomination bills and a corresponding decrease in large denomination bills with no corresponding currency transaction report filings;
o The rapid increase in the size and frequency of cash deposits with no corresponding increase in non-cash deposits.

Black Market Peso Exchange (BMPE) Activity
o Cash transactions and deposits (usually of monetary instruments with individual face values of less than $3,000) that appear to have been structured before reaching the bank;
o Suspicious activity in the accounts of non-resident aliens from countries and jurisdictions considered to be at high risk for money laundering. (These accounts are characterized by small cash deposits and checks written to purchase large ticket items, sometimes located in the Florida and Panama free trade zones. These accounts also lack typical payments for housing, utilities, and credit cards, etc.);
o Wire transfers, especially those that involve any type of import/export business and are to or from Colombia, Panama, Aruba or Mexico, for suspicious activity;
o Unusual check activity (e.g., structuring, followed by lump sum payments to U.S. appliance manufacturers or import/export companies in Florida and Panama).

Cash Intense Businesses (specific)

o Profit margin outside the norm for the customer's peer group and/or geographic area of operation;

o Sales per square foot significantly outside the norm for the customer's peer group and/or geographic area of operation;

o Significant overstatement of revenues (indicating that illegal money is mixed with legitimate money, thereby boosting total revenues);

o Large payments made to the owners or other related parties in the form of consulting fees, salaries, etc.;

o Ostentatious displays of wealth by owners or employees;

o Owners taking frequent trips out of the country;

o Involvement of payments and transmissions of funds out of the customer's account to or through various white collar professionals, e.g., accountants, lawyers, investment advisors, etc.;

o Transaction activity appearing to have no lawful business purpose (see examples below);

o Other cash intense related inconsistent activities:

- Customer operates a retail business and provides check cashing service and does not make large draws of cash against checks deposited. (This may indicate the customer has another source of cash);

- Unusual cash purchases of money orders and cashier's checks;

- Accounts with a large volume of deposits in cashier's checks, money orders, and/or wire transfers, when the nature of the account holder's business does not justify such activity;

- The accounts show frequent large bill transactions (i.e., deposits, withdrawals, monetary instrument purchases) without a business reason;

- A single, substantial cash deposit composed of many $50 and $100 bills.

- Frequent exchanges of small bills for large bills or vice versa;

- Sudden and inconsistent change in currency transactions or patterns;

- A business owner (e.g., a one-location store owner) who makes several deposits on the same day at different bank branches;

- The account shows unusually large deposits of U.S. food stamps (often used as currency in exchange for narcotics);

- The account sends and receives wire transfers (especially to/from bank-haven countries), without an apparent business reason or when inconsistent with the customer's business or history;

- The account receives many small incoming wire transfers or makes deposits using checks and money orders, and almost immediately wire transfers all but a token amount to another city or country, when such activity is not consistent with the customer's business or history;

- The account for the customer is at an address outside the bank's service area;
- A loan for the customer is collateralized by a certificate of deposit or other investment vehicle;
- The customer often visits the safety deposit box area immediately before making cash deposits just under a reportable threshold;
- The account or customer has frequent deposits of large amounts of currency wrapped in currency straps that have been stamped by other banks;
- The account or customer has frequent deposits of musty or extremely dirty bills.

Charities and NGOs

- Discrepancies between apparent sources of income and the amount of funds;
- Discrepancies between the size and pattern of financial activity and the stated purpose of the organization;
- Sudden upswings in the size and frequency of financial transactions, or funds are held in accounts for a prolonged period of time;
- Large and unexplained cash transactions;
- The absence of contributions to the charity from donors within the organization's home jurisdiction;
- The existence of foreign directors, particularly in combination with large outgoing transactions to the country of origin of such directors and especially if destination is a high-risk jurisdiction;
- The existence of a large number of NGOs with unexplained links: for example, several NGOs transfer money to each other or share the same address, same managers or personnel; or a large number of NGOs are related to the same community and use the services of the same gatekeeper;
- NGOs with little substance in relation to their stated purpose and financial flows (e.g., they appear to have little or no staff, suitable offices or telephone number).
- Operations in or transactions to or from high-risk jurisdictions could of course also be considered as a reason for higher scrutiny by financial institutions. It could also serve as a criterion for initiating increased attention by supervisory or other competent authorities;
- Incongruities between apparent sources and amount of funds raised or moved such as situations in which large amounts of funds are apparently raised within communities that have a very modest standard of living;
- A mismatch between the pattern and size of financial transactions on the one hand and the stated purpose and activity of the NGO on the other, for example (as mentioned above) a cultural association that after ten years of existence opens a bank account for handling the proceeds of a music festival and deposits a disproportionately large amount of money into the account;

  o A sudden increase in the frequency and amounts of financial transactions for the account of an NGO or the inverse, that is, the NGO appears to hold funds in its account for a very long period.

Correspondent Banking
  o The countries involved in the movement of funds, especially if the account holder is regularly sending funds to a high risk jurisdiction;
  o A pattern of transactions for a single account to multiple recipients;
  o Multiple transactions from different accounts to a single recipient;
  o Large or unusual transactions not consistent with the bank's expectations of the relationship;
  o Unusually large numbers of wire transfers;
  o Transactions conducted in bursts of activity within a short period of time;
  o Unexplained repetitive or unusual patterns of wires;
  o High number of rejected wires;
  o Behavior indicative of nested accounts or third-party financial institutions which have not clearly been identified;
  o The routing of transactions involving a respondent bank through several jurisdictions and/or financial institutions prior to or following entry into the Bank without any apparent purpose other than to disguise the nature, source, ownership or control of the funds;
  o Beneficiaries maintaining accounts at foreign banks that have been the subject of previous suspicious activity reporting due to suspicious wire or other activity.

Credit Transactions
  o A customer's financial statement makes representations that do not conform to accounting principles;
  o A transaction is made to appear more complicated than need be by the use of nonsensical terms, e.g., "prime bank note";
  o A customer requests loans secured by obligations of offshore banks;
  o A customer collateralizes a loan with a cash deposit;
  o A customer purchases CD's and uses them for collateral for a loan;
  o A customer wishes to collateralize a loan with cash deposited in an offshore institution;
  o A customer's loan proceeds are unexpectedly transferred offshore;
  o A large business customer presents financial documents not prepared by an accountant;
  o A business customer presents financial statements noticeably different form those of similar businesses;
  o A customer maintains an inordinately and unusual number of accounts for his type of business;
  o A business account does not show periodic or regular activity.

Cross Border
- U.S. bank increases sales or exchanges of large denomination U.S. bank notes to Mexican financial institution(s);
- Large volumes of small denomination U.S. banknotes being sent from Mexican casas de cambio to their U.S. accounts via armored transport or sold directly to U.S. banks. These sales or exchanges may involve jurisdictions outside of Mexico;
- Casas de cambio direct the remittance of funds via multiple funds transfers to jurisdictions outside of Mexico that bear no apparent business relationship with the casas de cambio. Funds transfer recipients may include individuals, businesses, and other entities in free trade zones;
- Casas de cambio deposit numerous third-party items, including sequentially numbered monetary instruments, to their accounts at U.S. banks;
- Casas de cambio direct the remittance of funds transfers from their accounts at Mexican financial institutions to accounts at U.S. banks. These funds transfers follow the deposit of currency and third-party items by the casas de cambio into their Mexican financial institution.

Currency Transaction Activity
- A sanitation company that makes numerous deposits of cash;
- A customer is accompanied by another customer and goes to different tellers to deposit sums just under the reporting limit;
- A customer opens several accounts in different names and makes cash deposits in each one under the reporting threshold;
- Unusually large deposits through night deposit boxes;
- A customer deposits or withdrawals of large amounts of cash for no apparent business purpose;
- A customer conducts large transactions at different branches on the same day;
- A customer consolidates account sums each just underneath the reporting limit and the n wires the funds internationally;
- A customer attempts to take part of a transaction back (over the threshold) after learning that there will be a report filed on the transaction;
- Multiple cash deposits just under the reporting limit at an ATM;
- Corporate account activity in cash;
- Customer deposits of currency in wrapped in straps stamped from other banks;
- Retail customers conducting an unusual amount of foreign currency transactions;
- Substantial deposit(s) of numerous $50 and $100 bills;
- The customer's account shows numerous currency or cashiers check transactions aggregating to significant sums.

Customer's Business or Occupation (inconsistent activity)

o   A customer opens several accounts for the type of business he or she purportedly is conducting and/or frequently transfers funds among those accounts;

o   A customer's corporate account(s) has deposits or withdrawals primarily in cash rather than checks;

o   The owner of both a retail business and a check cashing service does not ask for cash when depositing checks, possibly indicating the availability of another source of cash;

o   The customer engages in unusual activity in cash purchases of traveler's checks, money orders, or cashier's checks;

o   A large volume of cashier's checks, money orders, and/or wire transfers are deposited into an account in which the nature of the account holder's business would not appear to justify such activity;

o   A customer frequently makes large dollar transactions (such as deposits, withdrawals, or purchases of monetary instruments) without an explanation as to how they will be used in the business, or the purchases allegedly are for a business that generally does not deal in large amounts of cash;

o   A business account history that shows little or no regular, periodic activity; the account appears to be used primarily as a temporary repository for funds that are transferred abroad. For example, numerous deposits of cash followed by lump-sum wire transfers;

o   A customer's place of business or residence is outside the financial Institution's service area;

o   A corporate customer who frequently makes large cash deposits and maintains high balances, but does not use other banking services;

o   A retail business routinely makes numerous deposits of checks, but rarely makes cash withdrawals for daily operations;

o   A retail business has dramatically different patterns of cash deposits from similar businesses in the same general location;

o   The currency transaction patterns of a business experience a sudden and inconsistent change from normal activities;

o   The amount and frequency of cash deposits are inconsistent with that observed at the customer's place of business;

o   The business frequently deposits large amounts of cash, but checks or other debits drawn against the account are inconsistent with the customer's retail business;

o   Businesses that do not normally generate currency make numerous currency transactions (i.e., a sanitation company that makes numerous deposits of cash);

o   Financial transactions involving monetary instruments that are incomplete or contain fictitious payees, remitters, etc., if known;

o   Unusual transfer of funds among related accounts or accounts that involve the same principal or related principals;

o   A business owner, such as an owner who has only one store, who makes several deposits the same day using different bank branches.

Embassy and Foreign Consulate Accounts
- Official embassy business is conducted through personal accounts;
- Account activity is not consistent with the purpose of the account, such as pouch activity or payable upon proper identification transactions;
- Accounts are funded through substantial currency transactions;
- Accounts directly fund personal expenses of foreign nationals without appropriate controls, including, but not limited to, expenses for college students.

Foreign Correspondent Banking
- The countries involved in the movement of funds are high risk jurisdictions;
- A pattern of transactions for a single account to multiple recipients;
- Multiple transactions from different accounts to a single recipient;
- Large or unusual transactions not consistent with the bank's expectations of the relationship;
- Unusually large numbers of wire transfers;
- Transactions conducted in bursts of activity within a short period of time;
- Unexplained repetitive or unusual patterns of wires;
- High number of rejected wires;
- Identify behavior indicative of nested accounts or third-party financial institutions which have not clearly been identified. Nested accounts occur when a foreign financial institution gains access to the Bank by operating through a correspondent account belonging to another foreign financial institution;
- The routing of transactions involving a Respondent Bank through several jurisdictions and/or financial institutions prior to or following entry into the Bank without any apparent purpose other than to disguise the nature, source, ownership or control of the funds;
- Beneficiaries maintaining accounts at foreign banks that have been the subject of previous suspicious activity reporting due to suspicious wire or other activity.

Funds Transfer Activity
- Wire transfer activity to/from financial secrecy haven countries without an apparent business; reason or when it is inconsistent with the customer's business or history;
- Periodic wire transfers from a personal account(s) to bank secrecy haven countries;
- Large incoming wire transfers on behalf of a foreign client with little or no explicit reason;
- Frequent or large volume of wire transfers to and from offshore banking centers;
- Large, round dollar amounts;
- Funds transferred in and out of an account on the same day or within a relatively short period of time;

o   Payments or receipts with no apparent links to legitimate contracts, goods, or services;
o   Transfers routed through multiple foreign or domestic banks;
o   Unexplained repetitive or unusual patterns of activity;
o   Deposits of funds into several accounts, usually in amounts of less than $3000, which are consolidated subsequently into one master account and transferred, often outside of the country;
o   Instructions to a financial institution to wire transfer funds abroad and to expect an incoming wire transfer of funds (in an equal amount) from other sources;
o   Regular deposits or withdrawals of large amounts of cash, using wire transfers to, from, or through countries that either are known sources of narcotics or whose laws are ineffective in controlling the laundering of money;
o   Many small incoming wire transfers of funds received or deposits made using checks and money orders, with all but a token amount almost immediately being wire transferred to another city or country, in a manner inconsistent with the customer's business or history;
o   Large volume of wire transfers from persons or businesses that do not hold accounts;
o   The customer's account has unexplained or sudden extensive wire activity, especially in accounts that had little or no previous activity;
o   The customer's account has a large number of wire transfers to unrelated third parties inconsistent with the customer's legitimate business purpose;
o   The customer's account indicates large or frequent wire transfers, immediately withdrawn by check or debit card without any apparent business purpose.

Insufficient and/or Suspicious Customer Information
o   An individual customer is unwilling or unable to provide identification or information;
o   An individual customer provides different identification or information each time he or she conducts a transaction:
   ▪   Different name or different spelling of name;
   ▪   Different address or different spelling or numeration in address;
   ▪   Different identification types;
       •   An individual customer without a local address, who appears to reside locally because he or she is a repeat customer;
       •   A legitimate ID that appears to have been altered;
       •   An identification document in which the description of the individual does not match the customer's appearance (e.g. different age, height, eye color, sex);
       •   An expired identification document;

- An individual customer who presents any unusual or suspicious identification document or information;
  - A business customer that is reluctant to provide complete information regarding:
    - the type of business;
    - the purpose of the transaction;
    - or, any other information requested by a bank officer or representative.

Insurance

- The purchase of an insurance product that appears to be inconsistent with a customer's needs;
- Any unusual method of payment, particularly by cash or cash equivalents (when such method is, in fact, unusual);
- The purchase of an insurance product with monetary instruments in structured amounts;
- The early termination of an insurance product, especially at a cost to the customer, or where cash was tendered and/or the refund check is directed to an apparently unrelated third party;
- The transfer of the benefit of an insurance product to an apparently unrelated third party;
- Little or no concern by a customer for the investment performance of an insurance product, but much concern about the early termination features of the product;
- The reluctance by a customer to provide identifying information when purchasing an insurance product, or the provision of minimal or seemingly fictitious information;
- The borrowing of the maximum amount available soon after purchasing the product;
- Money from a recently-purchased policy or contract was distributed:
  - as a partial or full surrender;
  - as part of the *free-look pe*riod;
  - as a loan;
  - through a falsified claim.
- A transaction is sought that is not appropriate to standard market activities;
- A transaction request is made by, or payment is received from, a third party or one whose identity is not disclosed or whose relationship to the owner is unclear;
- A large, single-premium policy is requested, which would be paid through a foreign financial institution;
- The owners or beneficiaries of the policy or contract:
  - Are foreign nationals;
  - Do not wish to disclose the identity of the ultimate beneficiary; or,
  - Are reluctant to reveal information requested in an application or other document.

- The premiums were paid with wired funds, and the customer has asked that the institution immediately transfer the funds to a third party via check or wire transfer;
- The owner of the policy or contract requested that funds be transferred to a third party in a country sanctioned by the U.S. Office of Foreign Assets Control;
- The customer's business history is elusive, inconsistent or non-existent;
- The policy or contract history has a pattern of repeated loans that are paid promptly;
- The customer makes payments (premium payments, etc.) under the policy with:
  - cash
  - multiple cashier's checks;
  - third-party payments;
  - money orders;
  - third-party payer checks of under US$10,000.
- There is a sudden flurry of extensive wire activity;
- Large or frequent wire transfers are made to the policy and withdrawn immediately;
- Premiums are paid by third parties;
- A broker pays the customer's premiums out if his own account and is reimbursed later by the customer (in cash, etc.);
- Repeat premium policy purchases by the same client;
- A customer attempts to borrow maximum cash value of a single premium policy soon after purchase;
- The purchaser of the policy is unemployed, yet purchases high regular premium/numerous policies/single premium policy(ies);
- Client has an abnormal number of single premium policies which do not make sense when considering his/her's known financial capabilities, occupation/business;
- A request to purchase a large single premium policy or series of small single premium policies by an unknown client or by an existing policyholder whose current policies are of only small regular premium amounts;
- Clients making large Top-Ups (supplementary payments) or a series of Top-Ups which when bearing in mind the client's occupation and financial commitments (including premium payments under existing policies) are considered to be excessive;
- Where a proposer has the habit of applying for numerous single premium policies but then cancels such proposals during the Cooling Off Period and, hence, obtains refunds via a check from an insurance company which he/she can use to buy further investments. (Why is he in the first place buying numerous small policies?);
- Clients paying an abnormal number of premiums/Top-Ups in a short period of time e.g. 12 months;

- Clients insisting to enter into a policy with a premium, whether regular or single premium which appears to be considerably beyond their means;
- Where a client surrenders his/her Single Premium policy and requests the proceeds to be forwarded to a Bank to pay off a loan (especially if the policy has only been recently purchased);
- Where a single premium or a large regular premium policy or a series of small single/regular premium policies are surrendered or a request for a surrender value is requested soon after the issuing of the policy e.g. two years;
- A proposer who does not seem interested in the estimated maturity values but makes enquires on estimated surrender values;
- Where a proposer for a single premium policy indicates at proposal stage that he/she will surrender the policy soon after it is issued (e.g. 1 or 2 years);
- An intermediary who has an abnormal number of clients surrendering Single Premium policies at a very early stage e.g. within the first 2 years of the policy;
- Nominated Beneficiaries were the same ones who had paid the premium;
- Nominated Beneficiaries are high risk clients or come from high risk countries;
- There is no apparent relationship between the beneficiary and the policyholder;
- The source of funds is unclear.

Know Your Employee
- Lavish lifestyle cannot be supported by an employee's salary;
- Absence of conformity with recognized systems and controls, particularly in private banking;
- Reluctance to take a vacation.

Lending
- Purpose of loan is not recorded;
- Proceeds of loan are used for a purpose other than the purpose recorded;
- Prepayment of interest on deposit accounts where such deposit accounts are used as collateral for loans;
- Anytime a bank seriously considers a loan request where the bank would have to obtain brokered deposits to be able to fund the loan should be viewed with suspicion;
- Promise of large dollar deposits in consideration for favorable treatment on loan requests. (Deposits are not pledged as collateral for the loans);
- Out-of-territory lending;
- Cash-secured loans;
- Loans that do not fit the customer's general business profile;
- Premature cancellation of debt, particularly with cash.

Monetary Instrument Activities
- o The instruments were purchased on the same or consecutive days from different locations;
- o The instruments are numbered consecutively in amounts just under $3,000 or $10,000;
- o The payee lines are left blank or made out to the same person (or to only a few people);
- o The instruments contain little or no purchaser information;
- o The instruments bear the same stamp symbol or initials;
- o The instruments were purchased in round denominations or repetitive amounts;
- o A customer frequently makes large dollar transactions (such as deposits, withdrawals, or purchases of monetary instruments) without an explanation as to how they will be used in the business, or the purchases allegedly are for a business that generally does not deal in large amounts of cash;
- o Financial transactions involving monetary instruments that are incomplete or contain fictitious payees, remitters, etc., if known;
- o A person or business that does not hold an account and that purchases a monetary instrument with large denominated bills;
- o Unusual monetary instrument or check activity associated with international brokered deposits.

Non-Cash Transactions
- o Deposits of a large number of traveler's checks in the same denomination and sequence;
- o A Customer deposits money orders bearing strange markings;
- o A Customer deposits large numbers of consecutively numbered money orders of large dollar amounts;
- o A Customer deposits checks and/or money orders not consistent with the nature of his business;
- o A Customer's funds are moved quickly out of her account via payment methods inconsistent with the established purpose or ownership of the account.

Non-Resident Aliens
- o Accounts characterized by small cash deposits and checks written to purchase large ticket items, sometimes located in the Florida and Panama free trade zones. These accounts also lack typical payments for housing, utilities, and credit cards, etc. (i.e., indicative of Black Market Peso Exchange (BMPE);
- o Structured deposits, including frequent deposits in round-dollar amounts, between $2,000 and $10,000;
- o Funds transfer activity to or from high-risk geographies;
- o A large volume of transaction activity with low average monthly account balances;
- o Checks drawn in large or round-dollar amounts;

o   The absence of ATM and point-of-sale transactions and of checks written for small odd-dollar amounts;

o   A high volume of incoming and outgoing wire transfers from various domestic and international accounts held in the names of unrelated individuals and corporations;

o   A high volume of check structuring activity;

o   The deposit of sequential and otherwise structured checks from multiple sources unaffiliated with the account;

o   Accounts controlled by NRAs but held in the name of offshore corporations;

o   Accounts controlled by domestic businesses that sell or export goods to South American customers, but generally receive payments from United States sources;

o   Individual accounts held by NRAs and US residents being used to transmit funds for unrelated persons;

o   A foreign person or entity opening a domestic account in a manner designed to avoid foreign laws or regulations;

o   A foreign person or entity opening a domestic account in a manner that makes it difficult to trace account transactions to the beneficial owner.

OFAC (the bank must block transactions that):

o   Are by or on behalf of a blocked individual or entity;

o   Are to or through a blocked entity;

o   Are in connection with a transaction in which a blocked individual or entity has an interest.

Offshore Lending

o   A large volume of cashier's checks or money orders deposited to an account where the Loans made on the strength of a borrower's financial statement reflects major investments in and income from businesses incorporated in bank secrecy haven countries;

o   Loans secured by obligations of offshore banks;

Pouch Activities

o   The instruments contained in the pouch were purchased on the same or consecutive days from different locations;

o   The instruments contained in the pouch are numbered consecutively in amounts just under $3,000 or $10,000;

o   The instruments contained in the pouch show payee lines left blank or made out to the same person (or to only a few people);

o   The instruments contained in the pouch detail little or no purchaser information;

o   The instruments contained in the pouch bear the same stamp symbol or initials;

o   The instruments contained in the pouch are purchased in round denominations or repetitive amounts.

Real Estate
- A customer attempts to buy with funds from a high risk country;
- A seller requests that proceeds be sent to a high risk country;
- A customer acts as an intermediary for an undisclosed party and will not say why or comment on his or her relationship to the person;
- A customer wants to use cash for the purchase of real estate;
- A customer in a transaction presents suspicious identification documents;
- A customer attempts to buy real estate in another name for no apparent reason;
- A customer buys and sells the same property quickly;
- A customer buys much for no apparent purpose;
- A prospective buyer or seller has documents reflecting something other than

Securities Transactions
- A customer engages in transactions in penny stocks or *Reg S* securities that have been used in connection with fraudulent schemes;
- A customer makes a deposit for the purpose of a long term investment purchase, then shortly thereafter, liquidates the position and transfers the funds out of the account.

Shell Company Activity
- A bank is unable to obtain sufficient information or information is unavailable to positively identify originators or beneficiaries of accounts or other banking activity (using Internet, commercial database searches, or direct inquiries to a respondent bank);
- Payments to or from the company have no stated purpose, do not reference goods or services, or identify only a contract or invoice number;
- Goods or services, if identified, do not match profile of company provided by respondent bank or character of the financial activity; a company references remarkably dissimilar goods and services in related funds transfers; explanation given by foreign respondent bank is inconsistent with observed funds transfer activity;
- Transacting businesses share the same address, provide only a registered agent's address, or have other address inconsistencies;
- Unusually large number and variety of beneficiaries are receiving funds transfers from one company;
- Frequent involvement of multiple jurisdictions or beneficiaries located in high-risk offshore financial centers;
- A foreign correspondent bank exceeds the expected volume in its client profile for funds transfers, or an individual company exhibits a high volume and pattern of funds transfers that is inconsistent with its normal business activity;
- Multiple high-value payments or transfers between shell companies with no apparent legitimate business purpose;
- Purpose of the shell company is unknown or unclear.

Structuring

- A customer, or group of customers, attempt to hide the size of a large cash transaction by breaking it into multiple, smaller transactions by, for example, conducting the smaller transactions:
  - At different times on the same day;
  - With different MSB cashiers on the same day or different days;
  - At different branches of the same MSB on the same or different days;
- A customer, or group of customers, conduct several similar transactions over several days, staying just under reporting or record keeping limits each time;
- A customer is reluctant to provide information needed for a reporting or record keeping requirement, whether required by law or by company policy;
- A customer who is reluctant to proceed with a transaction after being informed that a report must be filed or a record made;
- A customer breaks down a single large transaction into smaller transactions after being informed that a report must be filed or a record made;
- A customer presents different identification each time a transaction is conducted;
- A customer spells his/her name differently or uses a different name each time he/she initiates or receives a money transfer or purchases traveler's checks;
- Any individual or group that forces or attempts to force a Bank employee not to file any required reporting forms or create a record required by law or company policy;
- By the same send customer, each transfer in an amount just under $3,000 (or other relevant threshold);
- By multiple send customers initiated at one branch location within minutes of each other, each transfer in an amount just under $3,000 (or other relevant threshold);
- A customer cashing multiple instruments (money orders, traveler's checks, cashiers' checks, foreign drafts) that appear to have been purchased in a structured manner (e.g. each in an amount below $3,000).

Trade Finance

- A customer seeks trade financing for commodities whose stated prices are well above or below market rates;
- A customer makes a letter of credit beneficiary change just prior to payment;
- A customer changes the place of payment in a letter of credit to an account in a country other than the beneficiary's stated location;
- A customer using a standby letter of credit as a performance bond without the normal reference to an underlying project, or in favor of unusual beneficiaries;

o   A steel company that starts dealing in paper products, or an information technology company that starts dealing in bulk pharmaceuticals);

o   Customers conducting business in high-risk jurisdictions;

o   Customers shipping items through high-risk jurisdictions, including transit through non-cooperative countries;

o   Customers involved in potentially high-risk activities, including activities that may be subject to export/import restrictions (e.g., equipment for military or police organizations of foreign governments, weapons, ammunition, chemical mixtures, classified defense articles, sensitive technical data, nuclear materials, precious gems, or certain natural resources such as metals, ore, and crude oil);

o   Obvious over or under pricing of goods and services;

o   Obvious misrepresentation of quantity or type of goods imported or exported.

o   Transaction structure appears unnecessarily complex and designed to obscure the true nature of the transaction;

o   Customer requests payment of proceeds to an unrelated third party;

o   Shipment locations or description of goods not consistent with letter of credit.

o   Documentation showing a higher or lower value or cost of merchandise than that which was declared to customs or paid by the importer;

o   Significantly amended letters of credit without reasonable justification or changes to the beneficiary or location of payment. Any changes in the names of parties should prompt additional OFAC review.

Terrorist Financing Defined

The motivation behind terrorist financing is ideological, as opposed to profit-seeking, which is generally the motivation for most crimes associated with money laundering. Terrorism is intended to intimidate a population or to compel a government or an international organization to do or abstain from doing any specific act through the threat of violence. An effective financial infrastructure is critical to terrorist operations. Terrorist groups develop sources of funding that are relatively mobile to ensure that funds can be used to obtain material and other logistical items needed to commit terrorist acts. Thus, money laundering is often a vital component of terrorist financing.

Terrorists generally finance their activities through both unlawful and legitimate sources. Unlawful activities, such as extortion, kidnapping, and narcotics trafficking, have been found to be a major source of funding. Trends observed of terrorist groups over time, however, support the notion that high risk activities, such as kidnapping or bank robbery become counterproductive to groups' long term efforts to raise money. Additionally, the financing of terrorist activities like those in Madrid and London, both essentially self-financed by independent cells through drug dealing and legitimate employment (respectively), illustrates the difficulty of establishing a terrorism nexus with other suspicious financial activity that may be detected by a financial institution.

Other observed activities include:
  o   Smuggling, fraud, theft;
  o   Robbery, identity theft;
  o   Use of conflict diamonds; and,
  o   Improper use of charitable or relief funds.

In the last case, donors may have no knowledge that their donations have been diverted to support terrorist causes. Other legitimate sources have also been found to provide terrorist organizations with funding, including foreign government sponsorship and business ownership.

FinCEN Analysis of SAR Filings

As part of its support to law enforcement, FinCEN routinely prepares referral packages developed from SARs and other BSA information. After September 11th, FinCEN reviewed such referrals to evaluate whether any of those cases could possibly involve mechanisms to fund terrorist activities. Five such cases revealed that traditional methods of money laundering were used and at least one of the following other indicators was involved:

  o   Movement of funds through state sponsors of terrorism and countries listed as having highly active anti-American terrorist activities;
  o   Use of unfamiliar charity/relief organization as a link in transactions;
  o   Wire transfer activities to and from multiple relief and/or charitable organizations, domestic and foreign; and/or,
  o   The individual or entity involved is identified on one of the lists of suspected terrorists, terrorist organizations, or associated individuals or entities.

While these indicators alone may not indicate terrorist funding, when combined with the common indicators of financial crime and money laundering, investigators may find this information useful and determine that additional scrutiny is warranted. Additionally, when one or several of the potentially suspicious factors exists in regard to a specific financial transaction (especially when the individual or entity may appear on one of the lists of suspected terrorists, terrorist organizations, or associated individuals or entities), an investigator would have cause to increase his scrutiny of the transaction and any associated individuals or entities.

The following methods have been used by organized crime and drug traffickers for decades to launder their illegal proceeds. Some of the common indicators of money laundering and other financial crime include:

- Financial activity inconsistent with the stated purpose of the business;
- Financial activity not commensurate with stated occupation;
- Use of multiple accounts at a single bank for no apparent legitimate purpose;
- Importation of high dollar currency and traveler's checks not commensurate with stated occupation;
- Significant and even dollar deposits to personal accounts over a short period;
- Structuring of deposits at multiple bank branches to avoid BSA requirements;
- Refusal by any party conducting transactions to provide identification;
- Apparent use of personal account for business purposes;
- Abrupt change in account activity;
- Use of multiple personal and business accounts to collect and then funnel funds to a small number of foreign beneficiaries;
- Deposits are followed within a short period of time by wire transfers of funds;
- Deposits of a combination of monetary instruments atypical of legitimate business activity (business checks, payroll checks and social security checks); and,
- Movement of funds through countries or territories with lax anti-money laundering controls.

See the Terrorist Financing Red Flags section for a more complete listing of associated red flags.

Note: Transactions to or from jurisdictions associated with terrorist activity, or conducted by persons with possible affiliations with jurisdictions associated with terrorist activity should not be the only factors that prompt the filing of a SAR. However, this information may be relevant and should be considered in conjunction with other relevant information in deciding whether a SAR is warranted (as set forth in 31 CFR 103.18 and the regulations prescribed by the bank regulatory agencies, such as a lack of any apparent legal or business purpose to a transaction or series of transactions.)

Resources that should be consulted about jurisdictions potentially associated with terrorism include:

- o   The State Department's list of State sponsors of terrorism;
- o   The Treasury Department's Office of Foreign Assets Controls (OFAC) lists of foreign terrorists; and,
- o   The FATF's list of Non-cooperative Countries and Territories (when any exist).

SARs identifying terrorist financing as the suspicious activity decreased 25% since 2004. However, in the first six months of 2007, Terrorist Financing filings increased 19% from the corresponding six-month period in 2006.

Terrorist Financing Red Flags

Since September 11, it has become clear that it can be difficult to definitively identify terrorist fund raising activities separate and apart from traditional money laundering and financial crime activities. Currently, there is no exhaustive or exclusive list of terrorist indicators that the government is able to provide. FinCEN and law enforcement continue to develop indicative and distinct typologies which may be associated with terrorist financing. The following activities in and of themselves might not be terror financing related. However, they have been identified as activities employed by terrorists.

- Funds are generated by a business owned by persons of the same origin or by a business that involves persons of the same origin from high-risk countries (e.g., countries designated by national authorities and FATF as non-cooperative countries and territories);
- The stated occupation of the customer is not commensurate with the type or level of activity;
- Persons involved in currency transactions share an address or phone number, particularly when the address is also a business location or does not seem to correspond to the stated occupation (e.g., student, unemployed, or self-employed);
- Regarding nonprofit or charitable organizations, financial transactions occur for which there appears to be no logical economic purpose or in which there appears to be no link between the stated activity of the organization and the other parties in the transaction;
- A safe deposit box opened on behalf of a commercial entity when the business activity of the customer is unknown or such activity does not appear to justify the use of a safe deposit box;
- Financial activity inconsistent with the stated purpose of the business;
- Financial activity not commensurate with stated occupation;
- Use of multiple accounts at a single bank for no apparent legitimate purpose;
- Importation of high dollar currency and traveler's checks not commensurate with stated occupation;
- Significant and even dollar deposits to personal accounts over a short period;
- Structuring of deposits at multiple bank branches to avoid BSA requirements;
- Refusal by any party conducting transactions to provide identification;
- Apparent use of personal account for business purposes;
- Abrupt change in account activity;
- Use of multiple personal and business accounts to collect and then funnel funds to a small number of foreign beneficiaries;
- Deposits are followed within a short period of time by wire transfers of funds;
- Deposits of a combination of monetary instruments atypical of legitimate business activity (business checks, payroll checks and social security checks); and,

o   Movement of funds through FATF designated non-cooperative countries or territories (NCCTs) or those with lax anti-money laundering controls.

Account Profile of 9–11 Hijackers

Through reconstruction of available financial information, the FBI established how the hijackers responsible for the September 11th attacks received their money and how money was moved out of accounts. The 19 hijackers opened 24 domestic bank accounts at four different banks. The following financial profile was developed from the hijackers' domestic accounts:

o   Accounts were opened with cash/cash equivalents in the average amount of $3,000 to $5,000;

o   Identification used to open the accounts were visas issued through foreign governments;

o   Accounts were opened within 30 days after entry into the U.S;

o   All accounts were normal checking accounts with debit cards;

o   The hijackers tended to open accounts in groups of three or four individuals;

o   Some of the accounts were joint accounts;

o   Addresses used usually were not permanent (i.e., mail boxes) and changed frequently;

o   The hijackers often used the same address/telephone numbers on the accounts;

o   No savings accounts or safe deposit boxes were opened;

o   The hijackers opened their accounts at branches of large, well known banks;

o   Twelve hijackers opened accounts at the same bank.

Transaction Profile of 9–11 Hijackers

o   Some accounts directly received/sent wire transfers of small amounts from/ to foreign countries such as United Arab Emirates (UAE), Saudi Arabia, and Germany;

o   Hijackers made numerous attempts of cash withdrawals that often exceeded the limit of the debit card;

o   High percentage of withdrawals was from debit cards;

o   Low percentage of checks was written;

o   Numerous balance inquiries were made;

o   After a deposit was made, withdrawals occurred immediately;

o   There was no discernible pattern with the timing of deposits/disbursements;

o   Account transactions did not reflect normal living expenses for rent, utilities, auto payments, insurance, etc.;

o   Funding for daily expenditures was not evident from transactions;

o   Overall transactions were below reporting requirements;

o   Funding of the accounts was by cash and overseas wire transfers;

o   ATM transactions occurred with more than one hijacker present (uninterrupted series of transactions involving several hijackers at the same ATM);

o   Debit cards were used by hijackers who did not own the accounts.

International Activity of 9–11 Hijackers

- o Three of the hijackers supplemented their financing by opening foreign checking accounts and credit card accounts at banks located in the UAE;
- o While in the U.S., two of the hijackers had deposits made on their behalf by unknown individuals;
- o Hijackers on all four flights purchased traveler's checks overseas and brought them into the U.S. These traveler's checks were partially deposited into their U.S. checking accounts;
- o Three of the hijackers (pilots/leaders) continued to maintain bank accounts in Germany after moving to the U.S;
- o Two of the hijackers (pilots/leaders) had credit cards issued by German banks and maintained those cards after moving to the U.S.;
- o One of the hijackers (pilot/leader) received substantial funding through wire transfers into his German bank account in 1998 and 1999 from one individual;
- o In 1999, this same hijacker opened an account in UAE, giving power of attorney over the account to the same individual who had been wiring money to his German account;
- o More than $100,000 was wired from the UAE account of the hijacker to the German account of the same hijacker in a 15-month period.

FinCEN Analysis of SAR Filings and other BSA information

After September 11th, FinCEN reviewed referral packages developed from SARs to evaluate whether any of those cases could possibly involve mechanisms to fund terrorist activities. Five such cases revealed that traditional methods of money laundering were used and at least one of the following other indicators was involved:

- o Movement of funds through state sponsors of terrorism and countries listed as having highly active anti-American terrorist activities [6];

Table 3: Countries Designated as State Sponsors of Terrorism

Country	Designation Date
Cuba	March 1, 1982
Iran	January 19, 1984
Sudan	August 12, 1993
Syria	December 29,1979

- o Use of unfamiliar charity/relief organization as a link in transactions;
- o Wire transfers activity to and from multiple relief and/or charitable organizations, domestic and foreign; and/or,
- o The individual or entity involved is identified on one of the lists of suspected terrorists, terrorist organizations, or associated individuals or entities.

While these indicators alone may not indicate terrorist funding, when combined with the common indicators of financial crime and money laundering (listed below), the banks' investigators may find this information useful and determine that additional scrutiny is warranted. Additionally, when one or several of the potentially suspicious factors exists in regard to a specific financial transaction especially when the individual or entity may appear on one of the lists of suspected terrorists, terrorist organizations, or associated individuals or entities, a financial institution would have cause to increase its scrutiny of the transaction and any associated individuals or entities.

The following methods have been used by organized crime and drug traffickers for decades to launder their illegal proceeds. Some of them are common indicators of money laundering and other financial crime (noted in the Money Laundering Red Flags section) and include:

- Financial activity inconsistent with the stated purpose of the business;
- Financial activity not commensurate with stated occupation;
- Use of multiple accounts at a single bank for no apparent legitimate purpose;
- Importation of high dollar currency and traveler's checks not commensurate with stated occupation;
- Significant and even dollar deposits to personal accounts over a short period;
- Structuring of deposits at multiple bank branches to avoid BSA requirements;
- Refusal by any party conducting transactions to provide identification;
- Apparent use of personal account for business purposes;
- Abrupt change in account activity;
- Use of multiple personal and business accounts to collect and then funnel funds to a small number of foreign beneficiaries;
- Deposits are followed within a short period of time by wire transfers of funds;
- Deposits of a combination of monetary instruments atypical of legitimate business activity (business checks, payroll checks and social security checks); and,
- Movement of funds through FATF designated non-cooperative countries or territories (NCCTs).

Terrorist Exclusion List (TEL)

The Secretary of State is authorized to designate groups on its TEL in consultation with, or upon the request of the Attorney General. An organization can be placed on the TEL if the Secretary of State finds that the organization:

- o   Commits or incites to commit, under circumstances indicating an intention to cause death or serious bodily injury, a terrorist activity;
- o   Prepares or plans a terrorist activity;
- o   Gathers information on potential targets for terrorist activity; or
- o   Provides material support to further terrorist activity.

Currently, the TEL [7] includes the following organizations:

1. Afghan Support Committee (a.k.a. Ahya ul Turas; a.k.a. Jamiat Ayat-ur-Rhas al Islamia; a.k.a. Jamiat Ihya ul Turath al Islamia; a.k.a. Lajnat el Masa Eidatul Afghania)
2. Al Taqwa Trade, Property and Industry Company Ltd. (f.k.a. Al Taqwa Trade, Property and Industry; f.k.a. Al Taqwa Trade, Property and Industry Establishment; f.k.a. Himmat Establishment; a.k.a. Waldenberg, AG)
3. Al-Hamati Sweets Bakeries
4. Al-Ittihad al-Islami (AIAI)
5. Al-Manar
6. Al-Ma'unah
7. Al-Nur Honey Center
8. Al-Rashid Trust
9. Al-Shifa Honey Press for Industry and Commerce
10. Al-Wafa al-Igatha al-Islamia (a.k.a. Wafa Humanitarian Organization; a.k.a. Al Wafa; a.k.a. Al Wafa Organization)
11. Alex Boncayao Brigade (ABB)
12. Anarchist Faction for Overthrow
13. Army for the Liberation of Rwanda (ALIR) (a.k.a. Interahamwe, Former Armed Forces (EX-FAR))
14. Asbat al-Ansar
15. Babbar Khalsa International
16. Bank Al Taqwa Ltd. (a.k.a. Al Taqwa Bank; a.k.a. Bank Al Taqwa)
17. Black Star
18. Communist Party of Nepal (Maoist) (a.k.a. CPN(M); a.k.a. the United Revolutionary People's Council, a.k.a. the People's Liberation Army of Nepal)
19. Continuity Irish Republican Army (CIRA) (a.k.a. Continuity Army Council)
20. Darkazanli Company
21. Dhamat Houmet Daawa Salafia (a.k.a. Group Protectors of Salafist Preaching; a.k.a. Houmat Ed Daawa Es Salifiya; a.k.a. Katibat El Ahoual; a.k.a. Protectors of the Salafist Predication; a.k.a. El-Ahoual Battalion; a.k.a. Katibat El Ahouel; a.k.a. Houmate Ed-Daawa Es-Salafia; a.k.a. the Horror Squadron; a.k.a. Djamaat Houmat Eddawa Essalafia; a.k.a. Djamaatt Houmat Ed Daawa Es Salafiya; a.k.a. Salafist Call Protectors; a.k.a. Djamaat Houmat Ed Daawa Es Salafiya; a.k.a. Houmate el Da'awaa es-

Salafiyya; a.k.a. Protectors of the Salafist Call; a.k.a. Houmat ed-Daaoua es-Salafia; a.k.a. Group of Supporters of the Salafiste Trend; a.k.a. Group of Supporters of the Salafist Trend)

22. Eastern Turkistan Islamic Movement (a.k.a. Eastern Turkistan Islamic Party; a.k.a. ETIM; a.k.a. ETIP)
23. First of October Antifascist Resistance Group (GRAPO) (a.k.a. Grupo de Resistencia Anti-Fascista Premero De Octubre)
24. Harakat ul Jihad i Islami (HUJI)
25. International Sikh Youth Federation
26. Islamic Army of Aden
27. Islamic Renewal and Reform Organization
28. Jamiat al-Ta'awun al-Islamiyya
29. Jamiat ul-Mujahideen (JUM)
30. Japanese Red Army (JRA)
31. Jaysh-e-Mohammed
32. Jayshullah
33. Jerusalem Warriors
34. Lashkar-e-Tayyiba (LET) (a.k.a. Army of the Righteous)
35. Libyan Islamic Fighting Group
36. Loyalist Volunteer Force (LVF)
37. Makhtab al-Khidmat
38. Moroccan Islamic Combatant Group (a.k.a. GICM; a.k.a. Groupe Islamique Combattant Marocain)
39. Nada Management Organization (f.k.a. Al Taqwa Management Organization SA)
40. New People's Army (NPA)
41. Orange Volunteers (OV)
42. People Against Gangsterism and Drugs (PAGAD)
43. Red Brigades-Combatant Communist Party (BR-PCC)
44. Red Hand Defenders (RHD)
45. Revival of Islamic Heritage Society (Pakistan and Afghanistan offices -- Kuwait office not designated) (a.k.a. Jamia Ihya ul Turath; a.k.a. Jamiat Ihia Al- Turath Al-Islamiya; a.k.a. Revival of Islamic Society Heritage on the African Continent)
46. Revolutionary Proletarian Nucleus
47. Revolutionary United Front (RUF)
48. Salafist Group for Call and Combat (GSPC)
49. The Allied Democratic Forces (ADF)
50. The Islamic International Brigade (a.k.a. International Battalion, a.k.a. Islamic Peacekeeping International Brigade, a.k.a. Peacekeeping Battalion, a.k.a. The International Brigade, a.k.a. The Islamic Peacekeeping Army, a.k.a. The Islamic Peacekeeping Brigade)
51. The Lord's Resistance Army (LRA)
52. The Pentagon Gang
53. The Riyadus-Salikhin Reconnaissance and Sabotage Battalion of Chechen Martyrs (a.k.a. Riyadus-Salikhin Reconnaissance and Sabotage Battalion, a.k.a. Riyadh-as-Saliheen, a.k.a. the Sabotage and Military Surveillance

Group of the Riyadh al-Salihin Martyrs, a.k.a. Riyadus-Salikhin Reconnaissance and Sabotage Battalion of Shahids (Martyrs))

54. The Special Purpose Islamic Regiment (a.k.a. the Islamic Special Purpose Regiment, a.k.a. the al-Jihad-Fisi-Sabililah Special Islamic Regiment, a.k.a. Islamic Regiment of Special Meaning)

55. Tunisian Combat Group (a.k.a. GCT, a.k.a. Groupe Combattant Tunisien, a.k.a. Jama'a Combattante Tunisien, a.k.a. JCT; a.k.a. Tunisian Combatant Group)

56. Turkish Hizballah

57. Ulster Defense Association (a.k.a. Ulster Freedom Fighters)

58. Ummah Tameer E-Nau (UTN) (a.k.a. Foundation for Construction; a.k.a. Nation Building; a.k.a. Reconstruction Foundation; a.k.a. Reconstruction of the Islamic Community; a.k.a. Reconstruction of the Muslim Ummah; a.k.a. Ummah Tameer I-Nau; a.k.a. Ummah Tameer E-Nau; a.k.a. Ummah Tameer-I-Pau)

59. Youssef M. Nada & Co. Gesellschaft M.B.H.

Designated Foreign Terrorist Organizations (FTOs) [8]

The Office of the Coordinator for Counterterrorism in the State Department (S/CT) continually monitors the activities of terrorist groups active around the world to identify potential targets for designation *as Foreign Terrorist organizations*. When reviewing potential targets, S/CT looks not only at the actual terrorist attacks that a group has carried out, but also at whether the group has engaged in planning and preparations for possible future acts of terrorism or, retains the capability and intent to carry out such acts.

Current List of Designated Foreign Terrorist Organizations

1. Abu Nidal Organization (ANO)
2. Abu Sayyaf Group
3. Al-Aqsa Martyrs Brigade
4. Ansar al-Islam
5. Armed Islamic Group (GIA)
6. Asbat al-Ansar
7. Aum Shinrikyo
8. Basque Fatherland and Liberty (ETA)
9. Communist Party of the Philippines/New People's Army (CPP/NPA)
10. Continuity Irish Republican Army
11. Gama'a al-Islamiyya (Islamic Group)
12. HAMAS (Islamic Resistance Movement)
13. Harakat ul-Mujahidin (HUM)
14. Hizballah (Party of God)
15. Islamic Jihad Group
16. Islamic Movement of Uzbekistan (IMU)
17. Jaish-e-Mohammed (JEM) (Army of Mohammed)
18. Jemaah Islamiya organization (JI)
19. al-Jihad (Egyptian Islamic Jihad)
20. Kahane Chai (Kach)
21. Kongra-Gel (KGK, formerly Kurdistan Workers' Party, PKK, KADEK)
22. Lashkar-e Tayyiba (LT) (Army of the Righteous)
23. Lashkar i Jhangvi
24. Liberation Tigers of Tamil Eelam (LTTE)
25. Libyan Islamic Fighting Group (LIFG)
26. Moroccan Islamic Combatant Group (GICM)
27. Mujahedin-e Khalq Organization (MEK)
28. National Liberation Army (ELN)
29. Palestine Liberation Front (PLF)
30. Palestinian Islamic Jihad (PIJ)
31. Popular Front for the Liberation of Palestine (PFLP)
32. PFLP-General Command (PFLP-GC)
33. Tanzim Qa'idat al-Jihad fi Bilad al-Rafidayn (QJBR) (al-Qaida in Iraq) (formerly Jama'at al-Tawhid wa'al-Jihad, JTJ, al-Zarqawi Network)
34. al-Qa'ida
35. al-Qaida in the Islamic Maghreb (formerly GSPC)
36. Real IRA
37. Revolutionary Armed Forces of Colombia (FARC)

38. Revolutionary Nuclei (formerly ELA)
39. Revolutionary Organization 17 November
40. Revolutionary People's Liberation Party/Front (DHKP/C)
41. Shining Path (Sendero Luminoso, SL)
42. United Self-Defense Forces of Colombia (AUC)

FinCEN Terrorist Financing SAR Typologies

Investigators should be familiar with scenarios that provide illustrations of activities that could indicate terrorist financing activities. The following case studies were compiled by FinCEN by analyzing SARs from financial institutions:

Case I: Relief Organization in the Middle East
FinCEN identified 649 SARs filed by seven depository institutions reporting transactions totaling $9 million involving structured cash deposits and deposits of business, payroll and Social Security benefit checks. These SARs were filed during a 3-1/2 year period. Deposited funds were subsequently wire transferred within one or two days to a company located in the Middle East. The deposit and wire transfer activity involved 37 individuals conducting transactions through 44 accounts on behalf of four businesses. Two of the businesses were wire remittance companies; one was described as a relief organization at the same location as one of the wire remittance businesses; the fourth undescribed business, located in the Middle East, was the beneficiary of the wire transfer activity. The majority of the wire transfers were sent to two accounts in the Middle East. Other wire transfers were made to accounts at three different banks in foreign locations. The majority of the transactions (83%) were structured. Amounts of the deposits ranged from $350 to $636,790; most deposits fell between $2,000 to $8,000.

Case II: Relief / Charitable Organizations in the US
One bank filed three SARs that reported the activities of a relief organization operating in the U.S., whose stated primary purpose is the collection of donations and funds for worthwhile causes in Middle Eastern countries. Over an approximate 15-month period, the relief organization initiated wire transfers from its U.S. bank account totaling $685,560 through its primary account in a former Soviet Republic to its accounts in other former Soviet Republic countries. The relief organizations U.S. bank account also received wire transfers totaling $724,694 from unknown senders at a European bank and wired a total of $65,740 to a U.S. charitable organization. The filing institution deemed this activity inconsistent with the stated purpose of the account. FinCEN identified two other SARs filed by two banks regarding financial activity of the U.S. charitable organization. The SARs identified $445,325 wired to the U.S. charitable organization's account in the Middle East through the filing bank's U.S. correspondent bank. They also wired $18,000 to a media services business in the Middle East in 2001. Four different accounts were used. SARs also described structured cash deposits totaling $53,800, and check deposits totaling $121,705. FinCEN identified three additional accounts at three other banks through currency transaction reports (CTRs). Those CTRs reported cash deposits totaling $227,519 in 1994, 1999, and 2001.

Case III: Car Salesman
A total of nine SARs and 14 CTRs were filed regarding the personal account activities of a used car dealer/car salesman/exporter during the period September 1991 through December 1999. Early activity involved check cashing by the account holder. In early 1996, he began structuring his transactions weekly and sometimes daily, primarily making cash withdrawals and cashing negotiable instruments, apparently to avoid the CTR reporting requirements. SARs were filed reporting structured cash withdrawals that ranged from $3,000 to $9,900. This activity continued through mid-1999. Beginning in

September 1998 and continuing through December 1999, the individual's personal account began receiving large dollar wire transfers from jurisdictions in the Middle East. In 1999, large dollar wire transfers were generated from the account to the benefit of businesses and individuals in the Middle East and North America. Account activity including withdrawals, checks cashed and negotiable instruments cashed totaled $556,350; deposits and wire transfers received amounted to $1,447,888.90 and wire transfers sent amounted to $465,246. Total account activity reported in SARs and CTRs, was in excess of $2 million.

Case IV: Import / Export Business
FinCEN identified five SARs filed by one bank, two SARs filed voluntarily by a money services business (MSB) and many CTRs filed by two different east coast financial institutions. These filings identified significant cash deposits and wire transfer activity by a business described as an import/export business and as a leather goods store. Over an approximate one-year period (July 1999 through June 2000), wire transfers totaling $702,366 were sent from a corporate account at one bank to businesses and individuals in numerous jurisdictions, including two NCCTs, one country designated as a state sponsor of terrorism, and one country subject to a travel warning for a high level of anti-American terrorist activities. Wire transfer amounts varied from a high of $22,150 to a low of $3,000. During the same period, CTRs reflected cash deposits into this account at New York and Florida branches, totaling $616,231 and monetary instrument deposits totaling $238,986. The majority of the cash deposits occurred weekly and was structured below CTR reporting thresholds. Monetary instruments were deposited at three branch locations and included commercial and U.S. Postal money orders, and bank, personal, and business checks. An individual using a New York address attempted to make a $12,995 cash deposit into this account at a California branch in March 2000, but when asked for additional identifying data, the individual refused and stopped the transaction. Cash withdrawals totaling $13,500 and four negotiable instruments cashed totaling $55,300 was reported for a second corporate account at a different bank.

A SAR narrative filed by the same bank links this business via telephone number to a second business described as an import/export and wire service business. The individual with signature authority on the original corporate account made cash deposits totaling $920,649 to the account of the second business during a ten-month period in 1998. Another SAR, for what appears to be his personal account, reflects cash deposits at New York and Florida branches of the bank that totaled $26,770 during a three-month period in 1999. The bank filed SARs because the deposits were structured. During the same period, wire transfers totaling $30,000 were sent to an individual in an NCCT and a business in Europe.

Case V: Owner of Pharmaceutical Company
A SAR was filed reporting two same-day deposits ($3,500 and $9,900) made three hours apart to a savings account by a bank customer. The bank initiated a review of the customer's accounts. The review identified additional suspicious activity in four of his personal accounts, including the original savings account. From December 1999 through April 2001, 38 cash/non-cash deposits and one wire transfer deposit totaled $2,202,384. During the same time period, one withdrawal, two cashings of negotiable instruments, three wire transfers and two other debit transactions totaled $2,256,223. Of this total,

$2,040,370 flowed into the original suspect's savings account and $2,097,323 flowed out of the account. Cash and non-cash deposits were described as even dollar amounts ranging from $1,000 to $100,000. Wire transfer activity included a $25,000 wire transfer received from an individual and three (3) transfers totaling $100,000 sent to two different individuals. The SAR and related CTRs describe the individual as the owner/president of a pharmaceutical company and the owner/CEO of a biochemical lab.

In July 1996, this individual transported $11,200 into the U.S. from a Caribbean country and in December 2000, he transported $11,500 from the U.S. to Europe. In both instances, he claimed citizenship in a country subject to a travel warning for anti-American terrorist activity and provided a non-U.S. passport as identification. He is also cited as entering the U.S. a total of 32 times from March 1996 through August 2001. Identification provided, as cited in the entry records, was an alien registration number.

Money Laundering and Terrorist Financing Contrasts

Activity	Money Laundering	Terrorist Financing
Origin of Funds	Illegal sources	Combination of legal, legitimate and illegal sources
Source of Funds	Internally from within criminal organizations	Internally from self-funding revenue-generating cells (increasingly centered on criminal activity, primarily various types of fraud) Externally – from charitable benefactors and fund raisers, and sponsor states
Purpose of Funds	Enjoy criminal profits and spend legally Capital needed to continue the criminal enterprise is secondary	Primarily to obtain resources to provide for logistical needs, support, and funding of operations
Motivation	Financial Gain/Profit	Ideological Commitment
Purpose of Money Laundering	Funds of criminal activity are moved or concealed in order to disguise the link between the crime and the illegally generated funds	To obscure or disguise the links between the terrorist group and its legitimate funding sources
Methodology	Traditional Laundering: • Placement • Layering • Integration	Reverse Money Laundering: • Integration (Collection) • Layering • Placement (Use)
Conduits	Favors formal financial system	Favors cash couriers or informal financial systems such as alternative remittance and currency exchange firms
Degree of Detection Difficulty	Anticipated or expected pattern of transactions are inconsistent with the nature and purpose of account Significant, unexpected and unexplained change in the nature and behavior of the account	Legal sources of funding Size of transaction (small amounts) Nature of transaction (usually not complex – primarily wire transfers) Customer profile – e.g., foreign students (not necessarily identified as requiring enhanced scrutiny)

Activity	Money Laundering	Terrorist Financing
General Typologies	Suspicious transactions, such as deposits uncharacteristic of customer's wealth or the expected activity, which lead to relational links	Suspicious relationships, such as wire transfers between seemingly unrelated parties, which lead to transactional links
Transaction Amounts	Large amounts often structured to avoid reporting requirements	Small amounts usually below reporting thresholds
Financial Activity Profile	Complex web of transactions often involving shell or front companies, bearer shares, and offshore secrecy havens	No workable financial profile of operational terrorists exists, according to U.S. 9/11 Commission
Audit / Money Trail	Circular – money eventually ends up with person who generated it	Linear – money generated is used to propagate terrorist group and activities
Suspicious Activity Indicators	From traditional typologies	Very similar to those developed from traditional typologies Key Indicators: • Geographical origin and destination of funds • Comparison with lists

Section IV – Suspicious Activity Topics For Investigators

Introduction

The Issues and Guidance sections of the SAR Activity Reviews discuss current issues of common interest raised with regard to the preparation and filing of SARs. The discussion is intended to identify SAR-related issues and provide explanations so that filing organizations can reasonably address these issues. The Bank Secrecy Act Advisory Group conducted a search of FinCEN's SAR database to compile much of the statistical information presented in this section. Since SAR data is classified information, the compilation of the data is a *virtual* (and legal!) peak into that classified information.

Additional information presented in this chapter was pulled together to support the FinCEN data. The 2007 edition of the FFIEC Examination Manual, numerous other regulatory agency guidance, and NGO publications containing background information useful to investigators is presented here collectively.

Advance Fee Fraud (a.k.a 4-1-9 Schemes)

FinCEN has advised financial institutions that it is unnecessary to file SARs on *4-1-9* scams if there was no monetary loss involved.

SARs increasingly reference bank account solicitation letters coming from suspect individuals in Nigeria, South Africa, or Ghana representing themselves to be former or current high-level government officials, soldiers or influential professionals (or their spouses). The letters are typically directed at bank officials and/or specific customers (individuals or businesses) of banks, and request direct access to bank account and other identification information to arrange for a supposed large transfer of funds (typically tens of millions of dollars) from Nigeria, South Africa, or Ghana into the subject account. This type of advanced fee fraud is called a .419 scam, (the 419 refers to the section of the Nigerian penal law that deals with advanced fee fraud.

The 419 penal law was revised and expanded with the issuance in April 1995, of Presidential Decree No. 13 entitled Advance Fee Fraud and other Fraud Offenses Decree 1995.), but is often reported in SARs in the BSA/Structuring/Money Laundering category, since the letters usually seem to be soliciting assistance for clandestine currency flight. The large sums of funds available are often described as resulting from over-invoicing or paybacks on contracts (e.g., petroleum; oil; equipment supply; construction). Some Ghanaian letters claim to have money embezzled from the UNITA rebels in Angola in two trunks in Accra, Ghana. The requester may also typically indicate that they are not allowed to own or operate foreign accounts, since they are officials of the Nigerian or South African government, or expatriates from Angola or Sierra Leone. A substantial percentage fee (e.g., 20-30%) for the use of the account is typically offered to the recipient of the correspondence. In one example, the letter stated that the source of the funds is drug free and 100% risk free.

Institutions Receiving 4-1-9 Letters and emails
Many institutions are now the recipients of solicitations for advanced fee schemes, which have commonly been referred to as Nigerian, West African or 419 advanced fee schemes. A determination as to whether a SAR should be filed is that of the institution that receives the solicitation. Financial institutions should be aware that the United States Secret Service (USSS) has dedicated resources to this issue. If a financial institution receives an advanced fee scheme letter through the mail, e-mail, or fax, and the institution has not initiated any contact with law enforcement or the perpetrators of the attempted fraud, the letter should be forwarded to USSS using one of the following methods:

e-mail to: 419.fcd@usss.treas.gov

fax to: (202) 406-5031; or,

mail to:

> United States Secret Service
> Financial Crimes Division, (ATTN: 419)
> 950 H Street, Suite 5300
> NW Washington D.C. 20373-5802

If, however, the financial institution has been victimized by one of these schemes, all written documentation should be mailed to the USSS at the above address and a call should be placed to the Agency at (202) 406-5850.

The determination whether to file a SAR with respect to a particular transaction or other activity must be made by the financial institution.

The U.S. Department of State, Bureau of International Narcotics and Law Enforcement Affairs published an April 1997 report entitled Nigerian Advance Fee Fraud that provides examples of the various business schemes used by Nigerian criminals to fraudulently obtain funds from U.S. businesses. This report can be found at

> http://www.travel.state.gov

The United States Secret Service also has interesting information on these schemes in its report, which can be found at:

> http://www.treas.gov/usss/financial_crimes.shtml#Nigerian

Asset Rental Fraud

This is a fraudulent scheme designed to exaggerate or inflate the stated value of a borrower's assets. SAR filers have reported schemes where funds were temporarily deposited into a loan applicant's bank account for the time required to qualify for a loan. The funds came from and then withdrawn from the bank account after the loans were approved.(Funds came from friends or family, or even from mortgage brokers attempting to qualify an ineligible borrower.)

One elaborate asset rental fraud scheme reported by Kenneth Harney in the Baltimore Sun involved deposits of funds into bank accounts established in a prospective borrower's name, with the deposited funds being temporarily "rented" for a fee. The customary fee charged for this service was reportedly approximately five percent of the deposited funds. The service also may include verification of employment and income in any amount for an additional fee of one percent of the claimed annual income.

ATM Related

Criminal and money launderers in particular are known to use automated teller machines to facilitate their activities. Money launderers have found automated teller machines to be a convenient and relatively less risky way to structure transactions to avoid the various reporting requirements of the Bank Secrecy Act. Check fraudsters have also found that passing insufficiently funded checks through an automated teller machine provides them with a greater degree of anonymity.

The two prominent suspicious activities identified by FinCEN in 1999 (SAR Bulletin – Issue 1, June 1999):
- o The use of automated teller machines as a way of avoiding certain Bank Secrecy Act requirements (e.g., structuring); and,
- o Check fraud

still represent the primary trends of suspicious activities reported in current Suspicious Activity Report filings.

- **Continued Use of Automated Teller Machines to Avoid Bank Secrecy Act Reporting Requirements**
  As was noted by FinCEN in SAR Bulletin – Issue 1, automated teller machines continue to be used by some to avoid the Currency Transaction Report. It is also suspected that money launderers and other criminals are using automated teller machines to avoid filing Reports of International Transportation of Currency and Monetary Instruments.

- **Cross Border Currency Movements**
  Law enforcement investigations reveal that drug dealers frequently use domestic automated teller machines to deposit illicit proceeds into financial institution accounts and then withdraw the funds from automated teller machines located in their drug suppliers' countries of origin. This method is a way to avoid the risks associated with bulk cash smuggling and the enhanced scrutiny of law enforcement at the borders. This technique also facilitates avoidance of a Report of International Transportation of Currency and Monetary Instruments filing. This same method can be used to move virtually any other type of illicit proceeds.

  A recent analysis by FinCEN found that financial institutions located in Florida file the majority of Suspicious Activity Reports that report suspicious cash withdrawals from automated teller machines in foreign countries. This finding likely is due to Florida's close proximity to the Caribbean and Latin America as well as Miami's role as an international travel hub. Florida also has a renowned tourism industry and, consequently, a strong cash economy. Money launderers prefer to operate in cash intensive areas like south Florida hoping that the likelihood of *illegal* cash being detected will be significantly reduced.

In addition, Suspicious Activity Reports sampled in FinCEN's analysis identified various monetary instruments deposited into accounts, with funds withdrawn shortly thereafter from foreign automated teller machines. In some instances, cash combined with other monetary instruments were deposited during a single transaction. Some of those other monetary instruments included:

- ○ Personal checks;
- ○ Cashiers checks;
- ○ International money orders;
- ○ Other money orders; and
- ○ Funds from redeemed Certificates of Deposit.

Suspicious Activity Report filings reported that these types of deposits were followed quickly by daily maximum cash withdrawals through automated teller machines located in foreign countries. The majority of withdrawals cited were from automated teller machines located in Colombia. The size and number of the cash withdrawals within short time frames indicate possible money laundering.

- **Currency Reporting Requirement**
  FinCEN's recent analysis also found continued prominent reporting of automated teller machines being used to structure currency transactions in order to avoid the Currency Transaction Report filing requirements.

Suspicious Activity Reports indicated two prevalent patterns of structuring:
- ○ Customers making multiple cash deposits and/or withdrawals aggregating to sums over $10,000 on the same day at one or more automated teller machine locations; and,
- ○ Customers using a combination of same-day teller and automated teller machine activity.

Some examples of this type of activity are:
- ○ Automated teller machines only (The automated teller machine activity could apply to transactions occurring either for an account owned by one or more customers or among multiple accounts owned by one or more customers.)
  - ▪ Four individuals deposit/withdraw $3,000 on the same day at seven different automated teller machines.(Most domestic financial institutions and host networks limit daily automated teller machine withdrawal amounts to between $300 and $500. However, each institution and host network, taking into consideration risk management and client relationship concerns, determines its own automated teller machine limits.)
  - ▪ One individual deposits/withdraws $3,000, several different times during the day, using the same automated teller machine.

- ○ Automated teller machine in combination with other types of transactions

- An individual cashes a check with a teller in a financial institution for $9000 followed by three $500 automated teller machine withdrawals.
- An individual deposits $8000 in cash with a teller in a financial institution followed by several $1,000 cash deposits through an automated teller machine.

In several instances, the filing financial institutions reported that the structured cash deposits consisted of all $100 bills or $20 bills. For example:

o   It is not uncommon for drug dealers to use $100 bills for bulk payments since it allows the cash to be concealed in smaller containers such as a brief case for easier and less detectable transport. Conversely,

o   Smaller denominations, such as $20 bills, are considered by law enforcement as *street money* for purchasing drugs.

o   Large deposits consisting of $20 bills at an automated teller machine also could represent funds withdrawn from another automated teller machine, with the successive transactions being an attempt to layer the movement of funds.

- **Check Fraud Violations**
  The majority of Suspicious Activity Reports citing check fraud violations in connection with automated teller machine usage involved insufficiently funded or *worthless* checks deposited in automated teller machines.("Worthless" is a term used in the Suspicious Activity Report narratives to describe, among other things, checks that are drawn on insufficient funds or closed accounts; stolen, forged or counterfeit checks (identity theft); or checks on which payment has been stopped.)

Many of the Suspicious Activity Reports sampled for this study reported that before these deposited checks were returned unpaid, the accounts were depleted through checks, point of sale debits, or cash withdrawals at automated teller machines, often resulting in a net loss to the bank. (The total loss amount related to check fraud conducted through automated teller machines is not readily available since some Suspicious Activity Report filers do not include a loss amount.) This type of activity can be spread across multiple accounts and involve multiple financial institutions.

What to do When Suspicious Activity is Suspected
When reporting suspicious activity involving automated teller machines:

o   File a complete and sufficient Suspicious Activity Report;

o   Be sure to include the dollar amount involved;

o   For depository institution filers, if applicable, include:

- the amount of loss prior to recovery (Item #36 on the Suspicious Activity Report form); and,
- The dollar amount of recovery (Item #37).

Automobile Industry

A search of the FinCEN SAR database revealed 1,765 SARs containing the terms:

- o Used cars
- o Car dealership
- o Automobile dealership
- o Automobile sales
- o Car sales

in the narrative portion of the SAR.

The top three reported violations were:

1. BSA /Structuring/Money Laundering (864 SARs);
2. Consumer Loan Fraud (257 SARs); and
3. Check Fraud (175 SARs). Forty-one SARs reported no violation.

Approximately 350 (20%) of the SARs were reviewed. The following are summaries of these types of activities:

- **The most common scenario involved Structuring:**

   - o Individuals working in the automobile retail industry withdrew and/or deposited cash just under the CTR reporting requirements. Some individuals did so with unusual frequency within a short period of time(days) at various bank branches within close proximity. The SARs indicated that these transactions were unusual for that type of business. One SAR reported a used car dealer making numerous cash deposits, twice daily and all under $10,000, at different area bank branches of the same bank. Deposits for one month totaled $750,000. The owner of this car dealership also owns a grocery market. Within one day of each deposit, checks drawn on the car dealership account were written to the grocery market. These checks temporarily depleted the dealership account. Another SAR described a small used car dealer located in a poor neighborhood that typically maintained just 10-12 used cars on the lot on any given day. During a two-month period, the car dealer made deposits of cash and checks totaling over $410,000. The cash deposits were always made under CTR reporting requirements.

   - o While attempting to conduct a transaction, some customers altered the cash amount transacted to fall below the CTR reporting requirements when informed a CTR would be completed.

   - o Individuals structured deposits and claimed the funds were derived from profits they made, on their own, buying and selling used cars. However, those individuals were not affiliated with any automobile retail business or formally involved in the automobile industry. The SARs described the suspicious activity but made no mention of similar withdrawals that may have been used to acquire the used cars. Suspects claimed to have acquired the funds by selling used cars but there was no account activity that would suggest how they initially obtained the vehicles.

o   Customers purchased cars by submitting structured checks/money orders.

- **Consumer Loan Fraud was also a frequently reported violation:**

    o   Incidents of consumer loan fraud primarily involved the submission of false or forged statements by loan applicants in their attempt to purchase a car. These applicants were both automobile dealers and retail purchasers. Both dealers and retail consumers submitted loan applications with false financial information, addresses, phone numbers, social security numbers, and forged signatures. Dealers, in applying for a loan, knowingly understated the automobile mileage to the lending institution. This fraudulently inflated the value of the vehicle and resulted in a larger than justified loan.

    o   SARs also reported out-of-trust sales, by used car dealers, of vehicles in their possession whose acquisition was financed by various financial institutions. Some car dealers altered lien information on duplicate titles in order to obtain a 'clear' certificate of title. These vehicles would then be sold with a loss incurred by the lending institution. The banks advanced payment for the vehicles but failed to receive payment when they were sold.

    o   Automobile dealers used personal information of their customers, without the knowledge or consent of those individuals, in order to obtain loans.

    o   SARs also reported the development of relationships between bank employees and car dealerships. Some situations involved the inappropriate manipulation of loan applications by bank employees that enabled applicants for automobile loans to obtain credit in violation of bank guidelines. The bank employees earned commissions on these fraudulent loans and the automobile dealership made money on the sales.

- **Check Fraud was the third most frequently reported violation:**

    o   SARs reported that checks, later returned for "insufficient funds available," were used to purchase automobiles from various car dealerships.

    o   Some SARs reported the theft of checks from car dealerships and then fraudulently negotiated by unauthorized individuals, in some cases by former employees.

    o   Other reports indicated that stolen, forged, and counterfeit checks were used to make payments on vehicles at various dealerships.

    o   Forged reproductions of a bank's counter-checks were made payable to a used car dealer located in a Gulf State. It is believed that these checks were computer generated.

- **Identity Theft was also reported:**

    o   Individuals used someone else's social security number and personal data in order to obtain a car loan in that person's name. Fake identification (driver's license) was also used and forged signatures were employed. Some SARs reported that employees of the automobile dealerships were aware of this fraud. One incident involved a car salesman providing customers a "reference number" so they could qualify for the loan. This "reference number" appeared to be someone else's social security number.

o   An unknown suspect established fraudulent bank accounts using the identities of numerous individuals. The only connection established between the victims was that each of them purchased automobiles from the same automobile dealership. The suspect deposited counterfeit checks into these accounts. The suspect then withdrew funds from these accounts via debit cards. The cash was then used to purchase postal money orders.

- **Commercial Loan Fraud also occurred involving automobile dealerships:**

  o   Banks advanced loan funds to car dealers via floor plan lines of credit secured by the automobiles in inventory. This collateral was later sold, out-of-trust, and the proceeds were not applied to the loan, thus creating a loss for the lender.

  o   SARs reported that multiple suspects applied for used vehicle loans via the internet. After normal screening, the loans were approved and drafts were sent. These funds were intended to purchase used cars. No payments were received on the loan and attempts to repossess the vehicles were futile. Vehicle Identification Numbers (VIN) given were found to be non-existent. Attempts to locate the suspects failed. One SAR reported that the New Jersey State Police are currently investigating approximately 100 cases of this type of fraud.

- **Check Kiting schemes were also reported:**

  o   Owners of car dealerships were utilizing the float by writing checks on various accounts at different banks.

Boat and Yacht Industry

A search of the SAR database revealed 61 SARs containing the terms:

- Boat sales;
- Boat dealership;
- Yacht sales; or,
- Yacht dealership

in the narrative portion of the SAR. The top three reported violations were: BSA/ Structuring/Money Laundering (28 SARs); 2) Consumer Loan Fraud (14 SARs); and 3) Commercial Loan Fraud (12 SARs). One SAR reported no violation. Violation amounts ranged from $0 to $28,500,000. Twenty-seven SARs reported a violation amount between $10,000 and $99,999. Twenty SARs were between $100,000 and $999,999. The violation amount on eight SARs exceeded $1,000,000. A total of 13 SARs were forwarded directly to federal, state or local law enforcement or regulatory authorities. The following are summaries of these types of activities.

- **The most common scenario involved Structuring:**

  o Individuals working in the boat retail industry withdrew and/or deposited cash just below the CTR reporting requirements. Some individuals conducted these transactions with unusual frequency within short period of time (days) at various bank branches within close proximity. The SARs indicated that the transactions were unusual for that type of business. It was noted that many deposits were regularly made, even during the boat sale off-season. Cash is not typically used to purchase boats. One boat dealer deposited over $255,000 from January 2002 to May 2002. Forty-three deposits were made, typically ranging from $5,000 to $9,000 (none over $10,000). Another SAR revealed that the owners and employees of a particular boat dealer purchased cashier's checks, with cash, at a bank with which they had no relationship, and then deposited the cashier's checks in the dealership's business account at another bank. All transactions fell below $10,000 and were, believed by the filer, to be intended to avoid CTR reporting requirements.

  o When informed of CTR reporting requirements, while attempting to conduct a transaction, some customers would alter the cash amount transacted to fall below reporting requirements.

  o Individuals structured deposits and claimed the funds were derived from boat sales.

  o Customers purchased boats by submitting structured checks/money orders.

  o Customers purchased boats by submitting large, one-time payments (in some cases in excess of $100,000). During a two-month period in 2001, a yacht sales company received $2,685,000 in seven wire transfers from the same individual located in a Middle Eastern country.

o One internet-based yacht brokerage firm filed a SAR regarding a suspicious acting customer. The customer wished to purchase a $28.5 million yacht through the firm. The customer's behavior was erratic and the deal was never consummated.

- **Consumer Loan Fraud**

  o Primarily involved the submission of false or forged statements by loan applicants in their attempt to purchase a boat.

- **Commercial Loan Fraud also occurred involving boat dealerships:**

  o Several SARs reported boats may have been sold to more than one owner; serial numbers on boats were altered; and boats stored at the dealership/ marina by legitimate owners were represented as inventory. These violations were discovered during audits performed by the lender.

  o More than one bank financed the same boat (duplicate loans) maintained by a boat dealer. The invoices on these boats were later found to be fraudulent.

  o Boat dealers, maintaining large lines of credit, substantially overstated the value of their boat inventory. A large portion of the overstatement resulted from the out-of-trust sale of boats without forwarding the sale proceeds to the banks. It is believed that the borrowers may never have owned boats pledged to the loan.

  o Boat dealerships diverted sales proceeds due the financing institution and loans from the financing institution to improper uses.

Commercial Real Estate

A random sampling of Suspicious Activity Reports describing commercial real estate transactions revealed that:

- o   property management;
- o   real estate investment;
- o   realty; and
- o   real estate development companies

were the most commonly reported entities associated with money laundering and related illicit activity. Professions that customarily collect fees in real estate transactions, such as appraisers, inspectors, surveyors, and attorneys, were reported as primary subjects with less frequency.

Since 2003, the trend line in suspicious activity reporting associated with potential commercial real estate-related money laundering has risen steeply. The increase in filings has closely tracked similar trends seen in FinCEN's recently issued mortgage loan fraud assessment. The increase is likely attributable to the steep decline in interest rate charges on real estate loans, which occurred contemporaneously with the increase in filings. It remains to be seen whether this trend in relevant suspicious activity reporting reverses as rates on real estate loans rise and the real estate markets cool.

It will sometimes prove difficult to determine when subjects structure particular commercial real estate-related business transactions to promote money laundering. Examples of bank SAR filings that reported such occurrences may be instructive. These can be found in the FinCEN Report noted in the References section.

Structuring Activities Related to Commercial Real Estate
This table shows a breakdown (in descending order of incidence) of the sampled SARs describing commercial real estate-related businesses, professions and individuals potentially involved in suspected structuring:

Primary Subject Entity Potentially Involved in Structuring	Reported Occurrences (#)	Percentage of Total Occurrences (%)
Property Management Company	59	44.70
Real Estate Investment Company	40	30.30
Realty Company	11	8.33
Development Company	7	5.30
Real Estate Services Company	3	2.27
Title Company	3	2.27
Individual	2	1.52
Mortgage Company	2	1.52
Real Estate Agent	2	1.52
Escrow Company	1	<1.00
Loan Broker	1	<1.00
Real Estate Holding Company	1	<1.00
Total	**132**	**100**

Money Laundering Activities Related to Commercial Real Estate
Sixty-three of the 260 SAR narratives examined in the FinCEN study described activities deemed suspicious and are generally indicative of money laundering. The table below shows a breakdown of the SARs describing businesses, professions and persons potentially involved in activities generally indicative of money laundering.

Primary Subject Entity Potentially Involved in Money Laundering	Reported Occurrences (#)	Percentage of Total Occurrences (%)
Real Estate Investment Company	21	30.89
Property Management Company	20	29.41
Realty Company	10	14.71
Individual	7	10.29
Construction Company	6	8.82
Title Company	1	1.47
Mortgage Company	1	1.47
Loan Broker	1	<1.00
Real Estate Holding Company	1	<1.00
Total	68	100

International Transfers Related to Commercial Real Estate
Out of the 260 SAR filings, 45 described international movement of money related to commercial real estate. The Table below shows a breakdown of the SARs describing businesses, professions and persons potentially involved in international transfers of funds to facilitate money laundering or other related illicit financial activity.

Primary Subject Entity Potentially Involved in International Transfers Related to Commercial Real Estate	Reported Occurrences (#)	Percentage of Total Occurrences (%)
Real Estate Investment Company	19	42.23
Individual	11	24.44
Property Management Company	8	17.78
Real Estate Development Company	3	6.67
Construction Company	2	4.44
Realty Company	1	2.22
Real Estate Leasing Finance Company	1	2.22
Total	45	100.00

Convenience Checks

Credit card checks, also known as *convenience checks* or *courtesy checks*, are issued through a credit card company and linked to a credit card account. Customers find credit card checks convenient for use with merchants that do not accept credit cards, but do take checks. Credit card checks may be mailed to customers without the customer's request. They do not require activation, thereby creating a heightened risk for identity theft by providing thieves an opportunity to gain access to customer's information by simply stealing their mail. The thief only needs to sign the customer's name on the face of the check and present it to any merchant. Customers may first learn of the identity theft when reviewing their credit card bills.

(Note: A convenience check may be tied to a credit card account, but it does not give a customer the same kind of consumer protection as a credit card. Regulation Z in the Truth in Lending Act (TILA), effective April 1, 2004, offers certain consumer protections for credit transactions. Currently, a convenience check is not treated as a credit card under Regulation Z because it can be used only once and not "from time to time" as a single transaction. For additional information on Regulation Z go to: http://www.federalreserve.gov/boarddocs/press/bcreg/2004/20040326/attachment.pdf)

FinCEN conducted an assessment of Suspicious Activity Reports (SARs) filed during the period April 1, 1996 to March 31, 2007 with narratives containing three key search terms: *credit card checks*, *convenience checks*, and *courtesy checks*. The Bank Secrecy Act (BSA) database search produced 14,816 SARs. Depository institution SARs showed the top 5 reasons for filing of suspicious activity related to convenience checks were:

- o   Check Fraud 7,158 (30.61%)
- o   Credit Card Fraud 6,933 (29.64%)
- o   Other 3,299 (14.11%)
- o   Identity Theft 1,887 (8.07%)
- o   BSA/Structuring/Money Laundering 1,361 (5.82%)

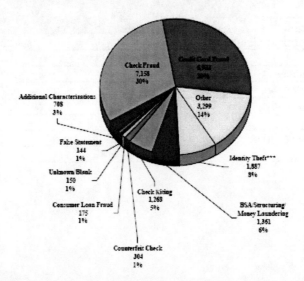

BSA/Structuring/Money Laundering violations – involved activities in which the subjects structured deposits and withdrawals of convenience, credit card, and courtesy checks. As soon as the funds were available, the suspect withdrew the funds, wrote checks, and made purchases. The financial institution sustained financial loss when the checks were later returned for insufficient funds.

Check Fraud – involved stolen convenience checks endorsed and deposited for illegal gain.

Credit Card Fraud – involved credit card "bust-out" schemes where the subjects opened credit accounts and quickly reached the credit limit. The subject then paid with a fraudulent convenience check to restore the credit balance and spent the limit again. Two hundred and ninety-nine reports indicated check fraud and identity theft and described activity where the accounts were established using the victims' names without their knowledge. In some cases subjects used their parents' identities, and in other cases subjects used the identities of deceased persons to establish credit card accounts.

Between April 1, 1996 through March 31, 2007, 14,670 depository institution SARs filed with the specific search terms Convenience Check, Credit Card Check, or Courtesy Check included in the narrative. Of those SARs 77% listed convenience check(s);
- 21% listed credit card check(s); and,
- 2% listed courtesy check(s).

The dollar ranges for those SARs is depicted below:

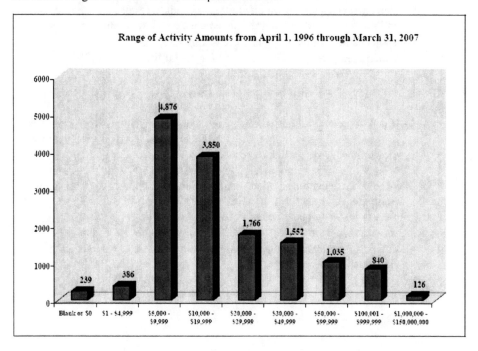

Range of Activity Amounts from April 1, 1996 through March 31, 2007

Depository Institution SAR Narrative Analysis

- A random sample of 1,745 (11.78%) narratives were analyzed to provide a statistical representation of the total SARs filed by depository institutions. A total of 2,218 distinct suspicious activities were reported on the sampled SARs. A total of 796 (35.89%) of the sampled narratives reported "check fraud." Specific activities described in those SARs include:
    - o Stolen convenience checks endorsed and deposited for illegal gain;
    - o Convenience checks counterfeited using computers, scanners, and copiers to create illegal checks;
    - o Checking accounts established using stolen identities and convenience checks at account opening. Checks subsequently issued from the account were returned for insufficient funds;
    - o Check kiting used in instances where the subject opened two or more accounts using convenience checks to create fraudulent balances;
    - o Convenience checks written on closed accounts.

- **A total of 762 (34.36%) of the sampled narratives reported "credit card fraud." Specific activities described in those SARs include:**
    - o Credit card bust-out schemes in which the subject opened a credit account and quickly reached the credit limit on the card, sometimes using credit card convenience checks for purchases. The subject then paid with a bad convenience check drawn on another account to restore the credit balance and spent the limit before the convenience check was returned again;
    - o Subject stole family member's credit card checks;
    - o Stolen credit card checks deposited for illegal financial gain.

- **A total of 321 (14.47%) of the sampled narratives described other types of fraud:**
    - o Check fraud and identity theft where credit card accounts were established in victim's names without their knowledge. The fraud was discovered when the victim was contacted for restitution;
    - o Misuse of position in which the employee of the financial institution established accounts and deposited credit card convenience checks that were later returned for insufficient funds. When the checks were returned, the employee had deleted any record of the account;
    - o New accounts were used for credit card fraud and bust-out schemes;
    - o Subjects used the accounts to make large purchases, sometimes with convenience checks.

- **A total of 272 (12.26%) of the sampled narratives reported "identity theft."**
  - ○ Children used their parents' identity to establish credit card accounts and subsequently received and used convenience checks issued by credit card companies;
  - ○ Subjects used the identity of deceased persons to establish credit card accounts and subsequently received and used convenience checks issued by credit card companies;
  - ○ Subjects illegally forged endorsements on credit card, convenience and courtesy checks that were stolen through the mail.

- **A total of 155 (6.99%) of the sampled narratives reported "BSA/Structuring/Money Laundering" as the suspicious activity:**
  - ○ Subjects structured deposits and withdrawals of the convenience, credit card and courtesy checks. As soon as the funds were available, the suspect withdrew the funds, wrote checks, and made purchases. The financial institution sustained financial loss when the convenience checks were later returned for insufficient funds.

Credit Union Cooperatives

Credit Union Cooperative Shared-Branching Model

Credit union cooperatives operate networks that provide Electronic Funds Transfer/Automated Teller Machine/Point of Sale (EFT/ATM/POS) and shared branching services to the cooperatives' member credit unions. Where applicable, cooperatives' EFT/ATM/POS networks enable members of participating credit unions to use other participating credit unions' ATMs without paying fees or on a reduced-fee basis. Shared branches allow members of participating credit unions to conduct transactions at either branches of the cooperative's other participating credit unions or facilities that are managed by the cooperative itself.

- **There are three types of shared branches:**
    1. **Outlet** – A facility owned and staffed by a credit union where members of other credit unions, within the same cooperative network, can conduct transactions.
    2. **Stand-Alone** – A facility owned and staffed by a credit union cooperative, where members of participating credit unions can conduct transactions.
    3. **Partnership Outlet** – A facility owned by a credit union or group of credit unions and staffed by employees of the cooperative, where members of participating credit unions can conduct transactions.

- **Credit unions belonging to shared-branching networks fall into two categories:**
    1. **Issuer** – Credit unions that allow their members to conduct account transactions, transfers, or payments at other outlets, partnership outlets, and stand-alones within the same shared-branching network.
    2. **Acquirer** (Issuer/Acquirer) – Issuers that serve as outlets by accepting and processing transactions from members of other credit unions within the same shared-branching network.

In a given transaction, the issuing credit union pays a fee to the acquiring credit union. If the transaction occurs at a shared-branching facility that is operated by the cooperative, the issuing credit union pays a fee to the cooperative. The cooperative annually distributes its income collected from fees to its stockholders. Credit union cooperative shareholders can be credit unions, corporate/industrial credit unions, state credit union leagues, or other credit union service organizations.

Synopsis of SAR Filing Activity: Credit Union Cooperatives

FinCEN researched SAR filings referencing credit union cooperatives for the period June 2004 through March 2007. The research addressed SARs filed by other financial institutions with narrative references to credit union cooperatives and terms related to terrorist financing, organized crime, fraud, scams, or money laundering. In addition, information about the cooperatives' structures and Bank Secrecy Act (BSA) compliance policies were reviewed. FinCEN's database queries produced 121 SARs with narrative references to credit union cooperatives and terms related to terrorist financing, organized crime, fraud, scams, or money laundering:

- Twenty-three depository institution SARs filed by credit union cooperatives;
- Four depository institution SARs and four SARs by Money Services Business (SAR–MSBs) that identified some name derivative of a credit union cooperative as a subject;
- Seventy-eight depository institution SARs and ten SAR–MSBs with narrative references to one of the cooperatives and terms related to fraud, scams, or money laundering; and,
- Other instances where credit unions apparently incorrectly filed a SAR–MSB and a SAR by Securities and Futures Industries (SAR–SF) that described shared-branching transactions.

The cooperatives' SAR filings demonstrated several errors including a potential lack of consistency in the use of filer names and Federal Employer Identification Numbers (FEINs). The twenty-three depository institution SAR filings contained sixteen different filer name variations, ten different filer FEINs, and seventeen different combinations of FEINs and filer names. Analysis identified other errors in 15 of the 23 depository institution SAR filings.

Fifty of the 121 (41.32%) SAR filings with some connection to the credit union cooperatives involved fraud or attempted fraud. Seven of the 23 filings (30.43%) by cooperatives involved alleged frauds.

Details on SARs Filed by Credit Union Cooperatives

Several facts about the 78 depository institution SARs and 10 SAR–MSBs with cooperative narrative references appear noteworthy. One SAR–MSB identified an elaborate plot to launder stolen funds using shared branches to deposit cash into a digital currency account holder's credit union account. Sixty-two of the 78 (79.49%) depository institution SARs and five of the ten (50%) SAR–MSBs identified credit union account holders as subjects. Thirty-nine of the 78 (50%) depository institution SARs alleged that a credit union account holder was attempting to launder funds. Eight of the ten SAR–MSBs involved money laundering as well.

Twenty-seven of the 78 (34.62%) depository institution SAR filings with narrative references to the credit union cooperatives involved transactions occurring at multiple shared-branching locations. Twenty-two of these 78 (28.21%) named members of participating credit unions as subjects. Fourteen SARs involving multiple shared branches contained narrative references to money laundering or structuring. Thirteen filings involving multiple shared branches had narrative references to frauds or attempted frauds.

Queries produced 23 depository institution SARs filed from June 2, 2004 through March 6, 2007 by the credit union cooperatives covered in this study. The reports had a total of 16 unique filer-name variations, 10 unique FEINs, and 17 unique combinations of the two.

At least 65.21 percent of SARs filed by credit union cooperatives contained other potential data quality problems. Approximately 30.43 percent of the total filings had either blank or incomplete narrative fields. Some filers attempted to place narratives in the Violation Type Other field. Some reports contained the wrong Branch Address, wrong Total dollar amount involved in known or suspicious activity, or lacked FEINs. Other filers inserted "please see attached" in the SAR narrative and listed Armed Robbery as the characterization of suspicious activity. As a reminder, when SAR forms are received at the Enterprise Computing Center–Detroit, only information that is in an explicit, narrative format is entered into the system; thus, tables, spreadsheets or other attachments are not entered into the SAR System database.

Table 4 displays the different characterizations of suspicious activity found in the 23 depository institution SAR filings (some reports contained multiple characterizations).

Table 4: SAR Filing Characterizations by Depository Institutions

Characterizations of Suspicious Activity	# of Reports with Characterizations	% of Reports with Characterizations
Other	8	34.78%
BSA/Structuring/Money Laundering	8	34.78%
Check Fraud	4	17.39%
Misuse of Position / Self Dealing	4	17.39%
Defalcation / Embezzlement	3	13.04%
Check Kiting	3	13.04%
Mysterious Disappearance	1	4.35%
Counterfeit Check	1	4.35%

Explanations of the covered cooperative depository institution SAR filings with "Other" as the characterization of suspicious activity included the following:

- "Armed Robbery"
- "Money Order Fraud"
- "Rejected Wire OFAC List"
- "OFAC Hit"
- "Avoid Filling Out CTR"
- "4 Separate Cash Deposits"
- "Deposited 9000.00 Cash In Acct He Holds"
- "Made Two Cash Deposits To An Account"

Depository Institution SARs with Credit Union Cooperatives Narrative References
Research identified 78 depository institution SAR narratives involving covered
cooperatives and terms related to fraud, scams, or money laundering that did not solely
involve unconfirmed structuring. Sixty-two of the 78 (79.49%) filings named members of
participating credit unions as subjects. Research did not locate any SARs where the filer
described a financial activity as being related to terrorist financing, terrorist groups, or
organized crime. Table 5 contains a summary of filer characterizations of suspicious
activity.

Table 5: SAR Narratives Referring to Credit Union Cooperatives

Characterization of Suspicious Activity	Count	% of Total	With Credit Union Member Subject	% of Total
BSA/Structuring/Money Laundering	45	48.39%	39	41.94%
Counterfeit Check	16	17.20%	12	12.90%
Check Fraud	12	12.90%	10	10.75%
Other	6	6.45%	4	4.30%
Check Kiting	5	5.38%	5	5.38%
Counterfeit Instrument (Other)	4	4.30%	1	1.08%
Wire Transfer Fraud	2	2.15%	2	2.15%
Debit Card Fraud	2	2.15%	2	2.15%
Credit Card Fraud	1	1.08%		
TOTAL	**93**	**100.00%**	**75**	**80.65%**

Thirty-four depository institution SAR narratives, or 43.59 percent of the total filings,
involved frauds or attempted frauds. Twenty-six of the SARs filed involving fraud or
attempted fraud, or 33.33 percent of the total filings, identified members of participating
credit unions as subjects. Seven filings described alleged 419 scams. Four of these seven
filings named members of participating credit unions as subjects. The remaining three
involved counterfeit instruments drawn on one of the cooperatives. In one instance the
individual allegedly was perpetrating a 419 scam and advised the potential victim to
attempt to cash a $6,500 counterfeit check at a specific shared branch.

Table 6 contains a summary of filings involving different types of fraud. The
characterizations in this table were drawn from descriptions of suspicious activities in
SAR narratives.

Table 6: Fraud SAR Narratives Referring to Credit Union Cooperatives

Characterization of Suspicious Activity	Count	% of Total	With Credit Union Member Subject	% of Total
Check Fraud	10	12.82%	9	11.54%
Counterfeit Check	9	11.54%	6	7.69%
Nigerian Scam and Check Fraud	4	5.13%	1	1.54%
Check Kiting	4	5.13%	4	5.13%
Counterfeit Checks and Debit Card Fraud	2	2.56%	2	2.56%
Nigerian Scam, Check Fraud and Counterfeit Money Orders	1	1.28%	1	1.28%
Nigerian Scam and Money Laundering	1	1.28%	1	1.28%
Nigerian Scam	1	1.28%	1	1.28%
Check Fraud and Money Laundering	1	1.28%	1	1.28%
ATM Fraud, Check Kiting, and Check Fraud	1	1.28%	1	1.28%
TOTAL	**34**	**100.00%**	**26**	**33.33%**

Sixty-one different financial institutions filed the 78 depository institution SARs discussed in this section. The 78 depository institution SAR narratives contained a total of eight different references to credit union cooperatives and affiliated entities covered in this study.

Debt Elimination Schemes

Debt Elimination Schemes can be financially devastating to consumers and can expose financial institutions to significant compliance and operational risks. Most of the debt elimination schemes reported in SARs or described in other sources, such as court documents and news reports, claim to be able to eliminate or cancel various types of debt, including mortgages; credit card balances; student, auto and small business loans. The underlying fraudulent claim and inducement in these schemes is that a debt can be eliminated or canceled simply by paying someone a small fee relative to the amount of debt to be eliminated. Many of the scams have been marketed on Internet web sites designed to appear legitimate and sophisticated. The scams take various forms, including those that:

- Falsely claim to pay the debt in some way;
- Claim to transfer the debt to some wealthy benevolent entity that does not exist or that exists but does not have adequate financial capacity; or,
- Falsely claim to have the debt declared invalid, either because the financial company is not permitted to lend money or because the documentation used by the lender is not valid.

The perpetrators of these schemes also frequently provide consumers and financial institutions with inaccurate or distorted information about applicable laws and the procedures to be followed for securing and paying off a loan. These schemes are not new, just the latest versions of the *up-front-fee scam*.

Banks and other financial institutions should periodically review their anti-money laundering programs to ensure that appropriate policies and procedures are in place to detect and report debt elimination schemes. Anti-money laundering policies, procedures, systems and training programs should take into account the unique risks posed by these practices. All of the requirements in applicable suspicious activity reporting regulations should be followed when reporting a suspected debt elimination scheme, including the minimum dollar thresholds for mandatory filing of a SAR. Financial institutions that become aware of debt elimination schemes that do not meet applicable dollar threshold requirements are not required to file SARs but may do so voluntarily.

Debt elimination schemes have also been reported in conjunction with mortgage fraud. See the Mortgage Loan Fraud section for additional information.

Endorsed Third Party Checks

An endorsed/third-party check is a check payable to someone other than the drawer who in turn transfers the check to a third party by endorsing the back of the instrument by writing "pay to the order of" to name a new holder. This action transfers the instrument to a new holder who has the same legal rights as the endorser. The new holder of the instrument is then free to negotiate the check themselves, either by endorsing the check and depositing it into an account, or by exchanging it for cash at a financial institution (bank, money services business, hawala or other type of alternative remittance or underground banking system, etc.) The Uniform Commercial Code allows the transfer of one check to a new owner any number of times.

Many individuals, small businesses, and even some large enterprises have legitimate reasons for using third-party checks for their transactions, particularly in parts of the world where the financial services infrastructure is not as developed as it is in the United States and where there is high demand for the U.S. dollar. At the same time, there is a potential for abuse. Endorsed third-party checks have been used to commit fraud, money laundering, tax evasion and other criminal offenses in the United States and abroad. For example, such checks are commonly used in the black market peso exchange and in other currency black markets in the Middle East, Africa, and the Americas. Such practices are commonly encountered in cases that involve a range of criminal activities. For these reasons, as well as the risk of non-payment, the practice of accepting endorsed/third-party checks is avoided by many financial institutions overseas and even discouraged or disallowed in some jurisdictions. Similarly, when money exchange companies or other financial institutions accept endorsed checks, they often charge a commission of three to five percent to cover the risk of non-payment. In other cases, third-party checks may be accepted for collection only, which delays the payment for several business days.

Suspicious Activity Report narratives have indicated that U.S. dollar third-party checks are being presented to banks located overseas, even though both the payee and payer appear unconnected to the area where these checks appear. Once negotiated, though, the checks become part of the international cash letter package sent to correspondent banks in the United States. Some of these third-party checks negotiated abroad and sent through the cash letter process might indicate one or more of the following crimes:

- o   Money laundering;
- o   Black market currency deals;
- o   Payment for smuggled or diverted goods;
- o   Tax evasion;
- o   Unlicensed/unregistered hawala/informal fund transfer business or settlement;
- o   Terrorist financing;
- o   Fraud; or
- o   Bribery / corrupt payments.

It is a common practice of financial institutions to flag transactions that make little or no commercial or economic sense. Regulatory authorities encourage this practice as part of a risk-based Bank Secrecy Act compliance program. This does not mean that a single flag proves that illegal activity has been committed, facilitated or covered up through particular checks. Instead, flags alert bank officials and regulators that something may be wrong and that they should exercise due diligence to ensure that their institution does not facilitate illegal activity and does not increase the possibility of reputational, financial or legal risks. In such instances, customer identification programs and banking business rules are particularly useful to avoid these risks.

To assist financial institution employees in preventing and reporting illegal transactions, a non-exhaustive list of possible indicators of endorsed/third-party check abuse is listed below as a guideline. These are some of the suspicious activities identified in Suspicious Activity Report filings for endorsed/third party checks negotiated abroad:

- o Checks payable to payees with no local connection to the city, area, or country where the checks were cashed or deposited (i.e., not payable to a person, organization or business with a local residence, office or business address);

- o Checks for unusually large amounts (i.e., certain threshold amounts, such as $50,000), especially when they appear unrelated to a particular business;

- o Business checks from a bank based in a jurisdiction different from the residence of the payer where there is no apparent connection between the issuer and beneficiary of the check (e.g., an importer in South America pays an exporter in Europe or the United States with a check drawn in the Middle East);

- o Checks written for amounts just below the currency reporting requirement limits ($10,000), which are then cashed out;

- o Checks from a source flagged for previously submitting problematic instruments (e.g., forged signatures, stolen checks, fraudulently obtained checks, suspected money laundering, terrorist finance or other financial crime connected checks);

- o Checks that appear to have no legitimate commercial purpose;

- o Multiple endorsed/third-party checks used for the settlement of a single purchase or transaction;

- o Checks in foreign currency deposited in jurisdictions/areas known to be vulnerable to abuse;

- o Checks on which more than one type of handwriting appears for the original item (e.g., one for the amount and another for the date or payee);

- o Checks in the same name made payable to the same payee, but with different signatures on each check;

- o Checks made out to different payees, but bearing the same handwriting endorsing them;

- o Checks with the payee line left blank;

- o Deposits of multiple endorsed/third-party checks; or

- o Checks dated five or six months before the deposit date.

Identity Theft

Identity Theft, which first appeared on the Suspicious Activity Report in July 2003 has continued to rise as a reported violation - originally debuting as number 20 and now in 2008, ranked 8th.

SAR narratives generally indicate that the most common ways to become the victim of identity theft are through the loss or theft of a purse or wallet, mail theft, and fraudulent address changes. There are also numerous instances of insider knowledge; i.e., persons who may share a residence, relatives, or even bank employees stealing the identity of another person. These individuals have easy access to personal information such as a checkbook bearing account numbers, Social Security Numbers (SSN) and business records.

Often, the SARs do not describe how an individual perpetrator came to obtain a victim's identifying information. In the cases where a relative was involved, it was usually an adult child of the victim. SARs describe young adults applying for credit cards or bank accounts (usually via the Internet) using their parents' pertinent information except for changing the date of birth to reflect their own. Once the perpetrator has obtained personal information, that person will open a bank account in the victim's name (or access a current account). The perpetrator will then begin depositing fraudulent, worthless or counterfeit checks into the account. Most deposits are carried out via automated teller machines (ATMs). Before checks are cleared, the perpetrator will withdraw cash on the account via ATMs. Check deposits usually average between $2,000 and $3,000 each with the total activity amounting to $20,000-$30,000. In some instances, the fraudster will deposit empty envelopes, with a dollar amount annotated, into an ATM.

Numerous narratives describe the fraudulent use of another individual's SSN to obtain car loans. In most cases, the assumed SSN, along with other identifying data, is used to purchase or lease high-end automobiles such as Jaguar, BMW, Mercedes Benz, Lexus, and sports utility vehicles. Most of the loans in this category average approximately $30,000. Loans are usually easily approved. Almost across the board, the bank becomes alerted to the scheme because the perpetrator will immediately default on the loan payments. It is a daunting task for the bank to ascertain who actually purchased or leased the vehicle in question. If the vehicle is recovered, it is normally auctioned off so that the bank can recover some of the loss.

Another common scenario described in the narratives is mail intercepts. An individual will steal an unwitting victim's mail to obtain bank checks or convenience checks issued by credit card companies. The thief will then write checks against the victim's account. The victim does not become aware of the intrusion until receipt of a monthly statement from the bank or credit card company.

Another common depiction is that of the perpetrator informing the bank of a change of address for an account holder. Once new checks are printed with the change of address they are mailed to the individual who requested the address change. Again, this goes unnoticed by the victim until the victim realizes that he/ she has not received a monthly statement from the bank.

Perhaps not as common, but described enough in the narratives to warrant mentioning, are individuals preying upon the elderly either by ingratiating themselves to the person in order to obtain personal information, or by a more overt method such as pick-pocketing.

Also indicated as a means of obtaining information are the use of SSNs or other personal identifiers of deceased individuals. Some banks report fraud rings operating in their jurisdictions. Washington, Texas, and North Carolina banks report fraud rings apparently based in Nigeria taking over the identities of numerous customers. The members of the fraud rings deposit fraudulent checks into the accounts of these individuals, and then withdraw the money in the form of money orders or via debit cards at ATMs. A bank in Delaware uncovered a fraud ring operating out of New York. The bank identified 75 accounts that were linked by four different phone numbers. Individuals making phone calls from these numbers reported lost or stolen debit cards issued on these accounts. The bank issued new cards and convenience checks that were intercepted at JFK Airport in New York. The intercepts were accomplished by members of the fraud rings, who then redirected the cards and checks to cooperating merchants in Saudi Arabia.

Over a one-year period, a bank in North Carolina investigated 113 suspect applications for business loans. In all instances, an application for a loan of $100,000 per business was made. Many of the applications appear to have similar handwriting or had been typed on the same typewriter. Not all of the applications have the same suspected area of fraudulent information. There are multiple irregularities in residence/business addresses, individuals' names, incorporation documents, mail drops, tax preparers, tax returns, and credit bureaus. It is suspected that most of the guarantors for these loans have been victimized by identity theft. According to the SARs filed by this bank, the bank stands to lose close to $7 million.

Another similar ring uncovered in California involved leases for as many as 400 vehicles through multiple financial institutions. The vehicles were also linked to a group dealing in large quantities of drugs. Individuals obtained leases using fraudulent income documents (primarily W–2s) then subleased the cars to individuals in other states. It appears that the ring leaders convinced unsuspecting third parties to allow their names and SSNs to be entered as signatories on the leases. The individuals signed blank credit applications and were told that by doing so they would receive a certain percentage of the profit on these investments. Rarely is a vehicle recovered.

SAR Filing for Identity Theft

Criminal activity related to Identity Theft has historically manifested itself as credit or debit card fraud, loan or mortgage fraud, or false statements to the institution, among other things. As a means of better identifying and tracking known or suspected criminal violations related to Identity Theft, a banking organization should, in addition to reporting the underlying fraud (such as credit card or loan fraud) on a SAR, also indicate within the narrative of the SAR that such a known or suspected violation is the result of Identity Theft. Specifically, when Identity Theft is believed to be the underlying cause of the known or suspected criminal activity, the reporting institution should, consistent with the existing SAR instructions, complete a SAR in the following manner:

- o   In **Part III, Box 35**, check all appropriate boxes that indicate the type of known or suspected violation being reported and, in addition, in the *Other* category, write in "Identity Theft"
- o   In **Part V**, explain what is being reported, including the grounds for suspecting Identity Theft in addition to the other violations being reported.
- o   In the event the only known or suspected criminal violation detected is the Identity Theft, then write in Identity Theft, as appropriate, in the *Other* Category in Part III, Box 35.
- o   Provide a description of the activity in **Part V** of the SAR.

Identity Fraud

Identity fraud refers to the loan applicant's use of a non-existent social security number or a number taken from the social security death index, along with the use of the borrower's true personal identifiers (name, date of birth, address).

Often seen in loan fraud cases, a loan applicant intends to use the Social Security number to qualify for a loan, either because the borrower does not have a number or because the borrower's credit rating associated with their true number is inadequate for approval. (Note: Identity theft, on the other hand, is an attempt to obtain credit in another person's name.)

Identity Fraud problems are also discussed later in this section under Taxpayer ID Problems.

Informal Value Transfer Systems (IVTS)

IVTS is a term used to describe money or value transfer systems that operate informally to transfer money. In the past, some of those informal networks were labeled by various terms including "alternative remittance systems" and "underground banking." Depending on the ethnic group, IVTS are called by a variety of names including, for example, *hawala* (Middle East, Afghanistan, Pakistan); *hundi* (India); *fei ch'ien* (China); *phoe kuan* (Thailand); and *Black Market Peso Exchange* (South America).

U.S. citizens and persons residing in this country, who are from nations where the use of IVTS is commonplace, employ the system for various reasons. In countries lacking a stable financial sector or containing substantial areas not served by formal financial institutions, IVTS may be the only method for conducting financial transactions. For example, foreign aid money going to Afghanistan is being disbursed through IVTS due to a lack of a banking infrastructure in that country. Individuals and organizations often use IVTS due to inadequate payment systems, foreign exchange or capital controls, or because the formal financial sector is not readily accessible, is significantly more expensive, or is more difficult to navigate.

Indicators of Misuse of IVTS in Terrorist Financing

While the majority of IVTS activity is legitimate in purpose (IVTS traditionally serves the purpose of remitting funds of expatriate communities to their home countries), some of these systems have been used to facilitate the financing of terrorism. The very features that make the systems attractive to legitimate customers — efficiency, convenience, trust, speed, anonymity, and the lack of a paper trail — also appeal to terrorists and terrorist organizations. Also, criminals use the networks to launder dirty money, make illicit payments, and commit other offenses such as tax evasions and customs violations.

- **The following activities may be suspicious and indicate misuse of IVTS:**

    o   Transactions divergent from the normal activity (or expected low income) of a business entity or customer including:

    o   sudden influxes of activity and/or unexplained funds deposits;

    o   high volumes of financial transactions in comparison with those of other same scale businesses located and operating in the area (e.g., grocery stores; travel agencies; boutiques; import/export businesses; shipping and trading companies; restaurants; jewelry stores or businesses; textile stores or businesses); or;

    o   large and/or mixed deposits of cash and monetary instruments, inconsistent with the expected type of transactions for the business.

    o   Unusually high levels of cash shipments detected in conjunction with a small business operation;

    o   Transactions involving unusual business trade connections (e.g., small scale auto parts dealer sending aggregate wire transfers to a precious metal dealer or agricultural importer);

- o Separate (or lack of) records kept for certain clients and/or large transactions;

- o Account activity involving only deposits and one-way wire transfers;

- o Varying methods of funds delivery and/or collection;

- o Unusually high volume or patterns of incoming express/priority mail.

- In March 2003, FinCEN issued Advisory 33,3 which provided a general overview of informal value transfer systems (IVTS) and indicators of such activity. As part of the Advisory, FinCEN provided instructions to financial institutions regarding the filing of IVTS related SARs. The guidance instructed depository institutions to check the "Other" box in Part III, Line 35(s) on Form TD F 90–22.47 and note the abbreviation "IVTS" in the space following the box in instances where the financial institution had reason to believe the activity to be IVTS related. Some financial institutions have followed that guidance and, in doing so, have provided valuable and more easily retrievable information to FinCEN and law enforcement regarding IVTS trends and patterns. Depository institutions should continue to follow the guidance in Advisory 33 for reporting IVTS related suspicious transactions.

- Most IVTS operations are considered money services businesses (MSBs) by virtue of the funds/value transfer services they provide to their customers. Financial institutions often identify IVTS operations when exercising effective due diligence on customers who claim to be money remitters yet fail to provide adequate proof that the business is registered with the Department of the Treasury or appropriately licensed in respective states where such licenses are required. The type of account activity exhibited by such entities also provides significant insight into the identification of illegal and informal MSBs that may be providing IVTS services. The SARs analyzed for this study provided a number of such indicators:

  - o Use of personal accounts to facilitate the negotiation of cash and third party checks followed by outgoing wire transfers;

  - o Account activity inconsistent with the type of account held by a customer and/or volume of activity anticipated by the filing institution (according to the expected levels conveyed to the institution by the account holder);

  - o Account holder occupation inconsistent with the type and volume of financial activity affecting an account; e.g., unemployed, housewife, etc.;

  - o Large volume deposits of cash, checks, and other types of monetary instruments immediately followed by wire transactions abroad;

  - o Structured cash transactions through the use of multiple transactors at multiple branches of the financial institution where the suspect account is maintained;

  - o Account holders using their personal accounts to act as possible agents of wire remitter businesses;

o   Personal accounts used as *layering* points involving wire transfers sent into those accounts from unregistered and/or unlicensed MSBs and then transferred abroad;

o   Cash intensive businesses (for example, restaurants) providing transfer services to groups of people by accepting cash to facilitate payments to customers' family members residing in a foreign country;

o   Businesses conducting structured cash deposits and drawing checks from their account to purchase bulk phone cards and/or stored value cards for possible resale;

o   Similarly, a subject engaged in the suspected operation of an unlicensed MSB conducting numerous outgoing wire transmissions out of his personal account, in addition to drawing checks from his account to pay for phone cards;

o   Use of possible shell companies and multiple accounts to facilitate the structuring of cash, deposit of money orders, and the negotiation of third party checks, followed by wire transfers from the accounts to high risk countries;

o   Deposits of cash into accounts and subsequent outgoing overseas wire transfers by unregistered and/or unlicensed MSBs conducted on behalf of expatriate workers wishing to send money back home to their families; an account is typically maintained to service customers in one state or locale, while the actual account holder (or an agent) conducts the remittance transactions from another state. In one reported instance, foreign cruise line employees transferred cash to an unlicensed MSB via an intermediary who carried the cash from the ship and deposited it into the unlicensed MSB account at a nearby bank branch on shore. The account holder was actually located several states away and transferred the funds to an associate in a foreign country for further dispersal to relatives of the cruise line employees, also residing in the foreign country.

o   Multiple wire transfers sent from unregistered and/or unlicensed MSBs to benefit a single beneficiary located in a foreign country; and

o   Unlicensed and/or unregistered MSBs sending large volumes of wire transfers to a single personal account within the United States; transactors in multiple states conduct cash deposits into the same personal account.

Hawala and Black Market Peso Exchange

Hawala

The term hawala simply means transfer in Arabic and is commonly associated with IVTS activities that occur in southwest Asia and the Middle East. Since September 11th, the financial community has acquired a better understanding of hawala and other IVTS(s) located in the United States and throughout the world, as well as observing their nexus with bank accounts.

- The following extracts were taken from SARs associated with hawala and similar types of IVTS related activity:

  o A wire transfer company was identified as a hawala by the filing financial institution. The company sent a large volume of wire transfers to an Arabian Gulf nation.

  o A financial institution identified a customer who accepted large volumes of money orders and other monetary instruments deposited into his personal account. When questioned about the activity, the customer indicated he provided services, through his brother residing in a south Asian country, to local expatriates wishing to send merchandise to their families in their home country. The customer further indicated he accepted payment from his customers either by money order or cashier's check. When his customers provided these payments, the suspect customer contacted his brother to release the merchandise to the particular family member abroad.

  o A former banking employee was suspected of acting as an unlicensed money transmitter on behalf of his brother located in a West African nation. He would collect cash from local members of the community that would be deposited into his personal account, followed by wire transfers to trading companies in Asia and North America.

  o An account held by a clothing and jewelry store was identified with large cash deposits and numerous deposits of checks and other monetary instruments. Once a month, a large wire transfer from the account was sent to a Southeast Asian country.

  o Street vendors, all expatriates of a south Asian country, deposited cash into accounts, from which the balances were subsequently wire transferred to a businessman residing in the south Asian country. When further questioned, the street vendors indicated they were conducting this operation because only certain individuals could maintain accounts in the receiving country.

  o An unregistered and/or unlicensed entity was identified as making several large cash deposits into its account, in addition to negotiating several checks drawn on personal accounts from all over the country. The funds were further transferred to a trading company located in an Arabian Gulf country.

  o Two "students" were identified as the joint holders of a checking account. Several checks issued from a number of Arabian Gulf nations, including cultural offices, were deposited into the account. Checks were also drawn on the account made payable to other subjects, as well as other varied types of debit activity occurring through the account.

o   A money exchange entity was identified as structuring over $3 million into an account within a one-month period. The account was set up to allow members of a local ethnic community to send funds to their families in a Southeast Asian country.

o   Two SARs, filed on the SAR–MSB form, mentioned "hawala" in the narrative. The SARs identified a customer who visited multiple branches of the same money transmitter service to send funds to a south Asian country. Each transaction was under $3,000 and was forwarded to the same payee on multiple days.

Black Market Peso Exchange (BMPE)

For additional information on BMPE, see FinCEN Advisory Issue 12, Black Market Peso Exchange Update, issued June 1999, (http://www.fincen.gov/advis12.pdf) and, FinCEN Advisory Issue 9, Black Market Peso Exchange, issued November 1997, (http://www.fincen.gov/advisu9.pdf).

• The type of activities revealed in SARs filed on BMPEs include the following:

o   Several accounts maintained at a financial institution were used to deposit bulk cash through domestic ATM transactions. Shortly after the deposits, numerous cash withdrawals of the funds were initiated via ATMs in Colombia.

o   An account holder engaged in agricultural activity was identified as remitting a total of $400,000 to numerous financial institutions located in Central America. The subject was suspected by the filing bank as engaging in possible BMPE operations based on secondary information received by the financial institution.

Insurance

As of May 2007, the SAR regulation includes several definitions that limit its applicability. FinCEN has defined an "insurance company" to be any person engaged in the business of issuing or underwriting "covered products." A covered product includes an annuity contract, a permanent life insurance contract, or any insurance product that possesses a cash value or investment feature. The practical result is that the insurance company SAR regulation applies primarily to life insurance companies and not traditional property and casualty or health insurance companies.

The regulation contains additional limitations on the scope of insurance products that must be reviewed for suspicious activity. Products that are offered to a group of persons but issued under a single contract are expressly excluded from the SAR regulation.[9] Therefore, group annuity and group life contracts are not required to be included within the scope of an insurance company's SAR process. This risk-based recognition of money laundering within the insurance world is very important as it allows the insurance industry to focus its limited resources on areas with more money laundering risk.

In addition to the definitional provisions noted above, the SAR regulation addresses two additional points that are unique to the insurance industry. First, it includes an exception from filing a SAR if the suspicious activity is associated with false or fraudulent information used to obtain a policy or make a claim (e.g., traditional insurance fraud). Again, this allows the insurance industry to focus on identifying and reporting suspicious activity that is indicative of money laundering or terrorist financing. The exception to the exception is that a SAR must still be filed if the false or fraudulent submission relates to terrorist financing or money laundering.

Second, the SAR regulation makes it clear that insurance companies are responsible for their agents (regardless of whether the agent is employed by the insurance company or an independent agent). Therefore, the SAR process must be designed to address the activities of their agents and report associated suspicious activity detected by these agents. The regulation does permit insurance companies to partner with other financial institutions to make a joint filing of the suspicious activity. An issue the insurance industry is struggling to address is the integration of their agents into the AML Program and SAR regulations.

SAR Filings Related to Insurance

- **SARs noted by insurance companies included:**
  - Cash used to buy insurance policies;
  - The insurance agency/broker served clients who did not have bank accounts and paid premiums in cash;
  - Transactions inconsistent with the types expected in an insurance agency, such as:
    - Deposits of funds for which the companies were unable to discern the source or purpose;
    - Unusually large cash deposits;
    - Operating a loan service; and,
    - Wire transfers with no apparent business purpose.
  - Suspicions that insurance agencies were operating check cashing services;
  - Wire transfers to foreign jurisdictions with no apparent business purpose;
  - Unverifiable source of cash funds deposits from affiliated agencies;
- **Suspicious transactions involved insurance annuities in 48 (5%) of the sampled narratives in 2007. Filers characterized all of the suspicious activity in these reports as BSA/Structuring/Money Laundering.**
  - **Unknown Source of Funds** – SAR filers reported unknown or unverifiable sources of funds, such as cash, official checks, or sequential money orders, used to fund annuity purchases;
  - **Structuring** – Filers reported structured withdrawals of funds following deposits of annuity checks. This type of activity could indicate an effort to avoid BSA reporting requirements.
  - **Rapid Fund Withdrawal** – Filers reported rapid withdrawals of funds shortly after deposits of large insurance checks. The filers deemed this activity suspicious because the purpose of the large fund withdrawals could not be determined.
  - **Free Look Period** [10] – Two filers in 2007 reported the cancellation of annuity products and requests for refunds within the free look period. Although this activity may be a legitimate exercise of consumer rights, it also could represent a money laundering method, particularly if accompanied by other indicia of suspicion.
  - **Investment Fraud** – One filer in 2007 reported a client's pattern of closing accounts with one known insurance company and reopening new accounts shortly afterwards with the same company, each time with new ownership information.
  - **Money Laundering** – Filers in 2007 reported activities they believed could represent money laundering involving annuities such as:

- a non-resident alien attempted to purchase a multi-million dollar, single premium, immediate annuity product with a monthly payout of over $10,000;
- a report of an indictment for money laundering involving some annuity accounts; and,
- a report of the circular movement of cash between a subject's personal and business accounts and an annuity account opened with another institution.

o **Reported suspicious activity has involved deposits of checks issued from insurance companies or checks used as payments to insurance companies**.

- **Structuring** – Subjects structured cash withdrawals after deposits of checks drawn by insurance companies. This could represent an effort to avoid the BSA reporting requirements.

- **Funding of Insurance Policies with Cash** – SAR filers reported that insurance premiums were funded with cash or negotiable instruments such as money orders or official checks. This could represent a money laundering method.

- **Other types of reported activities included:**

  o **Viatical Settlements** – Four filers in 2007 reported suspicious activities involving viatical settlements. (In a viatical settlement, a person purchases the life insurance policy (or part of a policy) from the seller (often someone with a terminal or chronic illness) at a price that is less than the death benefit of the policy. The purchaser becomes the new owner or beneficiary of the life insurance policy, pays all future premiums, and collects the death benefit when the seller dies. Viatical settlements are legitimate investment products that can be abused to commit fraud against the insurance company and legitimate investors, as well as for money laundering. One subject guaranteed investment returns up to 80%. Another filer reported that the policy beneficiaries were primarily located in a foreign jurisdiction.)

  o **Advance fee fraud** – Between May 2002 and March 2004, two insurance companies filed 30 reports regarding e-mails requesting assistance in moving large sums of money. These emails were typical of advance fee fraud [11] schemes.

  o **Insurance loans** – A pattern of structured cash withdrawals and repayments involving a loan on an insurance policy. The subject withdrew just under $10,000 from the policy, replaced the funds within a few days, and then repeated the process a few days later.

  o **Insurance Fraud** – A depository institution reported applications for life insurance policies by three individuals from a foreign jurisdiction. The filer suspected something was wrong because the individuals obtained identification and opened bank accounts on the same dates that they submitted the insurance applications. The subjects were upset that the policies would not be issued on the day of the application.

o   **Terrorist Financing** – A foreign national applied for a life insurance policy. During the application process, the subject asked if the policy would pay if the insured committed suicide.

o   **Money Laundering** – A depository institution suspected that cash deposited to a customer's account originated from illegal drug sales proceeds. Funds from five debits from the customer's account, totaling over $250,000, were sent to an insurance company.

o   **Pre-Paid Insurance Policies** – Insurance filers reported possible methods of money laundering using pre-paid insurance policies. One report described the deposit of over $10,000 into a pre-paid insurance policy. The policy owner then requested a loan against that policy in an amount under $10,000. Another report described multiple subjects paying advance insurance premiums and then requesting refunds of the pre-paid amounts. A third report described a subject who sent 21 checks from different businesses (all with the same address) totaling over $40,000 to pre-pay premiums on his life insurance policy. The annual premium was over $10,000.

- **Money Services Businesses also filed SARs related to insurance:**

  ▪   Forty-nine percent of SARs filed reported the suspicious use of money orders that were made payable to insurance companies. The purchase of these money orders appeared to have been structured in order to avoid BSA reporting requirements.

  ▪   SARs also reported the use of official checks that were made payable to insurance companies. Fifteen percent of the SARs filed reported the structured purchase of official checks.

- **The Securities and Futures Industries reported insurance related BSA suspicious activities as follows:**

  o   Filers reported customers using numerous money orders to initially purchase insurance policies or annuities or to pay annual premium payments. Customers also used money orders to repay loans taken against their policies. One filer indicated that it was unusual to receive money orders as payments and that insurance premiums typically were paid by personal or business checks or electronic funds transfers. Activities described in the narratives included subjects:

    ▪   Purchasing money orders from more than one vendor;

    ▪   Purchasing money orders from different tellers at the same bank on the same day. Some money orders were also purchased at two or more of a bank's branches, usually on the same day; and

- Purchasing money orders prior to taking out loans against insurance policies. The money orders were then used to repay the loans.

- **Filers reported suspicious actions by applicants during the insurance or annuity application process. Actions by applicants included:**

  o Providing false information (e.g. name, social security number, citizenship, etc.) or providing information which could not be verified;

    - Failing to produce proper documentation to substantiate the information on the application. In some instances, upon being questioned about the information provided, applicants rescinded their applications;
    - Insisting that a rush should be placed on the application process; and,
    - Asking questions or making comments that raised the filer's suspicion.

- **SAR filers reported insurance agents, broker/dealers and/or registered representatives of insurance companies engaging in illegal activities concerning customer's insurance products. Insider actions by agents, broker/dealers or representatives included:**

  o Opening accounts in customers' names and making insiders the account beneficiaries. The named account owners usually were unaware of the policies. In some instances, representatives changed the beneficiary information on clients' policies to make themselves the beneficiaries;

  o Taking a portion of the funds, usually cash, given by customers for premium payments and depositing the funds into the insider's own bank accounts for personal use. One filer reported a registered representative for accepting cash from a family friend for the purchase of a fixed annuity. The cash was deposited into the representative's personal account so that the bank could prepare a cashier's check as payment for the annuity purchase;

  o Paying premiums on customers' (e.g. friends, family, unrelated clients) accounts with the insider's own money;

  o Engaging in Advance Fee Fraud scams. One representative sent e-mails from his employment account soliciting and offering to provide assistance to individuals involved in these types of scams;

  o Forging the signatures of clients on forms; and,

  o Submitting premium payments for policies, using money orders or personal checks, on behalf of clients from organizations or individuals that were not named as the intended premium payers as part of the application process and where no insurable or financial interest was apparent.

- **A securities firm in 2007 filed ten reports on immigrants associated with an insurance agent who sold numerous policies to these immigrants and their families**. The immigrants primarily traveled from one location to another, working in service jobs and earning minimal salaries. The filer believed the agent assisted the individuals in their pursuit of legal status in the United States. The agent, of the same nationality, admitted falsifying employment information on applicants; assisting in paying the individuals' premiums by converting cash into money orders; and accepting premium payment from third parties, usually family members but also other unrelated parties. The filer believed that none of the insured immigrants had legal status in the United States.

  o SAR filers reported large dollar amounts wired in and out of accounts involving annuity life accounts. Some of the wire activity involved annuity accounts in foreign jurisdictions.

- **Other reported activities included:**

  o SAR filers reported customers purchasing numerous policies or annuities, usually with large amounts of cash and then taking advantage of the free-look periods to cash out the instruments. Filers indicated that this activity was consistent with money laundering activities, although it may also have been a legitimate exercise of consumer rights.

  o SAR filers reported customers using structured cash payments to purchase annuities, pay premiums or repay loans taken out against a life insurance policy. Filers stated that the activity might indicate that its customers may have been trying to circumvent BSA reporting requirements. Reports also were filed for large cash deposits as well as when the filer was unable to determine the source of funds.

  o SAR filers reported customers using multiple payment methods, (e.g., cashier's check, personal check, money order, etc.) to pay premiums. One filer indicated that it was unusual to see multiple payment forms used in paying premiums.

  o SAR filers reported several customers structuring check deposits (teller check, bank check, traveler's check, cashier's check, and personal check) to pay for premiums, fund annuity accounts and repay loans against life insurance policies.

  o SAR filers reported customers treating annuity accounts like savings accounts. Customers deposited large sums of money into their annuity accounts and then made withdrawals, which sometimes left the account with a zero balance. On numerous reports, customers provided what the filers considered vague explanations for the activity. Deposits started again only to be followed by withdrawals. Similarly, customers were reported for opening life insurance policies and after a period of time, making numerous partial surrender/withdrawals with corresponding premium payments.

o   One filer in 2007 reported an applicant for making frequent small dollar premium remittances over a period of less than one year for life insurance policies that had yet to be issued. Numerous small dollar refund checks issued back to the applicant were never cashed. The applicant blamed it on an erroneous address and asked for the refund in one lump sum by wire, totaling thousands of dollars. Similarly, filers reported customers sending in larger payments than the expected amount due, resulting in refund checks issued back to customers.

o   SAR filers reported customers moving money between multiple products. Customers opened policies and then after a short period of time, asked for a surrender/withdrawal and used the funds to open another policy, sometimes with the same filer or with another policy issuer.

o   SAR filers reported customers making substantial surrender/withdrawals from either an annuity or life insurance policy. The filers found it suspicious when customers expressed little or no concern about the surrender/withdrawal charges assessed on the investment.

o   SAR filers reported customers depositing money into several insurance policies with various insurance companies.

o   SAR filers reported numerous instances when filers' representatives, while conducting routine reviews of clients, uncovered news articles concerning law enforcement investigations, arrests, indictments or guilty pleas for illicit acts, (e.g., money laundering, pornography, organized crime, racketeering, etc.), which involved the individuals. In some instances, a news article initiated a client review. Filers indicated reviews attempted to ascertain if clients used any funds derived from the illicit activities to pay insurance premiums.

International Cash Letter Clearing

In basic terms, an *international cash letter* functions as a method of inter-bank communication for processing transactions between banks located in different countries. The communication is in the form of a document (cash letter) that accompanies checks, drafts, money orders, and traveler's checks. When submitted for collection by a foreign correspondent depository bank to the U.S. clearing bank, the cash letter details the number of checks or other items sent as well as the total dollar amount of the included items. Upon receipt from a foreign correspondent bank, the U.S. clearing bank sends the monetary instruments for clearance or negotiation to the financial institution(s) upon which the individual items were originally drawn. The foreign bank's account at the U.S. clearing bank will then be credited for the total amount of the cash letter.

International cash letter processing through correspondent accounts is a standard banking service provided by some U.S. financial institutions to foreign financial institutions. An international cash letter is an inter-bank transmittal letter that accompanies checks or monetary instruments (such as money orders) sent from one bank to another internationally. Some banks that monitor their cash letter processes for suspicious activities have identified bulk movements of monetary instruments, which appear to be indicative of money laundering. Their observations are consistent with several recent law enforcement cases involving money laundering through bulk monetary instrument transactions. FinCEN is monitoring this reported activity to determine if it is indicative of a trend.

Investigations and SARs filed by financial institutions have revealed that monetary instruments, purchased in bulk with illicit proceeds, are sometimes cleared through cash letters. It is important to note that the clearing banks are several steps removed from the actual conversion of the illicit funds to monetary instruments. Their ability to nonetheless identify the indicia of suspicious activity in the course of clearing these instruments suggests there may be a vulnerability at the stage at which the instruments are actually issued (for example, sequentially numbered monetary instruments endorsed by the same person aggregating to a high value). Thus, monitoring of the cash letter process can yield important insights into not only trends in bulk movement of monetary instruments but also potential vulnerabilities at their point of sale.

The banking regulatory agencies have examination procedures requiring financial institutions to give enhanced scrutiny to cash letter processing, which has resulted in SAR filings. FinCEN's comprehensive study of IVTS provided examples of suspicious activity involving the international transport of monetary instruments. For example, BMPE schemes reveal narcotic proceeds clearing through correspondent accounts via checks, money orders, and other types of monetary instruments. FinCEN has found the SARs filed by financial institutions from their monitoring of cash letters to be valuable in identifying such activity.

- Following are some examples of activities involving bulk monetary instruments and cash letters:
  - o In a case involving the Kumar hawala, the United States Attorney for the Eastern District of New York recently charged nine defendants with participating in the Kumar Organization's unlicensed money transmitting

business. Kumar transmitted in excess of $32 million out of the United States between January 2001 and May 2003. The government alleged that in addition to illegal money transmissions, Kumar converted currency into monetary instruments, including money orders and checks, and sent these funds via courier service outside the United States. On a single day, May 25, 2002, Customs Inspectors at Newark/Liberty International Airport intercepted Kumar's courier packages destined for Canada containing approximately $100,000.

o Law enforcement agents in the San Francisco area report that lower volume hawalas re sending money orders overseas for negotiation.

o Law enforcement personnel at several major airports on the east coast have discovered large amounts of money orders in even amounts, and sequentially numbered, being sent regularly to a country in the Middle East.

International Lottery Schemes

Although there are several variations of the international lottery scam (The Federal Bureau of Investigation (FBI) recently posted an advisory regarding foreign lottery scams on its website (http://www.fbi.gov/page2/aug06/lotto_scams080906.htm), callers to the FinCEN's Regulatory Help-Line have most frequently reported a version involving monetary instruments and overseas wires. Generally, international lottery scam operators will contact individuals via the Internet, telephone, or mail and announce that the individuals have won cash prizes in a foreign lottery. The individuals also are informed that, before they can collect their winnings, they must pay certain fees, taxes, or other expenses. To "assist" with payment of these miscellaneous fees, the lottery scam operators will mail to the individuals checks or other monetary instruments, with instructions to cash the instruments. The individuals are told that, once instruments are cashed, the proceeds must immediately be wired to an entity or person located in another country. The lottery scam operators claim that when the proceeds have been received, the lottery scam operators will pay the individuals the supposed winnings. As is the case with most scams of this nature, there is a great sense of urgency expressed by the scam operators and the individuals are exhorted to "act now" in order to receive, and not forfeit, the winnings.

Financial institutions typically become aware of these scams when the individuals seek to deposit or cash the checks or monetary instruments or wire the proceeds. Callers to the Regulatory Help-Line have indicated that in some cases the monetary instruments presented clearly are bogus, e.g., containing obvious spelling errors or poorly created seals. In some instances, financial institutions have declined to negotiate the monetary instruments and advised the customer that the instruments are counterfeit or bogus. In other instances, the monetary instruments presented appear authentic and are cashed for the customer; later, however, the monetary instruments are returned as non-negotiable and either the bank or the customer suffers a monetary loss.

SAR Filing for International Lottery Schemes

Although FinCEN previously has provided guidance regarding the filing of SARs on other types of scams, financial institutions have sought clarification as to whether that previously issued guidance applies equally to international lottery scams. In The SAR Activity Review – Trends, Tips & Issues, Issue 7 (August 2004), FinCEN advised financial institutions that it was unnecessary to file SARs on 4-1-9 (advance fee fraud) scams if there was no monetary loss. However, FinCEN also advised financial institutions that they should consider filing a Suspicious Activity Report if there was a monetary loss to the financial institution or if the scam involved other illegal activity. In The SAR Activity Review – Trends, Tips & Issues, Issue 10 (May 2006), FinCEN reiterated this guidance for "third party receiver of funds" scams. The preceding guidance, given with regard to 4-1-9 and third party receiver of funds scams, applies to international lottery scams as well.

It may be difficult to clearly identify suspects in connection with international lottery and similar scams. Callers to the Regulatory Help-Line often indicate they have listed their customers as suspects on related SAR forms; however, generally, the customer should not be considered a suspect unless there is reason to believe that the customer knowingly cashed counterfeit monetary instruments or was otherwise complicit in the scam. In most circumstances, the customer is a victim of the scam, and unaware that participation in foreign lotteries is illegal or that the checks or other monetary instruments that they have received are counterfeit. Additionally, the names (such as the payee name) that appear on such checks or other monetary instruments typically are phony and do not indicate real suspects; however, if a Suspicious Activity Report is completed, it is recommended that the payee name be included in the Suspect/Subject field of the Form.

If counterfeit instruments are received via the U.S. postal system, financial institutions may report that to the U.S. Postal Inspection Service. If contact was initially made via the Internet, a complaint may be filed with the Internet Crime Complaint Center (http://www.ic3.gov/). Moreover, individuals who have been victimized by these scams may contact their local FBI office.

Mexico Related and Bulk Cash Smuggling

An increasingly prevalent money laundering threat involves the smuggling of bulk U.S. currency into Mexico in combination with the misuse of relationships with U.S. financial institutions by certain Mexican financial institutions, including Mexican casas de cambio. Mexican casas de cambio, unlike money services businesses in the United States, may act as brokers for financial transactions. For example, a casa de cambio as part of its routine business may direct payment to a U.S. manufacturer for export of commodities to Mexico.

Once U.S. currency is in Mexico, numerous layered transactions may be used to disguise its origins, after which it may be returned directly to the United States or further transshipped to or through other jurisdictions. The following activities, in various combinations, may be associated with this currency smuggling trend:

- o An increase in the sale of large denomination U.S. bank notes to Mexican institutions by U.S. banks;
- o Small denomination U.S. bank notes smuggled into Mexico being exchanged for large denomination U.S. bank notes possessed by Mexican financial institutions;
- o Large volumes of small denomination U.S. bank notes being sent from Mexican casas de cambio to their accounts in the United States via armored transport, or sold directly to U.S. banks;
- o Multiple wire transfers initiated by casas de cambio that direct U.S. financial institutions to remit funds to jurisdictions outside of Mexico that bear no apparent business relationship with that casa de cambio (recipients include individuals, businesses, and other entities in free trade zones and other locations associated with Black Market Peso Exchange-type activities);
- o The exchange of small denomination U.S. bank notes for large denomination U.S. bank notes that may be sent to jurisdictions outside of Mexico, including jurisdictions associated with Black Market Peso Exchange-type activities (The Black Market Peso Exchange (BMPE) is a large-scale money laundering system used to launder proceeds of narcotic sales in the United States by Latin American drug cartels by facilitating swaps of dollars in the U.S. for pesos in Colombia through the sale of dollars to Latin America businessmen seeking to buy U.S. goods to export. For additional information , see the Informal Value Transfer Systems section of this manual);
- o Deposits by casas de cambio to their accounts at U.S. financial institutions that include third-party items (including sequentially numbered monetary instruments); and;
- o Deposits of currency and third-party items by Mexican casas de cambio to their accounts at Mexican financial institutions and thereafter direct wire transfers to the casas accounts at U.S. financial institutions

While the activity highlighted above may not be indicative of criminal activity, U.S. financial institutions should consider this activity in conjunction with other information when determining whether to file a suspicious activity report in accordance with the standard for SAR reporting.

Recent Changes in the Laundering Cycle

More recently, US law enforcement agencies have reported a shift from past patterns where drug proceeds were transited through Mexico en route to Colombia or other Central and South American destinations. The shift has been made toward using techniques and schemes in which drug proceeds are cycled through Mexico directly back into the U.S. As reported in SARs filed by financial institutions, patterns of large wire transactions ($1.5 million or more per transaction) moving funds to U.S. payees from Mexican money exchange houses and other financial institutions have been observed that may at least, in part, be attributable to changes in the laundering cycle. Generally speaking, such changes in patterns are believed to stem from the heightened profile of Mexico-based criminal groups in drug trafficking in the U.S. which, in turn, creates a corresponding increased threat of money laundering activity linked to Mexico.

Mortgage Loan Fraud

Mortgage loan fraud can be divided into two broad categories: fraud for property and fraud for profit. Fraud for property generally involves material misrepresentation or omission of information with the intent to deceive or mislead a lender into extending credit that would likely not be offered if the true facts were known. The fraudulent activities observed in the SAR narratives describing fraud for property include:

o   Asset fraud;
o   Occupancy fraud;
o   Employment and income fraud;
o   Debt elimination fraud;
o   Identity theft; and,
o   Straw buyers (A straw buyer is someone who purchases property for another person in order to conceal the identity of the true purchaser).

Fraud for property is generally committed by home buyers attempting to purchase homes for their personal use. In contrast, the motivation behind fraud for profit is money. Fraud for profit is often committed with the complicity of industry insiders such as mortgage brokers, real estate agents, property appraisers, and settlement agents (attorneys and title examiners). Typical fraudulent activities associated with this category in the SAR filing sampling are:

o   Appraisal fraud;
o   Fraudulent flipping (Property flipping generally involves the buying and selling of the same property within a short period of time with the intention of making a quick profit.)
o   Straw buyers; and,
o   Identity theft.

Identity theft was frequently reported in conjunction with the commission of suspected mortgage loan fraud.

Reported Suspicious Activities in SAR Narratives
In the FinCEN 2006 study: Mortgage Loan Fraud: An Industry Assessment Based on SAR Analysis, the following was noted:

- **Loan Types**
  The purchase of residential property was the most frequently reported loan purpose (83.65%), followed by refinance, home equity, and second trust loans (12.17%). New construction loans made up a relatively small percentage of the sampled narratives (1.52%).

- **Material Misrepresentation (65.78%)**
  The following are the types of loan falsifications reported in the sampled SAR narratives:
  o   Altered bank statements;
  o   Altered or fraudulent earnings documentation such as W–2s and income tax returns;
  o   Fraudulent letters of credit;

- o Fabricated letters of gift;
- o Misrepresentation of employment;
- o Altered credit scores;
- o Invalid social security numbers;
- o Silent second trust; (A silent second trust occurs when the seller takes back a second down payment. The lender is not aware of the second trust.
- o Failure to fully disclose the borrower's debts or assets; or
- o Mortgage brokers using the identities of prior customers to obtain loans for customers who were otherwise unable to qualify.

- **Identity Fraud (23.12%)**
  Identity fraud refers to the loan applicant's use of a non-existent social security number or a number taken from the social security death index, along with the use of the borrower's true personal identifiers (name, date of birth, address). The loan applicant intends to use the Social Security number to qualify for a loan, either because the borrower does not have a number or because the borrower's credit rating associated with their true number is inadequate for approval. (Note: Identity theft, on the other hand, is an attempt to obtain credit in another person's name. It was noted on only 3.9% of the narratives.)

- **Misrepresentation of Loan Purpose / Misuse of Proceeds (12.26%)**
  The most commonly reported misrepresentation was occupancy fraud, which occurs when the borrower fails to occupy the property, although the loan application specified the property was the borrower's primary residence. Occupancy fraud was reported in 104 (80.62%) of these reports. Possible motivations for misrepresentation of the loan purpose are to purchase investment property with more favorable loan rates than would be available if a lender knew the property was intended for use other than as a primary residence, or to launder funds from illicit activity.

- **Appraisal Fraud**
  Appraisal fraud and fraudulent property flipping were described in 111 of the sampled reports (10.55%). Appraisal fraud is frequently associated with fraudulent property flipping. Filers indicated on 48 (42.34%) of these reports that they suspected the fraudulent activity was perpetrated with the collusion of mortgage brokers, appraisers, borrowers, and/or real estate agents/brokers.

  Lenders rely on accurate appraisals to ensure that loans are fully secured. Appraisal fraud occurs when appraisers fail to accurately evaluate the property, or when the appraiser deliberately becomes party to a scheme to defraud the lender, the borrower, or both. The Appraisal Institute and the American Society of Appraisers testified that "...it is common for mortgage brokers, lenders, realty agents and others with a vested interest to seek out inflated appraisals to facilitate transactions because it pays them to do so." Higher sales prices typically generate higher fees for brokers, lenders, real estate agents, and loan settlement offices, and higher earnings for real estate investors. Appraisal fraud has a snowball effect on inflating real estate values, with fraudulent values being entered into real estate multiple listing systems and then used by legitimate appraisers as comparable values for determining market values for neighborhood properties. Some commonly reported types of appraisal fraud found in the sampled narratives are:

o   Appraisers failed to use comparable properties to establish property values;
o   Appraisers failed to physically visit the property and based the appraisal solely on comparable properties, i.e., the actual condition of the property was not factored into the appraisal;
o   Appraisers participated in a fraud scheme such as flipping; or,
o   A licensed appraiser's name and seal were used by unauthorized persons.

- **Property Flipping**
Fraudulent property flipping is purchasing property and artificially inflating its value. The fraud perpetrators frequently use identity theft, straw borrowers and industry insiders to effect property flipping schemes. Ultimately, the property is resold for 50 to 100 percent of its original cost. In the end, the loan amount exceeds the value of the property and the lender sustains a loss when the loan defaults. The following fraudulent activities were reported in the sampled narratives that described property flipping.

o   Nearly 64 percent of sampled narratives described collusion by sellers, appraisers, and mortgage brokers in connection with property flipping.
o   Nearly 14 percent of the sampled narratives described the use of straw buyers.

- **Forged Documents**
Use of forged documents was reported on 20 (1.9%) of the sampled narratives, with correspondent lenders or mortgage brokers processing the loans described in five of those reports. The types of activity reported include the following:

o   Borrowers forged co-owners' signatures to loan documents (most often one spouse forging the other spouse's signature without prior knowledge or permission);
o   Loan closing services forged applicants' signatures on loan documents (possibly to expedite the loan process); or
o   Builders forged borrowers' names on loan draw documents.

- **Other Fraudulent Activity**
Other types of fraudulent activity reported in the sampled narratives included:

o   Loan closing services failed to properly disburse loan proceeds or pay off underlying property liens, including prior mortgage trusts.
o   Loan settlement offices were also reported for failure to pay insurance premiums from funds collected at settlement;
o   Borrowers signed multiple mortgages on the same property from multiple lenders. The mortgage settlements were held within a short period of time to prevent the lenders from discovering the fraud;
o   Loan closing services failed to record the mortgage in property land records;

o   Prior lenders failed to release home equity loans in land record offices after receiving mortgage pay-off, causing the new lender's loans to have a subordinate position. Homeowners continued to use the prior lines of credit in addition to the new loan to obtain an extension of credit that exceeded the property value;

o   Violations of the Mortgage Broker Practices Act by mortgage brokers who abused the terms of a power of attorney;

o   Mortgage brokers or correspondent lenders failed to ensure all loan documentation was properly signed;

o   Real Estate Settlement Procedures Act (RESPA) violations by lenders accepting kickbacks from mortgage brokers;

o   Non-arm's-length sales occurred when parties to the real estate transaction failed to disclose relationships between the buyers and sellers. Knowledge of a non-arm's-length sale would alert lenders to scrutinize loan packages more carefully;

o   Elder exploitation where older individuals were persuaded to sign loan documents without understanding borrower rights and responsibilities under applicable federal and state law;

o   Unofficial loan assumption occurred when property ownership was transferred without the knowledge of lenders. This could indicate that a straw buyer was used to obtain the loan, with the property title being transferred to the actual owner after the loan disbursement;

o   Theft of debit card or convenience checks associated with home equity lines of credit;

o   Fraudulent bankruptcy filings to stall or prevent foreclosure; and

o   Suspected use of real estate purchases to launder criminal proceeds.

- **Mortgage Related Debt Elimination Fraud**
  Examples of mortgage related debt elimination schemes reported by SAR filers have included borrowers attempting to pay off their mortgages with non-negotiable checks, or fake instruments such as bills of exchange or subrogation and security bonds. Filers described specious arguments in which the borrowers claimed the mortgage was invalid and the debt never existed. Borrowers who presented these specious arguments are believed to belong to groups that believe U.S. laws and regulations, along with banking regulations, do not apply to them.

  A typical debt elimination fraud scheme involved the presentation of numerous documents containing frivolous arguments that the subject mortgage was invalid. The arguments presented in the documents avowed that funds were never loaned, despite the fact that the borrower received the proceeds. Successful culmination of this scheme would result in the filing of a fraudulent mortgage discharge. The arguments relied on an unreasonable interpretation of Section 1–207 of the Uniform Commercial Code that has never been affirmed or supported by any court or governmental authority.

Other types of debt elimination schemes reported in the SARs were attempts to fraudulently release mortgage liens from municipal land records. Once the land title appeared clear of all mortgage debt, the homeowner could theoretically obtain another mortgage loan based on what appeared to be a clear title. The threat this fraud scheme presents is that a subsequent lender could believe it had a first priority lien on property when in reality there could be little or no equity to secure the loan.

Natural Disaster Relief Fraud

In the wake of natural disasters, such as Hurricanes, an unusually large amount of emergency financial assistance is distributed to victims. Some of the crimes associated with this assistance involve fraudulent schemes in which individuals apply for emergency assistance benefits to which they are not entitled and thereafter seek to deposit or obtain cash derived from the emergency assistance payments.

Possible signs of fraudulent activity that will assist financial institutions in identifying and combating natural disaster related benefit fraud may include:

- o   Deposits of multiple FEMA, Red Cross, or other emergency assistance checks or electronic funds transfers into the same bank account, particularly when the amounts of the checks are the same or approximately the same (e.g., $2,000 or $2,358).
- o   Cashing of multiple emergency assistance checks by the same individual.
- o   Deposits of one or more emergency assistance checks, when the accountholder is a retail business and the payee/endorser is an individual other than the accountholder.
- o   Opening of a new account with an emergency assistance check, where the name of the potential accountholder is different from that of the depositor of the check.

SAR Filing Related to Hurricane or Other Disaster Relief Fraud

To ensure that fraudulent transactions are identified by law enforcement as early as possible FinCEN requests that financial institutions use key terms in the narrative portion of all Suspicious Activity Reports filed in connection with disaster related benefit fraud. Examples of such key terms include

- o   "Katrina," (or name of the hurricane)
- o   "FEMA"
- o   "Red Cross"

If financial institutions encounter any of these situations, or other situations that they suspect may involve hurricane related benefit fraud or other potentially illicit transactions, they should immediately complete and file a Suspicious Activity Report and, in these instances, also contact their local office of the Federal Bureau of Investigation or the United States Secret Service.

Online Gaming Payments

In July, 2006, Congress passed the SAFE Port Act of 2006. (SAFE being an acronym for Security and Accountability For Every Port). Title VIII of the Act is known as the Unlawful Internet Gambling Enforcement Act (UIGEA). This part of the Act intended to prevent the use of certain payment instruments, credit cards, and fund transfers for unlawful Internet gambling, with the notable exceptions of:

- ○ Fantasy Sports;
- ○ Online Lotteries, and,
- ○ Horse/Harness Racing.

In an April 2008 Congressional hearing by The House Monetary and Technology Subcommittee, two regulators and four representatives from the banking industry made clear that there were several issues related to the law that made crafting and implementing regulations difficult and at odds with anti-money laundering compliance practices.

Federal Reserve Director Louise Roseman summed up the UIGEA's problems this way:

> "The construct [of the law] creates ambiguity between what is legal and illegal gambling. And the intent is for the payment system to be the enforcement mechanism. But the payment system is not well designed for this task." She went on to testify that "...the reason that online gambling transactions will be allowed through is that American banks aren't likely to receive assistance from foreign banks in enforcing the UIGEA."

> "Money laundering is a global concern," Roseman said in explaining why money laundering processes can't be applied to online gambling. "Banks around the world cooperate. But the banking industries in countries where gambling is legal have no reason to work on this."

Wayne Abernathy, executive vice president for the American Bankers Association added in his testimony that:

> "The UIGEA takes banks beyond the role of reporting suspicious activities, and makes financial institutions the police, prosecutors, and judges in place of real law enforcement officers."

The practical constraints that regulators are facing makes it unlikely that regulations will be issued by The Federal Reserve or the Treasury Department in 2008. Further, as of this writing, the US has been found in violation of treaty obligations with Antigua by the World Trade Organization by not granting full market access to online gambling companies based in the island nation. In April 2007, U.S. Congressman Barney Frank introduced a bill to overturn the gambling aspects of the Act.

Online/Internet Banking

The common types of violations reported in SARs referencing Internet banks are:
- Check Fraud
- Counterfeit Check
- BSA/Structuring/Money Laundering
- Identity Theft
- Credit Card Fraud
- Other: Unauthorized ACH Debits
- Check Kiting

Trends and Patterns

The mostly commonly reported violations consisted of many different scenarios. The following is a synopsis of the reported activity.

- The vast majority (90%) of SARs reporting check fraud or counterfeit checks involved accounts opened through a bank's Internet website using identities of real persons. Small opening deposits, usually around $100 and consisting of cash, money orders or third-party checks, were conducted in person or mailed to the bank. Shortly thereafter, worthless or counterfeit checks were deposited into the accounts. Some characteristics of those checks included:

  - Alteration to the payee line;
  - Checks chemically washed or otherwise altered; and,
  - Computer generated counterfeit checks.

- Before the fraudulent items were detected and returned, ATM/ debit card withdrawals, point-of-sale transactions, or the transfer of funds via the Internet to another account at a different bank, depleted the deposited funds.

- Frequent, sometimes more than one a day, cash deposits were made to an account followed by online transfers from the receiving account to another account (i.e., moving funds electronically from a checking account to a money market account or from a savings account to a business account). One SAR revealed cash deposits, followed by pre-authorized online withdrawals by an international money transmitter.

Many SARs citing identity theft report the use of individuals' personal information (i.e., social security numbers, personal identification numbers) to access and steal funds in existing bank accounts through on-line transactions, change mailing addresses, order checks on-line, open new depository accounts, or obtain fraudulent loans or credit and debit cards through financial institutions' Internet websites. Frequently, reported activity involves suspects who gained access to victims' accounts to establish online bill payment services. Once activated, the SARs citing identity theft reported the use of individuals' personal information (i.e., social security numbers, personal identification numbers) to access and steal funds in existing bank accounts through on-line transactions, change mailing addresses, order checks on-line, open new depository accounts, or obtain fraudulent loans or credit and debit cards through financial institutions' Internet websites.

Frequently, reported activity involved suspects who gained access to victims' accounts to establish online bill payment services. Once activated, the suspects were able to authorize payments from the victims' accounts to the suspects' creditors.

Financial institutions have reported computer intrusion or hacking attempts perpetrated randomly upon accounts or institution websites, possibly to access customer accounts or information. Often, suspects made numerous attempts within a short time period to penetrate the institutions' firewalls.

Pretext Calling

The fraudulent use of an individual's personal identifying information, such as social security number, date of birth, or bank account number, to commit a financial crime like credit card, check, loan or mortgage fraud –which is commonly referred to as *identity theft*– is a growing problem. One way that wrongdoers improperly obtain personal information of bank customers so as to be able to commit identity theft is by contacting a bank, posing as a customer or someone authorized to have the customer's information, and through the use of trickery and deceit, convincing an employee of the bank to release customer identifying information. This practice is referred to as *pretext calling*.

Banking organizations can take various steps to safeguard customer information and reduce the risk of loss from identity theft. These include:
   o   Establishing procedures to verify the identity of individuals applying for financial products;
   o   Establishing procedures to prevent fraudulent activities related to customer information; and,
   o   Maintaining a customer information security program.

Verification Procedures

Verification procedures for new accounts should include, as appropriate, steps to ensure the accuracy and veracity of application information. These could involve using independent sources to confirm information submitted by a customer; calling a customer to confirm that the customer has opened a credit card or checking account; or verifying information through an employer identified on an application form. A financial institution can also independently verify that the zip code and telephone area code provided on an application are from the same geographical area.

Fraud Prevention

To prevent fraudulent address changes, banking organizations should verify customer information before executing an address change and send a confirmation of the address change to both the new address and the address of record. If an organization receives a request for a new credit card or new checks in conjunction with a change of address notification, it should verify the request with the customer.

When opening a new account, a banking organization should, where possible, check to ensure that information provided on an application has not previously been associated with fraudulent activity. For example, if a banking organization uses a consumer report to process a new account application and the report is issued with a fraud alert, the banking organization's system for credit approval should flag the application and ensure that the individual is contacted before it is processed. In addition, fraud alerts should be shared across the organization's various lines of business.

Information Security

In early 2001, the Federal Reserve Board and the other federal banking agencies issued *Interagency Guidelines Establishing Standards for Safeguarding Customer Information.* The Guidelines require banking organizations to establish and implement a comprehensive information security program that includes appropriate administrative, technical, and physical safeguards for customer information. To prevent pretext callers from using pieces of personal information to impersonate account holders in order to gain access to their account information, the Guidelines require banks and other financial institutions to establish written policies and procedures to control access to customer information.

Other measures that may reduce the incidence of pretext calling include limiting the circumstances under which customer information may be disclosed by telephone. For example, a banking organization may not permit employees to release information over the telephone unless the requesting individual provides a proper authorization code (other than a commonly used identifier). Banking organizations can also use caller identification technology or a request for a call back number as tools to verify the authenticity of a request.

Banking organizations should train employees to recognize and report possible indicators of attempted pretext calling. They should also implement testing to determine the effectiveness of controls designed to thwart pretext callers, and may consider using independent staff or third parties to conduct unscheduled pretext phone calls to various departments.

SAR Filing for Pretext Calling

Criminal activity related to pretext calling or identity theft has historically manifested itself as credit or debit card fraud, loan or mortgage fraud, or false statements to the institution, among other things. As a means of better identifying and tracking known or suspected criminal violations related to pretext calling, a banking organization should, in addition to reporting the underlying fraud (such as credit card or loan fraud) on a SAR, also indicate within the narrative of the SAR that such a known or suspected violation is the result of pretext calling. Specifically, when pretext calling is believed to be the underlying cause of the known or suspected criminal activity, the reporting institution should, consistent with the existing SAR instructions, complete a SAR in the following manner:

- o   In **Part III, Box 35**, check all appropriate boxes that indicate the type of known or suspected violation being reported and, in addition, in the Other category, write in "Pretext Calling"
- o   In **Part V**, explain what is being reported, including the grounds for suspecting pretext calling in addition to the other violations being reported.
- o   In the event the only known or suspected criminal violation detected is the pretext calling, then write in Pretext Calling, as appropriate, in the Other Category in Part III, Box 35.
- o   Provide a description of the activity in **Part V** of the SAR.

Banking organizations should also assist their customers who are victims of identity theft and fraud by having trained personnel to respond to customer inquiries, by determining whether an account should be closed immediately after a report of unauthorized use and by prompt issuance of new checks or new credit, debit or ATM cards. If a customer has multiple accounts with the institution, it should assess whether any other account has been the subject of potential fraud.

Russian Political Activity

Law enforcement information indicates a steady increase in Russian organized criminal activity in the U.S. since the early 1990's. An analysis of Bank Secrecy Act (BSA) data indicates that SARs filed by U.S. financial institutions for suspected structuring/money laundering activity involving Russian transactors, owners or citizenship averages approximately $200 million per year. A correlation of SARs, Currency Transaction Reports (CTRs) and Currency and Monetary Instrument Reports (CMIRs) for Russian transactions indicates some level of financial activity in 45 states, with heavier concentrations in the metropolitan areas of New York, Boston, Washington D.C., Chicago, Miami, Los Angeles, San Francisco, and Seattle. There are also indications of unusual patterns of suspicious financial activity in Texas (i.e., San Antonio, Houston, Dallas/ Ft. Worth, El Paso, and along the U.S-Mexico border.)

On September 21, 1999, the U.S. House of Representatives Committee on Banking and Financial Services held its third hearing on Russian organized crime and corruption for the preceding twelve month period. Witnesses were heard who made allegations that corrupt Russian groups and individuals had infiltrated Western financial institutions. While most professionals in the AML field are familiar with the Bank of New York case involving Lucy Edwards, and while more stringent AML practices have been implemented by banks –especially since 2001, it is probably safe to assume that the practices described by those witnesses continue still today. The full text of the hearing is available on the internet.

Shell Corporations

Most shell companies are formed by individuals and businesses for legitimate reasons. However, these entities also have been used for illicit purposes. Lack of transparency in the formation and operation of shell companies may be a desired characteristic for certain legitimate business activity, but it is also a vulnerability that allows these companies to disguise their ownership and purpose.

Shell Company Overview

The term "shell company," as used herein, refers to non-publicly traded corporations, limited liability companies (LLCs), and trusts that typically have no physical presence (other than a mailing address) and generate little to no independent economic value. Most shell companies are formed by individuals and businesses for legitimate purposes, such as to hold stock or intangible assets of another business entity or to facilitate domestic and cross-border currency and asset transfers and corporate mergers. As noted in the 2005 U.S. Money Laundering Threat Assessment, shell companies have become common tools for money laundering and other financial crimes, primarily because they are easy and inexpensive to form and operate. and can be easily interlocked with other shell corporations located all over the world. If a shell corporation is established in a jurisdiction with strict secrecy laws, it can be almost impossible to identify the owners or directors of the corporation and therefore nearly impossible to trace illicit funds back to their true owner. This is precisely the effect the launderer, terrorist financier and tax evader seeks, and is why shell corporations are an effective means of interrupting the paper trail used by investigators.

Shell corporations typically exist only on paper. The corporation's formation documents may list a valid bank account and little more than the name and address of the lawyer or agent handling the incorporation, some officers, and perhaps a few shareholders. When criminals seek to utilize shell corporations to disguise ownership or other illicit activity, they will provide fictitious names or nominee names on the corporate formation documents. These accounts play very important roles in illicit money movements because they can be used to receive deposits and as transfer points to the accounts of other shell corporations, legitimate businesses or individuals. The incorporation documents give shell corporations the outward appearance of legitimate businesses, allowing their bank accounts to be used to receive structured cash deposits designed to avoid currency reporting requirements.

It should be noted that LLCs are a predominant form of business structure nationwide. Ownership and transactional information on these entities can be concealed from regulatory and law enforcement authorities. All states have laws governing the formation of limited liability companies; however, most states do not collect or otherwise require the disclosure to state governments of ownership information at the formation stage or thereafter. Furthermore, there are several ways, consistent with state laws, in which organizers of shell companies may obscure company structure, ownership, and activities. For example, many states' laws permit corporations, general partnerships, trusts, and other business entities to own and manage LLCs. This statutory feature enables an individual or business to further conceal involvement in the activities of a shell LLC. Layers of ownership can be devised which make it highly unlikely that relationships among various individuals and companies can be discerned, even if one or more of the owners is actually known or discovered.

Suspicious Activity Report Review

A review of FinCEN's database indicates that suspected shell corporations, like legitimate businesses, appear to establish customer relationships with financial institutions in other countries around the world—many of which are located in Eastern European countries:

- o 397 Suspicious Activity Reports filed between April 1996 (the time financial institutions were mandated to file Suspicious Activity Reports) and January 2004 involved shell corporations, Eastern European countries, and the use of correspondent bank accounts.
- o The aggregate violation amount reported in those 397 Suspicious Activity Report forms totaled almost $4 billion.

Many of these financial institutions, in turn, had established correspondent banking relationships with financial institutions in the United States.

Agents and Nominee Incorporation Services (NIS)

Agents, also known as intermediaries or nominee incorporation services (NIS), can play a central role in the creation and ongoing maintenance and support of shell companies. NIS firms are often used because they can legally and efficiently organize business entities in any state. Numerous agents and NIS firms advertise a wide range of services for shell companies, such as serving as a resident agent and providing mail-forwarding services. Organizers of shell companies also may purchase corporate office "service packages" in order to appear to have established a more significant local presence. These packages often include a state business license, a local street address, an office that is staffed during business hours, a local telephone listing with a receptionist, and 24-hour personalized voicemail.

International NIS firms have entered into marketing and customer referral arrangements with U.S. banks to offer financial services such as Internet banking and funds transfer capabilities to shell companies and foreign citizens. U.S. banks that participate in these arrangements may be assuming increased levels of money laundering risk.

Some agents and NIS firms also provide individuals and businesses in the United States and abroad a variety of nominee services that can be used to preserve a client's anonymity in connection with the formation and operation of shell companies. Such features, while legal, may be attractive to those seeking to launder funds or finance terrorism. These services include, for example:

- o Nominee Officers and Directors: Incorporators provide the shell company with nominees for all offices that appear in public records.
- o Nominee Stockholders: A beneficial owner may use nominee stockholders to further ensure privacy and anonymity while maintaining control through an irrevocable proxy agreement.
- o Nominee Bank Signatory: A nominee appointed as the company fiduciary (such as a lawyer or accountant) can open bank accounts in the name of the shell company. The nominee accepts instructions from the beneficial owners and forwards these instructions to the bank without needing to disclose the names of the beneficial owners.

Banks can serve as formation agents and, when so acting, are subject to all BSA requirements, including suspicious activity reporting.

Potential Indicators of Money Laundering and Other Risk Related Considerations
The use of shell companies provides an opportunity for foreign or domestic entities to move money by means of wire transfers or other methods, whether directly or through a correspondent banking relationship, without company owners having to disclose their true identities or the nature or purpose of transactions. A review of Suspicious Activity Report data reveals that shell companies in the United States have been used to move billions of dollars globally. Additionally, the following elements are cited repeatedly in Suspicious Activity Reports involving shell companies:

- o An inability to obtain –whether through the Internet, commercial database searches, or direct inquiries to the foreign correspondent bank whose customer is the originator or the beneficiary of the transfer, information necessary to identify originators or beneficiaries of wire transfers;
- o A foreign correspondent bank exceeds the anticipated volume projected in its client profile for wire transfers in a given time period, or an individual company exhibits a high amount of sporadic activity that is inconsistent with normal business patterns;
- o Payments have no stated purpose, do not reference goods or services, or identify only a contract or invoice number;
- o Goods or services of the company do not match the company's profile based on information previously provided to the financial institution;
- o Transacting businesses share the same address, provide only a registered agent's address, or raise other address-related inconsistencies;
- o An unusually large number and variety of beneficiaries receive wire transfers from one company;
- o Frequent involvement of beneficiaries located in high-risk, offshore financial centers;
- o Multiple high-value payments or transfers between shell companies with no apparent legitimate business purpose.

SAR Filing on Shell Corporations

If a financial institution discovers suspicious activities such as those listed above, it should file a SAR and:

- In the narrative, the term "shell," should be used, as appropriate;
- The preparer should provide all required and relevant information about the conductor(s) and transactions, including, as applicable, the names:
  - and account numbers of all originators and beneficiaries of domestic and international wire transfers;
  - and locations of shell entities involved in the transfers; and,
  - names of and information regarding any registered agents or other third parties.

Structuring

Structuring is the term used to describe the illegal act of dividing a large transaction into smaller amounts for the purpose of avoiding the currency transaction reporting requirements of 31 USC 5324. Structuring is defined in the BSA (31 CFR 103.63), which states that:

> **"A person structures a transaction if that person, acting alone, in conjunction with or on behalf of others, conducts or attempts to conduct one or more transactions in currency at one or more financial institutions, on one or more days, in any manner, for the purpose of evading the CTR filing requirements."**

"In any manner," includes, but is not limited to "the breaking down of a single sum of currency exceeding $10,000 into smaller sums, including sums at or below $10,000, or the conduct of a transaction, or series of currency transactions, including transactions at or below $10,000. The transaction(s) need not exceed the $10,000 CTR reporting threshold at any one financial institution on any single day in order to constitute structuring within the meaning of this definition."

Structuring Provisions of the BSA

31 USC 5324 prohibits certain actions by any person who acts with the purpose of evading:

- The Currency Transaction Reports reporting requirements of Section 5313; or,
- The reporting requirements of Section 5325 (reports required to be made or recorded upon the sale of certain monetary instruments); or,
- The reporting requirements of Section 5316 (Report on Exporting & Importing Currency and Monetary Instruments); or,
- The reporting or recordkeeping requirements imposed by any order issued under section 5326 (Targeting Orders); or
- The recordkeeping requirements under Section 21 of the Federal Deposit Insurance Act and Section 123 of Public Law 91–508 relating to funds transfers. (See 31 CFR 103.33.)

In order to successfully structure a series of transactions, the customer may:

- Obtain the cooperation of the financial institution and its owners;
- Obtain the cooperation of an employee;
- Lower the amount of the transaction to avoid any identification requirements;
- Use agents of larger financial institutions to complete the transactions (for example, when an individual goes to multiple money transmitter locations that happen to be agents for the same company);
- Use third parties as initiators or recipients of transactions to complete the transactions;
- Complete the transactions at a number of different financial institutions; or,
- Complete numerous small transactions over a number of days.

Red flags indicative of structuring should be considered in conjunction with the red flags for:

- ○ General Account Activity
- ○ Avoidance of Reporting or Record Keeping
- ○ Wire Transfers
- ○ Avoidance of Reporting or Record Keeping
- ○ Cash Intense Businesses
- ○ Cross Border Transactions
- ○ Currency Transactions
- ○ Monetary Instruments
- ○ Black Market Peso Exchange (BMPE) Activity

Taxpayer ID Problems

Institutions should use reasonable discretion to determine if problems with Taxpayer Identification Numbers are suspicious in nature or otherwise explainable and not suspicious. For example, an institution may suspect that a customer provided an incorrect Social Security Number if the Detroit Computing Center generates correspondence stating that a Currency Transaction Report filed by the institution contained a customer's name and Social Security Number that did not match. If the institution determines that a teller inadvertently transcribed numbers, its risk-based response would be different than if it determined that the customer made a false statement by intentionally rearranging or changing numbers in an attempt to circumvent the reporting requirement. Alternatively, an institution may have software applications or other resources that reveal the number belongs to another person, or a deceased person, in which case the motive for the transaction and the inherent nature of the transaction may be characterized more clearly as suspicious.

Institutions should note that there may be legitimate circumstances in which a person conducting a transaction would have no Taxpayer Identification Number (e.g., some foreign customers of the bank), or a changed identification number (e.g., some victims of identity theft, or a sole proprietorship that has become incorporated)[12]. Institutions should consider all of the available facts and circumstances surrounding such transactions when deciding whether or not it is suspicious.

Identity Fraud

Because an individual cannot have both an ITIN and an SSN, the above situation could be an indicator of identity theft or fraud. Financial institutions should review such circumstances carefully, and a SAR must be filed if applicable thresholds are met and if the institution knows, suspects, or has reason to suspect a possible violation of law or regulations. Financial institutions also voluntarily may file a SAR in instances where applicable thresholds are not met, but where similar suspicions arise [13].

Third Party Receiver of Funds Schemes

A prevailing type of scam, referred to as a *third party receiver of funds* scam, is similar to 4-1-9 schemes. It usually involves a third party wiring money order or check proceeds back to business entities located overseas.

Instead of being contacted by a person claiming to be a foreign government official located in a foreign jurisdiction, individuals are usually contacted via email or via online job postings by an entity that claims to be a legitimate business seeking financial transaction assistance in the United States. The business, usually an auction operation, will claim that due to banking restrictions placed on foreign entities, it can not easily engage in financial transactions in the United States. The business will request that the U.S. citizen cash checks or money orders on its behalf and then wire most of the proceeds back to the business. An individual may be referred to a business website that looks very professional, which tricks the individual into believing the business is legitimate.

Financial institutions become aware of the scam once a customer comes to cash the monetary instruments. Filers report that the monetary instruments presented are in some cases obviously fake, containing glaring spelling errors or poorly created seals. In these instances, financial institutions decline to negotiate the monetary instruments and advise the customer that the instruments are counterfeit. Other times, the monetary instruments presented appear authentic and are ultimately cashed for the customer. Later, the monetary instruments are returned as non-negotiable and either the bank or the customer must take a monetary loss.

SAR Filing for Third Party Receiver of Funds Schemes

Due to the slightly different nature of the third party receiver of funds scams in relation to the 4-1-9 and advance fee fraud scams, financial institutions have sought clarification on whether the third party receiver of funds scams could be treated in the manner that 4-1-9 or "advance fee fraud" scams are for SAR filing purposes. In previous guidance (The SAR Activity Review, Issue 7, August 2004), FinCEN advised financial institutions that the filing of a SAR was unnecessary for 4-1-9 or "advance fee fraud" if there was no monetary loss. FinCEN advised that a financial institution should consider filing a SAR if there was a monetary loss or if the scam involved another illegal activity (such as investment fraud, counterfeiting, forgery, misuse of a U.S. government seal, etc.).

Because the activities are similar, the guidance given with regard to 4-1-9 or advance fee fraud scams would apply to third party receiver of funds scams as well. If the counterfeit monetary instruments are received via the U.S. postal system, financial institutions and individuals may also report the receipt to the U.S. Postal Inspection Service:

U.S. Postal Inspection Service
Operations Support Group
222 S. Riverside Plaza
Suite 1250
Chicago, IL 60606-6100

Individuals who would like to report a third party receiver of funds scam may file a complaint via the Internet Crime Complaint Center, which is hosted by the FBI. The website address is http://www.ic3.gov.

Unregistered MSB Activity

The term "money services business" includes any person[14] doing business, whether or not on a regular basis or as an organized business concern, in one or more of the following capacities:

- Currency dealer or exchanger
- Check casher
- Issuer of traveler's checks, money orders or stored value
- Seller or redeemer of traveler's checks, money orders or stored value
- Money transmitter
- U.S. Postal Service.

An activity threshold of greater than $1,000 per person per day in one or more transactions applies to the definitions of: currency dealer or exchanger; check casher; issuer of traveler's checks, money orders or stored value; and seller or redeemer of travelers' checks, money orders or stored value. The threshold applies separately to each activity - if the threshold is not met for the specific activity, the person engaged in that activity is *not* an MSB on the basis of that activity.

No activity threshold applies to the definition of money transmitter. Thus, a person who engages as a business in the transfer of funds is an MSB as a money transmitter, *regardless* of the amount of money transmission activity.

Notwithstanding the previous discussion, the term "money services business" does not include:

- A bank, as that term is defined in 31 CFR 103.11(c), or
- A person registered with, and regulated or examined by, the Securities and Exchange Commission or the Commodity Futures Trading Commission.

For the complete regulatory definition of "money services business", see 31 C.F.R. 103.11 (uu).

Recently, there has been a trend by banks to shy away from opening accounts for MSBs. This is because of misunderstandings, both on the regulators' part and on bank compliance staffs' part. Since MSBs are regulated entities themselves, as cash intense businesses, one might draw the conclusion that they are in fact less risky to bank than other cash intense businesses. The regulatory guidance has made clear that banks are *not* expected to act as MSBs' de facto regulator. Therefore, if KYC, and where applicable, increased due diligence practices are soundly implemented, a bank should not have concerns about banking MSBs.

There is a definite regulatory concern, however, for cases where a business conducts MSB activity but is not registered to do so. Financial institutions must adopt policies, procedures and controls to detect and report such activity. Monitoring of transactions is usually the first defense for identifying unregistered MSB activity. Consideration of the type of activity in an account (e.g., cash transactions or international wires), patterns of activity (e.g., whether it reflects an ongoing fraud or other criminal activity), and the volume of activity and transaction amounts are foundational to detection. For example, *cash- in* activity would certainly be expected within limits (which you should try to define with your normal due diligence profiling for the customer); but cash-out activity by the same business might suggest that the business is cashing checks –an activity for which they may have to be registered as an MSB (depending on volume). Consider the same analysis for ACH, i.e., is the activity in or out? ACH *in* may suggest that the business is selling money orders or is perhaps operating an ATM machine.

An analysis of the narrative sections of the relevant depository institution SARs by FinCEN found reference to at least 13 different types of MSB related activities. When studying these SAR narratives for patterns, the sampling revealed *check cashing*—both over $1,000 for a customer on any day and nonspecific— as the activity most often reported, followed by money transmission (as illustrated in Table 1 below). Most notably, 15 SARs involved either indictments or arrests for alleged criminal behavior associated with the operation of the MSB or concerned activities strongly suggesting specific criminal activities.

For example, three SARs filed by three separate depository institutions reported the indictment of a corporation for acting as an unlicensed funds transmitter. This corporation sent over $3.2 billion from shell companies to offshore accounts over a five-year period beginning in 1997.

Another SAR narrative described a company whose owner was arrested in late 2004 for operating as an unlicensed money transmitter. This individual made frequent deposits to his company's account, usually through several small checks. The owner subsequently sent two or three funds transfers a month to beneficiaries located in India, Hong Kong, and South Africa. Indications are that this was a hawala-type operation involved in sending money either directly to India, or alternately to Hong Kong or South Africa to purchase gold to be subsequently smuggled into India.

A third SAR narrative described a customer's use of two different business accounts to transfer hundreds of thousands of dollars. The bank believed that the pattern of funds transfers indicated a fraudulent investment scheme. Bank research determined the customer had been arrested in the early 1990s on fugitive warrants from three different states for fraud related charges.

Geographic Distribution of Unregistered MSBs
Results of an analysis conducted by FinCEN in 2005 revealed:
- **Unregistered check cashers** to be most concentrated in the central United States
  - Ohio
  - Michigan
  - Texas
  - Tennessee
  - Illinois
- **Unregistered money transmitters** were found to be most concentrated on the East and West coasts
  - California
  - Washington
  - New Jersey

- o New York
- o Florida

Probable Money Laundering

Table 7 references 12 unregistered MSB related SARs that concern activities linked to suspected money laundering.

Table 7: Types of Reported Activities

Activity	Occurrences	Percentage of Total Reported Activities
Check cashing (Over $1,000 aggregate for any person on any day)	345	27.87%
Check cashing (Non-specific)	339	27.38%
Money transmission	309	24.96%
Money services businesses activities (Nonspecific)	131	10.58%
Informal Value Transfer Systems (Including hawala)	49	3.96%
Arrests, indictments, and illicit activities associated with the operation of unregistered money services business	15	1.21%
On Money Services Business Registration List without authorization date	13	1.05%
No apparent money services business activity	13	1.05%
Money laundering	12	0.97%
Currency exchange	7	0.57%
Black Market Peso Exchange-like activity	2	0.16%
Exchange of cashed third-party checks with related business for cash	2	0.16%
Registered money services business facilitating transfers for related unregistered money services business	1	0.08%
TOTALS	**1,238**	**100.00%**

Examples of Unregistered MSBs reported in SAR Narratives

An individual who received over $500,000 in wire transfers on a specific date in early 2005 and also purchased cashier's checks totaling $450,000. The next day he re-deposited one of the checks for $200,000 and issued 21 checks for $9,000 all to the same payee.

- o   These actions may be evidence of illicit proceeds.
- o   Issuance of the $9,000 checks also suggests they were intended to be cashed in a structured manner to evade currency transaction reporting requirements.

An individual who structured cash deposits into a personal account to transact same-day wire transfers to the same beneficiary located in Central America. The deposits totaled more than $100,000 and the wire transfers exceeded $145,000. The money was allegedly for craft items; however, a site visit to the individual's business by employees of the reporting institution cast doubt on whether the business activity could support the volume of purchases.

- o   In addition to the possibility of operating as an unregistered money transmission business, the business may also be engaged in laundering illicit receipts from unidentified sources.

SAR Filing for Unregistered MSB Activity

In April 2005, FinCEN and the federal banking agencies issued guidance to the banking industry on providing banking services to the MSB industry [15]. Among other topics, the guidance clarified that depository institutions should file SARs if they become aware that an MSB is operating in violation of the registration or state licensing requirements[16]. Depository institutions are reminded, however, that, as explained below, there may be legitimate reasons for an MSB to *not* be registered with FinCEN or licensed in certain states.

31 CFR §103.41(b)(3) grants a newly established MSB 180 days to comply with the registration requirement. Additionally, §103.41(a)(2) clarifies that a person who provides money services solely as the agent of another registered MSB is not required to register with FinCEN[17]. Similarly, certain types of MSBs in some states may not have licensing requirements.

Further, banking organizations are *not* expected to terminate existing accounts of MSBs based solely on the discovery that the customer is an MSB that has failed to comply with licensing and registration requirements (although continuing non-compliance by the MSB may be an indicator of heightened risk). There is no requirement in the BSA regulations that a banking organization must close an account that is the subject of a suspicious activity report. The decision to maintain or close an account should be made by a banking organization's management under standards and guidelines approved by its board of directors. However, if an account is involved in a suspicious or potentially illegal transaction, the banking organization should examine the status and history of the account thoroughly and should determine whether or not the institution is comfortable maintaining the account. If the banking organization is aware that the reported activity is under investigation, it is strongly recommended that the banking organization notify law enforcement before making any decision regarding the status of the account.

As set forth in the April 2005 Inter-agency Guidance, depository institutions must conduct a reasonable inquiry into a business' registration or licensing status before they can accurately determine whether a business is unregistered or unlicensed and thus should be the subject of a SAR. It should be clarified that a bank is not required to file a SAR if it makes a business decision to close an MSBs account based solely on the level of risk, and not on the business' registration or licensing compliance or other reportable activity. As the Inter-agency Guidance makes clear, requesting that the business provide copies of correspondence acknowledging their registration or licensing is one reliable method of verifying that an MSB has registered with FinCEN. There should be no conflict between this request and SAR confidentiality.

Section V – FinCEN SAR Filing Guidance

Introduction

FinCEN has issued voluminous guidance over the years with regard to SAR filings on specific topics. While financial institutions are required to comply with that guidance, it is often difficult to keep track of –or for that matter, find specific guidance.

This section provides detailed information on SAR filing guidance for topics covered in FinCEN guidance, the SAR Activity Review Issues, Federal Register, and other sources. Investigators should check this section to determine if there are any specific instructions they need to follow regarding their suspicious activity report content and filings.

Investigators should be sure to check FinCEN's website regularly for updated guidance.

SAR Reporting Timeline

A national bank is required to file a SAR no later than 30 calendar days after the initial detection of facts that may constitute a basis for filing a SAR. If no suspect can be identified, a national bank may delay filing by an additional 30 calendar days in order to identify a suspect(s). In no case shall reporting be delayed more than 60 calendar days after the date of initial detection. In situations requiring immediate attention or when there is an ongoing violation, the financial institution shall immediately notify by telephone, an appropriate law enforcement authority as well as the institution's federal functional regulator in addition to filing a timely SAR.

Generally, banks' automated transaction monitoring systems generate alerts that are indicative of unusual behavior outside either an absolute norm or a norm for a customer's peer group. The clock for SAR filing does not begin with the time an alert was generated, unless your institution's policies hold that to be the case. Most banks will undertake a review of an alert and escalate the alert for full investigation if warranted. Only after such steps determine that the identified unusual activity is indeed suspicious and worthy of reporting does the SAR clock start.

A word of caution here is necessary. Regulators will generally give financial institutions a reasonable period of time to determine whether an alert is worthy of an investigation, but that period of time should not be abused, lest the regulators view the whole detection-to-decision-to-reporting process to be overly burdened or broken.

Questioning Individuals With Regard to Suspicious Account Activity

When determining whether suspicious activity has occurred, institutions are responsible for examining all the facts, including the background and possible purpose of the transaction.[18] As part of an institution's due diligence to determine whether suspicious activity has occurred, reasonable investigation into the nature and purpose of the activity may be necessary. Institutions, however, have expressed concern over the perceived tension between questioning a customer about potentially suspicious activity and the institution's responsibility to maintain the confidentiality of SARs.[19]

FinCEN recognizes that under certain circumstances, institutions may discreetly question a customer about the nature and purpose of a transaction without revealing their intention to file a SAR. For example, to determine whether a customer's transactions are "designed to evade any [reporting] requirements,"[20] an institution may wish to ask a customer why he or she is making frequent cash deposits slightly below a certain reporting or record keeping threshold. If the customer provides an answer that reasonably satisfies the institution that the transaction is not designed to evade reporting requirements (e.g., her business has a verifiable insurance policy that covers up to $10,000 in currency in the event of a burglary), no SAR would be required. Financial institutions are encouraged to document SAR decisions, including final decisions not to file a SAR.

Institutions are reminded that any questioning should not risk tipping off the customer or otherwise disclose that a SAR is being filed. Ultimately, institutions will need to exercise discretion and judgment when determining how and when to inquire of customers about unusual activity.

Account Closure

The Financial Crimes Enforcement Network in June 2007 issued guidance for financial institutions with account relationships that law enforcement may have an interest in ensuring remain open notwithstanding suspicious or potential criminal activity in connection with the account (FIN–2007–G002).

Ultimately, the decision to maintain or close an account should be made by a financial institution in accordance with its own standards and guidelines. Although there is no requirement that a financial institution maintain a particular account relationship, financial institutions should be mindful that complying with such a request may further law enforcement efforts to combat money laundering, terrorist financing, and other crimes.

If a law enforcement agency requests that a financial institution maintain a particular account, the financial institution should ask for a written request. A written request from a federal law enforcement agency should be issued by a supervisory agent or by an attorney within a United States Attorney's Office or another office of the Department of Justice.

If a state or local law enforcement agency requests that an account be maintained, then the financial institution should obtain a written request from a supervisor of the state or local law enforcement agency or from an attorney within a state or local prosecutor's office. The written request should indicate that the agency has requested that the financial institution maintain the account and the purpose of the request. For example, if a state or local law enforcement agency is requesting that the financial institution maintain the account for purposes of monitoring, the written request should include a statement to that effect. The request should also indicate the duration for the request, not to exceed six months. Law enforcement may issue subsequent requests for account maintenance after the expiration of the initial request.

Although there is no recordkeeping requirement under the Bank Secrecy Act for this type of correspondence, FinCEN recommends that financial institutions maintain documentation of such requests for at least five years after the request has expired. If a financial institution is aware –through a subpoena, 314(a) request, National Security Letter, or similar communication– that an account is under investigation, FinCEN recommends that the financial institution notify law enforcement before making any decision regarding the status of the account.

If the financial institution chooses to maintain the account, it is required to comply with all applicable Bank Secrecy Act recordkeeping and reporting requirements, including the requirement to file Suspicious Activity Reports, even if the bank is keeping an account open or maintaining a customer relationship at the request of law enforcement.

Disclosure of SARs and Underlying Suspicious Activity

Federal law (31 U.S.C. 5318(g)(2)) prohibits the notification of any person that is involved in the activity being reported on a SAR that the activity has been reported. This prohibition effectively precludes the disclosure of a SAR or the fact that a SAR has been filed. However, this prohibition does not preclude, under federal law, a disclosure in an appropriate manner of the facts that are the basis of the SAR, so long as the disclosure is not made in a way that indicates or implies that a SAR has been filed or that the information is included on a filed SAR.

The prohibition against disclosure can raise special issues when SAR records are sought by subpoena or court order. The SAR regulations direct organizations facing those issues to contact their primary supervisor, as well as FinCEN, to obtain guidance and direction on how to proceed. In several matters to date, government agencies have intervened to ensure that the protection for filing organizations and the integrity of the data contained within the SAR database remain intact.

In some cases, customers may be innocently conducting an activity that they do not realize is illegal. Structuring transactions is the usual culprit. Customers may at times be ill advised by an accountant, financial advisor, or other person to break transactions into less than $10,000 amounts. Yet whether or not the structuring is conducted willfully, it is a crime for which the consequences to the customer may be severe. Rather than reporting the customer in a SAR, it may be prudent to alert the customer to the fact that the activity he is engaging in is reportable to the government by filing a CTR. Be very careful not to mention anything about a SAR.

The best way to inform clients is through a standard letter or brochure. Such brochures can be acquired commercially or easily prepared by your bank. It should simply state that:

- o Many customers do not know that financial institutions must file CTRs for cash transactions in excess of $10,000; and,
    - Are required to maintain records for the cash purchase of certain negotiable instruments in the range of $3,000 to $10,000.
- o Breaking cash deposits into smaller pieces to avoid the $10,000 reporting limit is a serious crime.

Make sure to have any such correspondence cleared by your bank's legal department.

Disclosure of SAR Documentation

Supporting documentation refers to all documents or records that assisted a financial institution in making the determination that certain activity required a SAR filing.

A financial institution must identify supporting documentation at the time the SAR is filed, and this documentation must be maintained by the institution for five years. The manner in which a financial institution maintains supporting documentation should be documented in the institution's anti-money laundering program written procedures.

What qualifies as supporting documentation depends on the facts and circumstances of each filing.
As indicated in each of the SAR forms, financial institutions should identify in the SAR narrative the supporting documentation, which may include, for example, transaction records, new account information, tape recordings, e-mail messages, and correspondence. While items identified in the narrative of the SAR generally constitute supporting documentation, a document or record may qualify as supporting documentation even if not identified in the narrative.

No Legal Process is Required for Disclosure of Supporting Documentation
The Right to Financial Privacy Act (RFPA) generally prohibits financial institutions from disclosing a customer's financial records to a Government agency without service of legal process, notice to the customer and an opportunity to challenge the disclosure. However 12 U.S.C. § 3413(b) provides that no such requirement applies when the financial institution provides the financial records or information to FinCEN or a supervisory agency in the exercise of its "supervisory, regulatory or monetary functions."

In addition, no such requirement applies when FinCEN or an appropriate law enforcement or supervisory agency requests either a copy of a SAR or supporting documentation underlying the SAR. Financial institutions must provide all documentation supporting the filing of a SAR upon request by FinCEN or an appropriate law enforcement or supervisory agency. (Supervisory agencies have independent statutory authority to examine all books and records of the financial institutions for which they are the appropriate regulator.) When requested to provide supporting documentation, financial institutions should take special care to verify that a requestor of information is, in fact, a representative of FinCEN or an appropriate law enforcement or supervisory agency. (Generally, such procedures include: independent employment verification with the requestor's field office or face-to-face review of the requestor's credentials.)

Disclosure of SARs to appropriate law enforcement and supervisory agencies is protected by the safe harbor provisions applicable to both voluntary and mandatory suspicious activity reporting by financial institutions.[21]

With respect to supporting documentation, rules under the BSA state explicitly that financial institutions must retain copies of supporting documentation, that supporting documentation is "deemed to have been filed with" the SAR, and that financial institutions must provide supporting documentation upon request. FinCEN has interpreted these regulations under the BSA as requiring a financial institution to provide

162 SAR Investigations – The Complete BSA/AML Desktop Reference

supporting documentation even in the absence of legal process. FinCEN understands that this is in accord with the RFPA, which states that nothing in the act "authorize(s) the withholding of financial records or information required to be reported in accordance with any Federal statute or rule promulgated thereunder."

Disclosures of SARs

As set forth in the October 2000 SAR Activity Review (Section 5 – Disclosure of SARs and Underlying Suspicious Activity), federal law (31 U.S.C. 5318(g)(2)) prohibits the notification to any person that is involved in the activity being reported on a SAR that the activity has been reported.

This prohibition extends to disclosures that could indirectly result in the notification to the subject of a SAR that a SAR has been filed, effectively precluding the disclosure of a SAR or even its existence to any persons other than appropriate law enforcement and supervisory agency or agencies.

In the rare instance when suspicious activity is related to an individual in the organization, such as the president or one of the members of the board of directors, the established policy that would require notification of a SAR filing to such an individual should not be followed. **Deviations to established policies and procedures so as to avoid notification of a SAR filing to a subject of the SAR should be documented, and appropriate uninvolved senior organizational personnel should be so advised.** The prohibition on notification of a SAR filing can raise special issues when SAR filings are sought by subpoena or court order. The SAR regulations direct organizations facing these issues to contact their primary supervisor, as well as FinCEN, to obtain guidance and direction on how to proceed. In several matters to date, government agencies have intervened to ensure that the protection for filing organizations and the integrity of the data contained within the SAR database remain intact.

SAR Disclosure to Self-Regulatory Organizations (SROs)

SROs such as the New York Stock Exchange and the National Association of Securities Dealers are *not* appropriate supervisory agencies under current law for purposes of SAR disclosure by financial institutions. This prohibition does not preclude, under federal law, a disclosure in an appropriate manner of the facts that are the basis of the SAR, so long as the disclosure is not made in a way that indicates or implies that a SAR has been filed or that information is included on a filed SAR.

Disclosure of SARs in Civil Litigation

As set forth in the October 2000 SAR Activity Review (Section 5 – Disclosure of SARs and Underlying Suspicious Activity), federal law (31 U.S.C. 5318(g)(2)) prohibits the notification to any person that is involved in the activity being reported on a SAR that the activity has been reported. This prohibition extends to disclosures that could indirectly result in the notification to the subject of a SAR that a SAR has been filed, effectively precluding the disclosure of a SAR or even its existence to any persons other than appropriate law enforcement and supervisory agency or agencies.

Self-regulatory organizations such as the New York Stock Exchange and the National Association of Securities Dealers are not appropriate supervisory agencies under current law for purposes of SAR disclosure by financial institutions. This prohibition does not preclude, under federal law, a disclosure in an appropriate manner of the facts that are the basis of the SAR, so long as the disclosure is not made in a way that indicates or implies that a SAR has been filed or that information is included on a filed SAR.

In the rare instance when suspicious activity is related to an individual in the organization, such as the president or one of the members of the board of directors, the established policy that would require notification of a SAR filing to such an individual should not be followed. Deviations to established policies and procedures so as to avoid notification of a SAR filing to a subject of the SAR should be documented and appropriate uninvolved senior organizational personnel should be so advised.

The prohibition on notification of a SAR filing can raise special issues when SAR filings are sought by subpoena or court order. The SAR regulations direct organizations facing these issues to contact their primary supervisor, as well as FinCEN, to obtain guidance and direction on how to proceed. In several matters to date, government agencies have intervened to ensure that the protection for filing organizations and the integrity of the data contained within the SAR database remain intact.

Disclosure of SAR Documentation

Disclosure of supporting documentation related to the activity that is being reported on a SAR does not require a subpoena, court order, or other judicial or administrative process. Under the SAR regulations, financial institutions are required to disclose supporting documentation to appropriate law enforcement agencies, or FinCEN, upon request.

The federal financial institution supervisors, as well as FinCEN, have always maintained that a request for the disclosure of a SAR in *civil* litigation pursuant to the federal discovery rules should be denied and the institution should identify for the court the relevant provisions of Title 31, Section 5318(g) of the United States Code (the BSA provision that prohibits disclosure). (However, institutions should never disobey the order of a court to make the disclosure, although they should appeal an adverse order and seek a stay when possible.)

It should be noted, however, that while there is now further judicial support for the proposition that SARs are not subject to disclosure in civil litigation, this does not apply to the underlying documentation (such as account statements, wire transfer records, etc.) that may evidence suspicious activity. In fact, in one of the cases the court specifically held that the prohibition from disclosure covered the SAR but not the underlying documentation. An institution that finds itself in the position as described herein should notify the court of the prohibition from disclosure and also, pursuant to the regulations of the federal financial institution supervisory agencies, notify its federal supervisor, or, if it has no such supervisor, notify FinCEN, that such a demand has been made.

SAR Filing for Grand Jury Subpoenas

Grand juries issue subpoenas in furtherance of conducting investigations of subjects and targets of their proceedings, and therefore the receipt of such a subpoena does not, by itself, require the filing of a SAR. Nonetheless, the receipt of a grand jury subpoena should cause a financial institution to conduct a risk assessment of the subject customer and also review its account activity. If suspicious activity is discovered during any such assessment and review, the financial institution should consider elevating the risk profile of the customer and filing a SAR in accordance with applicable regulations.

Unless there is something suspicious about the activities of a customer, apart from the service of the grand jury subpoena, a SAR should *not* be filed. If, however, a financial institution does prepare a SAR following the receipt of a grand jury subpoena, it should provide detailed information about the facts and circumstances surrounding the suspicious activity, rather than merely the fact that a subpoena was received.

Receipt of a grand jury subpoena also does not alter the standards for filing a SAR. Financial institutions should only file a SAR for transactions:

- Conducted or attempted by, at, or through the financial institution involving or aggregating at least $5,000 when the financial institution knows, suspects, or has reason to suspect that:
  - The transaction involves funds derived from illegal activity or is intended or conducted in order to hide or disguise funds or assets derived from illegal activities;
  - The transaction is designed to evade any requirements under the BSA;
  - The transaction has no business or apparent lawful purpose or is not the sort in which the particular customer would normally be expected to engage, and the bank knows of no reasonable explanation for the transaction after examining all the available facts; or,
  - The transaction involves use of the financial institution to facilitate criminal activity.

If a financial institution is served with any subpoena requiring disclosure of the fact that a Suspicious Activity Report has been filed or of the Report itself, except to the extent that the subpoena is submitted by an appropriate law enforcement or supervisory agency, the financial institution should neither confirm nor deny the existence of the Suspicious Activity Report. The financial institution should immediately notify the Office of Chief Counsel at FinCEN at:

(703) 905-3590

as well as the financial institution's federal functional regulator under that regulator's parallel requirement, if any.

Sharing SARs With Head Offices and Controlling Companies

FinCEN and the Federal Banking Agencies have issued guidance to confirm that under the Bank Secrecy Act and its implementing regulations:

- A U.S. branch or agency of a foreign bank may disclose a Suspicious Activity Report to its head office outside the United States; and,
- A U.S. bank or savings association ("depository institution") may disclose a Suspicious Activity Report to controlling companies [22] whether domestic or foreign.

A depository institution that files a Suspicious Activity Report may disclose to entities within its organization information underlying the filing (that is, information about the customer/suspect and transaction(s) reported). However, neither the Financial Crimes Enforcement Network nor the Federal Banking Agencies have taken a definitive position concerning whether a depository institution is permitted under the Bank Secrecy Act and Federal Banking Agency regulations to share or disclose to entities within its corporate structure, the Suspicious Activity Report itself or the fact that a Suspicious Activity Report was filed. (However, the Federal Banking Agencies' regulations require notification of the filing of Suspicious Activity Reports to boards of directors, whether domestic or global. See 12 C.F.R. § 353.3(f) [Federal Deposit Insurance Corporation]; 12. C.F.R. § 208.62(h) [Board of Governors of the Federal Reserve System]; 12 C.F.R. § 21.11(h) [Office of the Comptroller of the Currency]; 12 C.F.R. § 563.180(b)(9) [Office of Thrift Supervision])

FinCEN and the Federal Banking agencies have taken into account the need for a head office, controlling entity or party to discharge its oversight responsibilities with respect to enterprise-wide risk management and compliance with applicable laws and regulations. To fulfill those responsibilities, head offices and controlling entities or parties may have a valid need to review a branch's, office's, or depository institution's compliance with legal requirements to identify and report suspicious activity. Accordingly, FinCEN et. al., has determined that a U.S. branch or agency of a foreign bank may share a Suspicious Activity Report with its head office outside the United States for these purposes. Similarly, a U.S. bank or savings association may disclose a Suspicious Activity Report to its controlling company, no matter where the entity or party is located. In the event that a depository institution's corporate structure includes multiple controlling companies, the filing institution's Suspicious Activity Report may be shared with each controlling entity. (Note: It should be noted that the requirement that knowledge of a Suspicious Activity Report's filing may not be disclosed to the controlling entity or party remains, even under this guidance, if there is a reason to believe it may be disclosed to any person involved in the suspicious activity that is the subject of the Suspicious Activity Report.)

There may be circumstances under which a depository institution would be liable for direct or indirect disclosure by its controlling company or head office of a Suspicious Activity Report or the fact that a Suspicious Activity Report was filed. Therefore, the depository institution, as part of its anti-money laundering program, must have written confidentiality agreements or arrangements in place specifying that the head office or controlling company must protect the confidentiality of the Suspicious Activity Reports through appropriate internal controls.

The sharing of a Suspicious Activity Report with a non-U.S. entity raises additional concerns about the ability of the foreign entity to protect the Suspicious Activity Report in light of possible requests for disclosure abroad that may be subject to foreign law. These concerns will need to be addressed in the confidentiality agreements or arrangements. The recipient head office, controlling entities or parties may not disclose further any Suspicious Activity Report, or the fact that such report has been filed; however, the institution may disclose without permission underlying information (that is, information about the customer and transaction(s) reported) that does not explicitly reveal that a Suspicious Activity Report was filed and that is not otherwise subject to disclosure restrictions.

The Financial Crimes Enforcement Network and the Federal Banking Agencies are considering whether a depository institution may share a Suspicious Activity Report with an affiliate other than a controlling company or head office, both in instances where the affiliate is located inside the United States and where the affiliate is located abroad. Until such time that guidance is issued, depository institutions should not share Suspicious Activity Reports with such affiliates.

Filing SARs on Activity Outside the United States

Consistent with the SAR regulations, it is expected that financial institutions will file SARs on activity deemed to be suspicious even when a portion of the activity occurs outside of the United States or the funds involved in the activity originated from outside the United States. Although foreign-located operations of U.S. organizations are not required to file SARs, an organization may wish, for example, to file a SAR with regard to suspicious activity that occurs outside of the United States that is so egregious that it has the potential to cause harm to the entire organization. (It is, of course, expected that foreign-located operations of U.S. organizations that identify suspicious activity will report such activity consistent with local reporting requirements in the foreign jurisdiction where the operation is located.)

Insignificant SAR Filing Errors

FinCEN FAQs address whether institutions are required to correct previously filed Suspicious Activity Reports if they discover "insignificant" or "inconsequential" errors, particularly when they feel that the corrected data would be of little or no use to law enforcement. FinCEN reminds institutions that information of apparent insignificance to a filer who has observed only a small part of a larger pattern of suspicious activity may be valuable to law enforcement personnel seeking a greater awareness of the entire pattern of activity.

Financial institutions must file complete and accurate reports, and must correct any error they detect in accordance with the directions on the Suspicious Activity Report form.

When correcting an error on a previously filed report:
- Mark Box #1 ("corrects prior report"); and,
- Follow the directions to make the necessary changes.

Whenever a corrected report is filed, the filer should explain the changes in the report narrative.

National Security Letters and SAR Reporting

National Security Letters are written investigative demands, somewhat analogous to administrative subpoenas that can be issued by the Federal Bureau of Investigation in counter-intelligence and counter-terrorism investigations to obtain the following:

- Telephone and electronic communications records from telephone companies and Internet Service Providers (pursuant to the Electronic Communications Privacy Act, 18 USC 2709);
- Information from credit bureaus (pursuant to the Fair Credit Reporting Act, 15 USC 1681u); and,
- Financial records [23] from financial institutions [24] (pursuant to the Right to Financial Privacy Act of 1978, 12 USC 3401 et seq.).[25]

National Security Letters can also be issued by other federal government authorities for purposes of conducting foreign counter or positive-intelligence activities,[26] certain protective functions,[27] or intelligence or counter intelligence analyses related to international terrorism[28] to obtain financial records from financial institutions.[29]

National Security Letters are highly confidential investigative tools employed by the federal government. Financial institutions that receive National Security Letters must take appropriate measures to ensure the confidentiality of the letters. FinCEN encourages financial institutions to have procedures in place for processing and maintaining the confidentiality of National Security Letters.[30]

Mere receipt of a National Security Letter does not, by itself, require the filing of a Suspicious Activity Report by the financial institution receiving the letter.[31] Nonetheless, the National Security Letter is a piece of information that may be relevant to a financial institution's overall risk assessment of its customers and accounts. It is incumbent upon a financial institution to assess the information in accordance with its risk-based anti-money laundering program, policies and procedures, and to determine whether a Suspicious Activity Report should be filed based on the totality of information available to the institution. In any event, all regulatory suspicious activity triggers and dollar thresholds for filing Suspicious Activity Reports would apply. So, for instance, under FinCEN's suspicious activity reporting requirements at 31 CFR 103.18, banks are required to file a Suspicious Activity Report for:

- Transactions conducted or attempted by, at, or through the bank involving or aggregating at least $5,000, and the bank knows, suspects, or has reason to suspect that (1) the transaction involves funds derived from illegal activity or is intended or conducted in order to hide or disguise funds or assets derived from illegal activities;
- The transaction is designed to evade any requirements under the Bank Secrecy Act; or,
- The transaction has no business or apparent lawful purpose or is not the sort in which the particular customer would normally be expected to engage, and the bank knows of no reasonable explanation for the transaction after examining the available facts.[32]

If a financial institution does file a Suspicious Activity Report relating to information in a National Security Letter, no reference to the receipt or existence of the National Security Letter should be made in any part of the Suspicious Activity Report, including the narrative. Instead, the Suspicious Activity Report should reference only facts and activities underlying or derived from the information in the National Security Letter; only those facts and activities should be detailed in the report.

If a financial institution has questions about Suspicious Activity Report filing relating to National Security Letters, or about Suspicious Activity Reporting in general, it should contact FinCEN's Regulatory Help Line at:

(415) 720-7581

Financial institutions having a federal functional regulator may also wish to contact their federal functional regulator for questions relating to that regulator's suspicious activity reporting requirements and to procedures and records that the institution should maintain.

Questions regarding National Security Letters should be directed to the financial institution's local Federal Bureau of Investigation field office. Contact information for Federal Bureau of Investigation field offices can be obtained from the FBI's website.

Repeated SAR Filings on the Same Activity

One of the purposes of filing SARs is to identify violations or potential violations of law to the appropriate law enforcement authorities for criminal investigation. This is accomplished by the filing of a SAR that identifies the activity of concern. Should this activity continue over a period of time, it is useful for such information to be made known to law enforcement (and the bank supervisors). As a general rule of thumb, organizations should report continuing suspicious activity with a report being filed at least every 90 days. This will serve the purposes of notifying law enforcement of the continuing nature of the activity, as well as provide a reminder to the organization that it must continue to review the suspicious activity to determine if other actions may be appropriate, such as terminating its relationship with the customer or employee that is the subject of the filing.

For filing SARs related to ongoing activity, make sure that the following information is contained in the SAR Form (TD F 90–22.47):

Part III, Item 33 – The SAR must be completed in its entirety and should contain the following information:
   o   Date or range of dates of suspicious activity should be included by entering the *first known date* of suspicious activity (same date as reflected on the initial report) in the *From* field and the last occurrence date in the *To* field.

Part III, Item 34 – The total dollar amount involved in the known or suspicious activity must reflect an *aggregated total* of all transactions for multiple or related suspicious activities by the same individual or organization within the same reporting period (as identified in Item 33). (**Note:** Dollar values should be calculated on the basis of suspicious transactions as opposed to loss to the filing institution.)

Part V – Suspicious Activity Information Explanation/Description may reference prior SARs filed with corresponding dates and dollar amounts, in addition to a detailed explanation/description of the known or suspected violation of law or suspicious activity.

Reporting Terrorist Related Activity on a SAR Form

Financial institutions should contact the Financial Institutions Hotline to report suspicious activity that may relate to terrorism:

866-556-3974

FinCEN's guidance for reporting possible terrorist related activity is as follows:
1. Report the information on the SAR accurately and completely; and
2. Complete the narrative section by describing the suspicious transaction as completely as possible and include the following information, if applicable:
   - any correspondent bank name/account information;
   - names/locations of business entities;
   - names of cities, countries and foreign financial institutions linked to the transaction, especially if funds transfer activity is involved; and,
   - account numbers and beneficiary names.

Financial institutions reporting potential terrorist related activity on Form TD F 90–22.47 are requested to:
- **Check the *Other* box on Part III, Line 35(s) of the form; and,**
- **Note the word *terrorism* in the space following the box.**

In some situations, the suspicious activity may also involve money laundering; therefore, the institution should also check Box 35(a). All filers should ensure that the narrative includes as much detail as possible regarding the potential terrorist related and money laundering activities.

It is important to remember that a SAR should not be filed based on a person's ethnicity. In addition, a SAR should not be filed solely because a person appears to have the same name as individuals identified by the media as terrorists. Transactions to or from, or conducted by persons with possible affiliations with jurisdictions associated with terrorist activity should not be the only factor that prompts the filing of a SAR. However, this information may be relevant and should be considered in conjunction with other relevant information in deciding whether a SAR is warranted, as set forth in 31 CFR 103.18 and the regulations prescribed by the bank regulatory agencies, such as a lack of any apparent legal or business purpose to a transaction or series of transactions.

SAR Filings on 314a Matches

Overview: Information Sharing Between Law Enforcement and Financial Institutions – Section 314(a) of the USA PATRIOT ACT (31 CFR 103.100)

A federal law enforcement agency investigating terrorist activity or money laundering may request that FinCEN solicit, on its behalf, certain information from a financial institution or a group of financial institutions. The law enforcement agency must provide a written certification to FinCEN attesting that there is credible evidence of engagement or reasonably suspected engagement in terrorist activity or money laundering for each individual, entity, or organization about which the law enforcement agency is seeking information. The law enforcement agency also must provide specific identifiers, such as a date of birth and address, which would permit a financial institution to differentiate among common or similar names. Upon receiving a completed written certification from a law enforcement agency, FinCEN may require a financial institution to search its records to determine whether it maintains or has maintained accounts for, or has engaged in transactions with, any specified individual, entity, or organization.

Upon receiving an information request, a financial institution must conduct a one-time search of its records to identify accounts or transactions of a named suspect. Unless otherwise instructed by an information request, financial institutions must search their records for current accounts, accounts maintained during the preceding 12 months, and transactions conducted outside of an account by or on behalf of a named suspect during the preceding six months. The financial institution must search its records and report any positive matches to FinCEN within 14 days, unless otherwise specified in the information request. No details should be provided to FinCEN other than the fact that the financial institution has a match. A negative response is not required. A financial institution may provide a list of named suspects to a third-party service provider or vendor to perform or facilitate record searches as long as the institution takes the necessary steps, through the use of an agreement or procedures, to ensure that the third party safeguards and maintains the confidentiality of the information.

Investigators should be aware that a financial institution cannot disclose to any person, other than to FinCEN, the institution's primary bank regulator, or the federal law enforcement agency on whose behalf FinCEN is requesting information, the fact that FinCEN has requested or obtained information.[33]

A match with a named subject issued pursuant to the Section 314(a) process does not automatically require the filing of a SAR.
Section 314(a) requests seek to identify assets associated with a particular suspect. There may be nothing about the particular account or transaction found in response to a Section 314(a) request that is inherently illegal. A financial institution should review the account activity or transaction(s) relating to the named subject for suspicious activity, and, if appropriate, file a SAR predicated upon the totality of the circumstances and the account activity, in addition to reporting the Section 314(a) match to FinCEN.

SAR Filings on 314b Requests

Overview: Voluntary Information sharing – Section 314(b) of the USA PATRIOT Act (31 CFR 103.110)

Section 314(b) encourages financial institutions and associations of financial institutions located in the United States to share information in order to identify and report activities that may involve terrorist activity or money laundering. Section 314(b) also provides specific protection from civil liability. To avail itself of this statutory safe harbor from liability, a financial institution or an association must notify FinCEN of its intent to engage in information sharing and that it has established and will maintain adequate comply with the requirements of 31 CFR 103.110 will result in loss of safe harbor protection for information sharing and may result in a violation of privacy laws or other laws and regulations.

A notice to share information is effective for one year The financial institution should designate a point-of-contact for receiving and providing information. A financial institution should establish a process for sending and receiving information sharing requests. Additionally, a financial institution must take reasonable steps to verify that the other financial institution or association of financial institutions with which it intends to share information has also submitted the required notice to FinCEN. FinCEN provides participating financial institutions with access to a list of other participating financial institutions and their related contact information.

If a financial institution receives such information from another financial institution, it must also limit use of the information and maintain its security and confidentiality (see 31 CFR 103.110(b)(4)). Such information may be used only to identify and, where appropriate, report on money laundering and terrorist activities; to determine whether to establish or maintain an account; to engage in a transaction; or to assist in BSA compliance.

Investigators should be aware that the safe harbor *does not* extend to sharing of information across international borders. In addition, section 314(b) does not authorize a financial institution to share a SAR, nor does it permit the financial institution to disclose the existence or nonexistence of a SAR. If a financial institution shares information under section 314(b) about the subject of a prepared or filed SAR, the information shared should be limited to underlying transactional and customer information. A financial institution may use information obtained under section 314(b) to determine whether to file a SAR, but the intention to prepare or file a SAR cannot be shared with another financial institution. Financial institutions should establish a process for determining when and if a SAR should be filed.

Actions taken pursuant to information obtained through the voluntary information sharing process do not affect a financial institution's obligations to respond to any legal process. Additionally, actions taken in response to information obtained through the voluntary information sharing process do not relieve a financial institution of its obligation to file a SAR and to immediately notify law enforcement, if necessary, in accordance with all applicable laws and regulations.

SAR Filings Using the Other Category

The *Other* category currently ranks 3rd in the frequency of its selection amongst all available options on the SAR Form by filers. To select *Other* generally indicates that a suspected activity (in whole or in part) is not among the list of other summary characterizations currently made available in Part III of the SAR or described in Section III Definitions and Criminal Statutes.

Based on the variety of entries received over the years, the rationale of the *Other* fixed-field to act as a "catch-all" alternative in addition to and/or outside of the provided list of other summary characterizations has proven to be quite justified. In 2006 there were 59,440 instances where *Other* was designated as the Characterization of Suspicious Activity (in whole or in part). In their description of Other, filers frequently noted the following activities:

- Unregistered/ Unlicensed MSB;
- Tax Evasion;
- Fictitious Instrument(s);
- Wire Transfer Fraud;
- ITIN/SSN Fraud or Misuse;
- Unusual [Cash] Activity;
- Bank Fraud under 18 USC 1344;
- Fraudulent W–2;
- BSA/Structuring/Money Laundering;
- Phishing and/or Spoofing; and,
- Automated Clearing House (ACH) Fraud.

An examination by FinCEN of the details accompanying the selection of *Other* has indicated that many SARs are filed improperly. Improper entries included:
comment to See Attached (or similar);

- One-word descriptions that were too broad (e.g., Fraud; Scam); or,
- Fragmentary information in support of the selected characterization (e.g. Unusual Activity; Suspicious Fraud Ring; Money Orders);
- The description portion of the Other field was left blank.

In addition, there were descriptions noted that indicated the filing of Suspicious Activity Reports was unnecessary. For example, there were SARs that contained the following descriptions:

- Robbery;
- Insufficient Funds/Overdraft;
- Mail Fraud; Bank Error.

A SAR *is not required* for a: robbery or burglary committed or attempted as long as it is reported to appropriate law enforcement (see 31 CFR 103.17(c)(1)(i); 103.18(c); 103.19(c)(1)(i); and 103.21(c)).

Descriptions in other reports, though less common, included supporting explanations such as: *Non Fraud* or *No Fraud Found.*

A number of explanations for use of the *Other* category contained the phrase *Subpoena* or *Grand Jury Subpoena*. FinCEN has issued guidance on Grand Jury Subpoenas, indicating **the mere receipt of any law enforcement inquiry does not, by itself, require the filing of a Suspicious Activity Report**. Nonetheless, a law enforcement inquiry may cause a financial institution to review the activity for the relevant customer. It is incumbent upon a financial institution to assess all of the information it knows about its customer, including the receipt of a law enforcement inquiry, when determining whether a SAR should be filed. Further information regarding FinCEN's guidance on Grand Jury Subpoenas and Suspicious Activity Reporting may be found at: http://www.fincen.gov/sarreviewissue10.pdf.

Filers utilizing the *Other* fixed-field could be more accurate and descriptive by clearly designating a more appropriate category: Wire Transfer Fraud; BSA/ Structuring/Money Laundering; Counterfeit Instrument (Other); Mortgage Loan Fraud; or Identity Theft.

Quality Control

An examination of the details accompanying the selection of *Other* indicated that many SARs were filed improperly. Improper entries included:

- o Comment to See Attached (or similar);
- o One-word descriptions that were too broad (e.g., Fraud; Scam); or fragmentary information in support of the selected characterization (e.g. Unusual Activity; Suspicious Fraud Ring; Money Orders);
- o The description portion of the Other field was left blank.

In addition, there were descriptions that indicated the filing of Suspicious Activity Reports was unnecessary. For example, there were SARs that contained the following descriptions:

- o Robbery;
- o Insufficient Funds/Overdraft;
- o Mail Fraud; Bank Error.

A SAR is not required for a robbery or burglary committed or attempted as long as it is reported to appropriate law enforcement (see 31 CFR 103.17(c)(1)(i); 103.18(c); 103.19(c)(1)(i); and 103.21(c)).

Descriptions in other reports, though less common, included supporting explanations such as: *Non Fraud* or *No Fraud Found*.

A number of explanations for use of the Other category contained the phrase *Subpoena* or *Grand Jury Subpoena*. FinCEN has issued guidance on Grand Jury Subpoenas, indicating the mere receipt of any law enforcement inquiry does not, by itself, require the filing of a Suspicious Activity Report. Nonetheless, a law enforcement inquiry may cause a financial institution to review the activity for the relevant customer. It is incumbent upon a financial institution to assess all of the information it knows about its customer, including the receipt of a law enforcement inquiry, when determining whether a SAR should be filed. Further information regarding FinCEN's guidance on Grand Jury Subpoenas and Suspicious Activity Reporting may be found at: http://www.fincen.gov/sarreviewissue10.pdf.

Filers utilizing the *Other* fixed-field could be more accurate and descriptive by clearly designating a more appropriate category: *Wire Transfer Fraud; BSA/ Structuring/Money Laundering; Counterfeit Instrument (Other); Mortgage Loan Fraud;* or *Identity Theft*.

SAR Filing Related to OFAC SDNs and Blocked Persons

FinCEN issued final guidance in December 2004 (which revised previous guidance) to eliminate the need for duplicative reporting in cases where a financial institution identifies a verified match with individuals or entities designated by OFAC. (http://www.fincen.gov/sarguidanceofac.html)

As of December, 2004 FinCEN will deem its rules requiring the filing of suspicious activity reports to be satisfied by the filing of a blocking report with OFAC in accordance with OFAC's Reporting, Penalties and Procedures Regulations. OFAC will then provide the information to FinCEN for inclusion in the suspicious activity reporting database where it will be made available to law enforcement.

A financial institution that files a blocking report with OFAC due to the involvement in a transaction or account of a person designated as a:

o   Specially Designated Global Terrorist,
o   Specially Designated Terrorist, a Foreign Terrorist Organization,
o   Specially Designated Narcotics Trafficker Kingpin, or,
o   Specially Designated Narcotics Trafficker,

shall be deemed to have simultaneously filed a suspicious activity report on the fact of the match with FinCEN, in satisfaction of the requirements of the applicable suspicious activity reporting rule.

This interpretation *does not* affect a financial institution's obligation to identify and report suspicious activity beyond the fact of the OFAC match. To the extent that the financial institution is in possession of information not included on the blocking report filed with OFAC, a separate suspicious activity report should be filed with FinCEN including that information.

This interpretation also does not affect a financial institution's obligation to file a suspicious activity report even if it has filed a blocking report with OFAC, to the extent that the facts and circumstances surrounding the OFAC match are independently suspicious—and are otherwise required to be reported under existing FinCEN regulations. In those cases, the OFAC blocking report would not satisfy a financial institution's suspicious activity report filing obligation.

Further, nothing in this interpretation is intended to preclude a financial institution from filing a suspicious activity report to disclose additional information concerning the OFAC match (such a report would be a voluntary report under the statutes and regulations), nor does it preclude a financial institution from filing a suspicious activity report if the financial institution has reason to believe that terrorism or drug trafficking is taking place, even though there is no OFAC match.

Finally, this interpretation does not apply to blocking reports filed to report transactions and accounts involving persons owned by, or who are nationals of, countries subject to OFAC-administered sanctions programs. Such transactions should be reported on suspicious activity reports under the suspicious activity reporting rules if, and only if, the activity itself appears to be suspicious under the criteria established by the suspicious activity reporting rules.

SAR Filing When No Loss Has Occurred

Although the Suspicious Activity Report form has a field to indicate the amount of loss (if applicable) suffered by the reporting institution, whether a reporting institution actually suffers a loss is irrelevant. The determination of whether or not suspicious activity has occurred is independent of the fact that a loss may have been suffered.

For example, when cash deposits exceeding applicable thresholds are structured to avoid reporting requirements, the institution most likely will not suffer a loss, but it is required nonetheless to report such activity. (For additional information, see 31 U.S.C. § 5318(g)(1), 31 U.S.C. § 5324, 31 C.F.R. § 103.17(a)(2)(ii), 31 C.F.R. § 103.18(a)(2)(ii)).

SAR Filing Post Law Enforcement Contact

Questions have been raised from the financial industry regarding the necessity for the continued filing of SARs on continuing activity after law enforcement has contacted a financial institution with regard to a SAR filing. In some instances, after the filing of one or more SARs, law enforcement has contacted a financial institution requesting more specific information with regard to the suspect activity or requesting identified supporting documentation. In other instances, a law enforcement agency has contacted a financial institution to report that it does not intend to investigate the matter reported on the SAR.

If conduct continues for which a SAR has been filed, the guidance set forth in the October 2000 SAR Activity Review (See Section IV – Repeated SAR Filings on the Same Activity) should be followed even if a law enforcement agency has declined to investigate or there is knowledge that an investigation has begun. The filing of SARs on continuing suspicious activity provides useful information to law enforcement and supervisory authorities. Moreover, the information contained in a SAR that one law enforcement agency has declined to investigate may be of interest to other law enforcement agencies, as well as supervisory agencies.

SAR Filing When Requested by Law Enforcement to Maintain an Account

The Financial Crimes Enforcement Network (FinCEN) has issued guidance for financial institutions with account relationships that law enforcement may have an interest in ensuring remain open notwithstanding suspicious or potential criminal activity in connection with the account.

Ultimately, the decision to maintain or close an account should be made by a financial institution in accordance with its own standards and guidelines. Although there is no requirement that a financial institution maintain a particular account relationship, financial institutions should be mindful that complying with such a request may further law enforcement efforts to combat money laundering, terrorist financing, and other crimes.

If a law enforcement agency requests that a financial institution maintain a particular account, the financial institution should ask for a written request.

- o A written request from a federal law enforcement agency should be issued by a supervisory agent or by an attorney within a United States Attorney's Office or another office of the Department of Justice.
- o If a state or local law enforcement agency requests that an account be maintained, then the financial institution should obtain a written request from a supervisor of the state or local law enforcement agency or from an attorney within a state or local prosecutor's office.

The written request should:

- o Indicate that the agency has requested that the financial institution maintain the account and the purpose of the request. For example, if a state or local law enforcement agency is requesting that the financial institution maintain the account for purposes of monitoring, the written request should include a statement to that effect.
- o Indicate the duration for the request, not to exceed six months.

Law enforcement may issue subsequent requests for account maintenance after the expiration of the initial request.

Recordkeeping

Although there is no recordkeeping requirement under the Bank Secrecy Act for this type of correspondence, FinCEN recommends that financial institutions maintain documentation of such requests for at least five years after the request has expired.

Notification of Law Enforcement Regarding the Account

If a financial institution is aware —through a subpoena, 314(a) request, National Security Letter, or similar communication— that an account is under investigation, FinCEN recommends that the financial institution notify law enforcement before making any decision regarding the status of the account.

Filing SARs on Accounts

If the financial institution chooses to maintain the account, it is required to comply with all applicable Bank Secrecy Act recordkeeping and reporting requirements, including the requirement to file Suspicious Activity Reports, even if the bank is keeping an account open or maintaining a customer relationship at the request of law enforcement.

SAR Filing When No Law Enforcement Action Has Been Taken

A financial institution has an obligation to report suspicious activity as prescribed by regulation if the activity continues. FinCEN previously provided the following guidance about the subject of law enforcement contact.

As noted in the June 2001 issue of The SAR Activity Review, "If conduct continues for which a SAR has been filed, the guidance set forth in the October 2000 The SAR Activity Review (Section 5 – Repeated SAR Filings on the Same Activity) should be followed even if a law enforcement agency has declined to investigate or there is knowledge that an investigation has begun.

- FinCEN has advised financial institutions to report ongoing suspicious activity at least every 90 days.
- FinCEN encourages financial institutions to contact appropriate law enforcement directly if the activity reported warrants prompt attention.
- Additionally, financial institutions should contact the Financial Institutions Hot-Line, at:

(866-556-3974)

to report suspicious activity that may relate to terrorism.

Suspicious Activity Locations Other Than Your Financial Institution

By requiring the reporting of transactions conducted or attempted by, at, or through an institution, FinCEN recognizes that reportable activity does not necessarily happen at an institution's physical location. For example, a bank debit or credit card may be stolen and then used at retail locations to purchase goods or services, but never used at the institution. Such transactions would correctly be characterized as "conducted through" the bank, and assuming appropriate thresholds were met, would require reporting.

When suspicious activity occurs at a location other than your bank, the filer *should not* put the actual location of the activity in the Suspicious Activity Report fields normally used to indicate where activity occurred.[34] Instead, because these fields often are used by law enforcement to determine where supporting documentation is maintained, an institution should:

- o List the location of its supporting documentation and records as the address in this field;
- o In the Suspicious Activity Report narrative, indicate that this address is not the location of the activity, but rather where the records are being kept.
- o Any available information about the actual location of the suspicious activity, including (for the example above) the:
  - names of the retail businesses;
  - addresses; and,
  - contact information, should also be included in the narrative. The Suspicious Activity Report should be completed in this manner for any type of reportable suspicious activity occurring somewhere other than the financial institution. For all other transactions that occurred at the financial institution, normal filing procedures should be followed.

Section VI – FFIEC & FinCEN SAR Form and Narrative Guidance

SAR Form – TD F 90–22.47

In April 1996, a Suspicious Activity Report (SAR) was developed to be used by all banking organizations in the United States. A banking organization is required to file a SAR whenever it detects a known or suspected criminal violation of federal law or a suspicious transaction related to money laundering activity or a violation of the BSA.

In March 2007, the Financial Crimes Enforcement Network (FinCEN), the federal banking and thrift agencies and the NCUA announced the issuance of a revised *Suspicious Activity Report – FinCEN Form 111.* Initially mandated for use by the end of 2007, the implementation of Form 111 has been delayed. Therefore (as of April 2008), TD F 90-22.47 is still in use.

The guidance on the rear of the SAR Form details the circumstances for which a bank must file a SAR Form:

Banks, bank holding companies, and their subsidiaries are required by federal regulations to file a SAR with respect to:

- Criminal violations involving insider abuse in any amount:
  Whenever the bank detects suspected Federal criminal violations committed or attempted against the bank or conducted through the bank where the bank believes that it was either an actual or potential victim of a criminal violation or the bank has a substantial basis for identifying one of its directors, officers, employees, agents or aided in the commission of a criminal act, regardless of the amount in the violation.

- **Criminal violations aggregating $5,000 or more when a suspect can be identified:**
  Whenever the bank detects any known or suspected Federal violation, or pattern of violations, committed or attempted to be committed against the bank or through the bank aggregating $5,000 or more in funds or assets where the banks believes that it was either an actual or potential victim where the bank has a substantial basis for identifying a possible suspect or group of suspects. If it is determined that an alias is used then available information regarding the true identity of the suspect or group of suspects, as well as identifiers, such as drivers license or social security numbers, addresses and telephone numbers, must be reported.

- **Criminal violations aggregating $25,000 or more regardless of a potential suspect:**
  Whenever the national bank detects any known or suspected Federal criminal violations, or pattern of criminal violations, committed or attempted against the bank involving transactions conducted through the bank and involving or aggregating $25,000 or more in funds or assets where the bank believes that it was either an actual or potential victim of a criminal violation, or series of criminal violations, or that the bank was used to facilitate a criminal transaction, even though there is no substantial basis for identifying a possible suspect or group of suspects.

- **Transactions conducted or attempted by, at, or through the bank (or an affiliate) and aggregating $5,000 or more, if the bank or affiliate knows, suspects, or has reason to suspect that the transaction:**
    - May involve potential money laundering or other illegal activity (e.g., terrorism financing) or is intended or conducted in order to hide or disguise funds or assets derived from illegal activities including the ownership, nature, source, location, or control of such funds or assets as a plan to violate or evade any law or regulation or to avoid any transaction reporting requirement under Federal Law;
    - Is designed to evade the BSA or its implementing regulations
    - Has no business or apparent lawful purpose or is not the type of transaction that the particular customer would normally be expected to engage in, and the bank knows of no reasonable explanation for the transaction after examining the available facts, including the background and possible purpose of the transaction

  (Note: A transaction includes a deposit; a withdrawal; a transfer between accounts; an exchange of currency; an extension of credit; a purchase or sale of any stock, bond, certificate of deposit, or other monetary instrument or investment security; or any other payment, transfer, or delivery by, through, or to a bank.)

- **Additional guidance is also detailed regarding Computer Intrusion:**
  For purposes of this report, "computer intrusion" is defined as gaining access to a computer system of a financial institution to:
    - Remove, steal, procure, or otherwise affect funds of the institution or the institution's customers;
    - Remove, steal, procure or otherwise affect critical information of the institution including customer account information; or,
    - Damage, disable or otherwise affect critical systems of the institution.

  (For purposes of this reporting requirement, computer intrusion *does not* mean attempted intrusions of websites or other non-critical information systems of the institution that provide no access to institution or customer financial or other critical information.
    - A financial institution is required to file a suspicious activity report no later than 30 calendar days after the date of initial detection of facts that may constitute a basis for filing a suspicious activity report. If no suspect was identified on the date of detection of the incident requiring the filing, a financial institution may delay filing a suspicious activity report for an additional 30 calendar days to identify a suspect. In no case shall reporting be delayed more than 60 calendar days after the date of initial detection of a reportable transaction.
    - This suspicious activity report does not need to be filed for those robberies and burglaries that are reported to local authorities, or (except for savings associations and service corporations) for lost, missing, counterfeit, or stolen securities that are reported pursuant to the requirements of 17 CFR 240.17f-1.

Suspicious Activity Report

July 2003
Previous editions will not be accepted after December 31, 2003

ALWAYS COMPLETE ENTIRE REPORT
(see instructions)

FRB:	FR 2230	OMB No. 7100-0212
FDIC:	6710/06	OMB No. 3064-0077
OCC:	8010-9,8010-1	OMB No. 1557-0180
OTS:	1601	OMB No. 1550-0003
NCUA:	2362	OMB No. 3133-0094
TREASURY:	TD F 90-22.47	OMB No. 1506-0001

1

1 Check box below only if correcting a prior report.
☐ Corrects Prior Report (see instruction #3 under "How to Make a Report")

Part I Reporting Financial Institution Information

2 Name of Financial Institution

3 EIN

4 Address of Financial Institution

5 Primary Federal Regulator
a ☐ Federal Reserve   d ☐ OCC
b ☐ FDIC   e ☐ OTS
c ☐ NCUA

6 City

7 State

8 Zip Code

9 Address of Branch Office(s) where activity occurred   ☐ Multiple Branches (include information in narrative, Part V)

10 City

11 State

12 Zip Code

13 If institution closed, date closed
___/___/_____
MM   DD   YYYY

14 Account number(s) affected, if any
a _____ Closed? ☐ Yes ☐ No
b _____ ☐ Yes ☐ No
c _____ Closed? ☐ Yes ☐ No
d _____ ☐ Yes ☐ No

Part II Suspect Information   ☐ Suspect Information Unavailable

15 Last Name or Name of Entity

16 First Name

17 Middle

18 Address

19 SSN, EIN or TIN

20 City

21 State

22 Zip Code

23 Country

24 Phone Number - Residence (include area code)
(   )

25 Phone Number - Work (include area code)
(   )

26 Occupation/Type of Business

27 Date of Birth
___/___/_____
MM   DD   YYYY

28 Admission/Confession?
a ☐ Yes   b ☐ No

29 Forms of Identification for Suspect:
a ☐ Driver's License/State ID   b ☐ Passport   c ☐ Alien Registration   d ☐ Other _____
Number _____   Issuing Authority _____

30 Relationship to Financial Institution:
a ☐ Accountant   d ☐ Attorney   g ☐ Customer   j ☐ Officer
b ☐ Agent   e ☐ Borrower   h ☐ Director   k ☐ Shareholder
c ☐ Appraiser   f ☐ Broker   i ☐ Employee   l ☐ Other _____

31 Is the relationship an insider relationship?   a ☐ Yes   b ☐ No
If Yes specify: c ☐ Still employed at financial institution   e ☐ Terminated
d ☐ Suspended   f ☐ Resigned

32 Date of Suspension, Termination, Resignation
___/___/_____
MM   DD   YYYY

Part III	Suspicious Activity Information	2

33 Date or date range of suspicious activity
From ___/___/___ To ___/___/___
  MM DD YYYY   MM DD YYYY

34 Total dollar amount involved in known or suspicious activity
$ | | | | | | | | | | .00

35 Summary characterization of suspicious activity:

a ☐ Bank Secrecy Act/Structuring/ Money Laundering
b ☐ Bribery/Gratuity
c ☐ Check Fraud
d ☐ Check Kiting
e ☐ Commercial Loan Fraud

f ☐ Computer Intrusion
g ☐ Consumer Loan Fraud
h ☐ Counterfeit Check
i ☐ Counterfeit Credit/Debit Card
j ☐ Counterfeit Instrument (other)
k ☐ Credit Card Fraud

l ☐ Debit Card Fraud
m ☐ Defalcation/Embezzlement
n ☐ False Statement
o ☐ Misuse of Position or Self Dealing
p ☐ Mortgage Loan Fraud
q ☐ Mysterious Disappearance
r ☐ Wire Transfer Fraud
t ☐ Terrorist Financing
u ☐ Identity Theft

s ☐ Other _____
(type of activity)

36 Amount of loss prior to recovery (if applicable)
$ | | | | | | | .00

37 Dollar amount of recovery (if applicable)
$ | | | | | | | .00

38 Has the suspicious activity had a material impact on, or otherwise affected, the financial soundness of the institution?
a ☐ Yes   b ☐ No

39 Has the institution's bonding company been notified?
a ☐ Yes   b ☐ No

40 Has any law enforcement agency already been advised by telephone, written communication, or otherwise?

a ☐ DEA
b ☐ FBI
c ☐ IRS

d ☐ Postal Inspection
e ☐ Secret Service
f ☐ U.S. Customs

g ☐ Other Federal
h ☐ State
i ☐ Local

j ☐ Agency Name (for g, h or i) _____

41 Name of person(s) contacted at Law Enforcement Agency

42 Phone Number (include area code)
( )

43 Name of person(s) contacted at Law Enforcement Agency

44 Phone Number (include area code)
( )

Part IV	Contact for Assistance

45 Last Name

46 First Name

47 Middle

48 Title/Occupation

49 Phone Number (include area code)
( )

50 Date Prepared
___/___/___
  MM DD YYYY

51 Agency (if not filed by financial institution)

| Part V | Suspicious Activity Information Explanation/Description | 3 |

Explanation/description of known or suspected violation of law or suspicious activity.

This section of the report is critical. The care with which it is written may make the difference in whether or not the described conduct and its possible criminal nature are clearly understood. Provide below a chronological and **complete** account of the possible violation of law, including what is unusual, irregular or suspicious about the transaction, using the following checklist as you prepare your account. **If necessary, continue the narrative on a duplicate of this page.**

a Describe supporting documentation and retain for 5 years.
b Explain who benefited, financially or otherwise, from the transaction, how much, and how.
c Retain any confession, admission, or explanation of the transaction provided by the suspect and indicate to whom and when it was given.
d Retain any confession, admission, or explanation of the transaction provided by any other person and indicate to whom and when it was given.
e Retain any evidence of cover-up or evidence of an attempt to deceive federal or state examiners or others.

f Indicate where the possible violation took place (e.g., main office, branch, other).
g Indicate whether the possible violation is an isolated incident or relates to other transactions.
h Indicate whether there is any related litigation; if so, specify.
i Recommend any further investigation that might assist law enforcement authorities.
j Indicate whether any information has been excluded from this report; if so, why?
k If you are correcting a previously filed report, describe the changes that are being made.

For Bank Secrecy Act/Structuring/Money Laundering reports, include the following additional information:
l Indicate whether currency and/or monetary instruments were involved. If so, provide the amount and/or description of the instrument (for example, bank draft, letter of credit, domestic or international money order, stocks, bonds, traveler's checks, wire transfers sent or received, cash, etc.).
m Indicate any account number that may be involved or affected.

Tips on SAR Form preparation and filing are available in the SAR Activity Review at www.fincen.gov/pub_reports.html

Completing the SAR Form

At the top of any SAR form is the statement, "Always complete entire report." On some parts of the SAR Form, this is appended with a statement that "items denoted by an asterisk (*) are considered critical."

What constitutes *completing* a SAR?

A SAR form has been completed when all of the available information has been entered and responses such as "none" or "not available" have been entered in any blank critical field. These responses are words, phrases, or codes that inform FinCEN that data for that item is unavailable or not applicable, and has not been simply overlooked by the filer. Items are considered critical when they contain important information required for law enforcement investigations, such as:
  o   Subject name;
  o   Subject identifying number and address;
  o   Type of suspicious activity; and,
  o   A detailed narrative.

These responses are needed for several reasons:
  1.   First, they tell law enforcement and data collectors that the filer considered the item;
  2.   Second, such responses indicate the requested information was not available at the time of filing, did not exist, or did not apply to the suspicious activity; and, T
  3.   Third, such responses assist in the processing of BSA data by eliminating the need to correspond with the filers to obtain what appears to be missing information.

The following are responses commonly used in SARs to clarify what appears to be missing data, their definitions, and examples of how they are used:
  o   **None** – The requested information does not exist
  o   **Not Applicable** – The requested information is not relevant to the subject or suspicious activity
  o   **Unknown** – The filer does not know the requested information.
  o   **XX** – This applies only to two digit fields such as state or country. This is the same code already in use by institutions that are approved for Magnetic Media filing.

General Tips for Using these Types of Responses in SARs:
  o   If the SAR instructions require a specific response for an item, use that response. For example, a list of country codes may show "XX" as the abbreviation used for a country that is unknown to the filer. This is the case for the Casino SAR form. Therefore, filers that do not know which country the suspicious activity is related to should put "XX" in the country code item.
  o   Do not further abbreviate responses such as "unknown" as it could cause further confusion. For example, "unknown" abbreviated as "UK" may

mislead law enforcement into thinking the suspicious activity is related to the United Kingdom.

o   Critically important fields of information such as: subject name; subject identifying number and address; type of suspicious activity; and the narrative, etc., should have "unavailable" in the field if no information is indeed available. Doing so will eliminate the need for the processing center to contact the filer asking for what might appear to be an oversight.

SARs are only as valuable as the data reported on them. Reports that do not identify a suspect, do not identify one of the "Types of Suspicious Activity" and do not provide a narrative, are of little use to law enforcement. Therefore, filers are reminded to pay particular attention to these fields and to supply as much information as possible regarding the identity of the listed suspect(s).

It's worth restating – SARs are only as valuable as the data reported on them. Fields of information left blank are of no use to law enforcement and may actually cause more confusion. If certain data is unavailable, does not exist, or is not applicable, law enforcement wants to know it. Using one of the above terms will clear up any ambiguity.

SAR Form Line-by-Line Instructions

- **Item #1**
  - If correcting a previously filed report, check the box.
  - Complete report in its entirety and include the corrected information.
  - Describe changes that are being made in Part V, line k.
- **Item #2**
  - Enter the full *legal trade name* of your bank
- **Item #3**
  - Enter your bank's nine digit Employer Identification Number without any alpha characters or substitutes.
- **Item #4**
  - Enter the address of the institution listed in Item 2.
  - Use only a P.O. Box if no street address is known.
- **Item #5**
  - One of these boxes must always be marked to reflect your financial institution's primary federal regulator.
- **Item #6**
  - Enter the financial institution's location.
- **Item #7**
  - Use the appropriate two letter state abbreviation.
  - If the state is unknown, place XX in this field.
- **Item #8**
  - The first five digits of the zip code are mandatory; the last four digits should be included if known, or otherwise, left blank.
- **Item #9**
  - If different than information provided in Box #4, enter the address of the branch or office where the activity occurred.
  - If suspicious activity occurred at more than one branch, check the box indicating the multiple branches and include the address information in Part V of the narrative of the SAR.
- **Item #10**
  - Enter the city where the branch entered in Item #9 is located.
- **Item #11**
  - Use the appropriate two letter state abbreviation.
  - If the state is unknown, place XX in this field.
- **Item #12**
  - List the corresponding zip code.
  - The last four digits may be left blank if they are unknown.

- **Item #13**
  - o If the financial institution is now closed, enter the date it was closed; otherwise, leave this box blank.
  - o Dates should be entered using the format *mm/dd/yyyy*, e.g., 07/15/2007.
    - ▪ A zero should precede any single digit number.
    - ▪ If a portion of the date is unknown, then zeros should be entered into that portion i.e. 01/00/2000.
- **Item #14**
  - o Enter the account number(s) that were affected by the suspicious activity.
    - ▪ If no accounts were affected please indicate with N/A.
    - ▪ Do not leave blank!
    - ▪ If more than four accounts are involved, provide additional information in Part V.
  - o Additionally, indicate by checking the appropriate box whether the account is still open or closed.
  - o Numbers should be entered as USD "$0,000,000" (rounded to the nearest dollar no notation of cents should be made).
- **Items #15–17**
  - o If the suspicious activity involves an individual, enter the individual's last name in Item 15, first name in Box 16, and middle name or initial in Item #17.
    - ▪ If no middle name or initial is known enter *N/A* or *Unknown*.
    - ▪ If an *organization* is involved in the suspicious activity:
      - ● Enter the entity name in Item 15 and leave Items 16 and 17 blank.
    - ▪ If knowledge of a separate doing business as (dba) name exists:
      - ● Enter after the business name in Box 15 followed by the phrase *DBA* and the name of the business, e.g., Car's Inc. DBA Johnny's Auto Sales.
  - o If additional space is required beyond Box 15, use Items #16 and 17.
  - o If more than one suspect is involved, additional copies of page 1 should be produced.
  - o If alias names are discovered, indicate such in Part V.
- **Item #18**
  - o Include the permanent address of the individuals or entities listed in Items #15, 16 and 17.
  - o A Post Office box should only be listed if there is no known street address.
  - o If a foreign address is the address utilized, it should be listed.
  - o If no address can be located, reflect as unknown.

- **Item #19**
  - ○ Enter the appropriate number or *unknown*
- **Item #20**
  - ○ Enter the city pertaining to the address in Item #18.
- **Item #21**
  - ○ Use the appropriate two letter state abbreviation.
  - ○ If the state is unknown, place XX in this field.
- **Item #22**
  - ○ List the corresponding zip code. The first five digits are mandatory.
  - ○ The last four digits may be left blank if they are unknown.
- **Item #23**
  - ○ Write full name of the country (if other than U.S.) that corresponds to the suspect information.
  - ○ If the country is the United States, enter US.
- **Item #24**
  - ○ Enter the home phone number for the individual, including area code.
  - ○ If unknown, enter *unknown*.
- **Item #25**
  - ○ Enter the workplace phone number for the individual, including area code.
  - ○ If unknown, enter *unknown*.
- **Item #26** – This item is often misunderstood. FinCEN is looking for more specific information, i.e. Safeway Store would be "Retail Grocery". Be as specific as possible.
  - ○ Fully identify the occupation, profession or business.
- **Item #27**
  - ○ Dates should be entered using the format *mm/dd/yyyy*, e.g., 07/15/2007.
  - ○ A zero should precede any single digit number.
  - ○ If a portion of the date is unknown, then zeros should be entered into that portion e.g., 01/00/2000.
- **Item #28**
  - ○ If the suspect has made an admission, for example to someone in the bank's retail group or to an investigator, check box *a*.
  - ○ If not, check box b.
- **Item #29**
  - ○ Do not leave blank, if unknown enter unknown
  - ○ Check the appropriate form of identification presented by the suspect.
  - ○ Include the identification number and issuing authority.
  - ○ For Box *d*, *Other*, provide a short explanation;
    - ▪ If more space is required, enter the details in Part V.

- **Item #30**
  - ○ Check the appropriate box.
    - ▪ More than one box may be checked.
  - ○ If the *Other* box is checked, provide a brief explanation.
  - ○ If more space is required, use Part V.
- **Item #31**
  - ○ Select box *a* or *b*
  - ○ Do not leave blank
- **Item #32**
  - ○ Indicate the date of status change occurring in Item #31
- **Item #33**
  - ○ If the SAR is an initial SAR, then:
    - ▪ Enter the first and last date of the suspicious activity.
      - ● If only one date applies, use the *From Date*.
      - ● It is not necessary to enter anything in the *To Date*.
  - ○ If multiple or related activity was conducted, report all activity on one SAR using the *From* and *To Dates*.
  - ○ If the activity is continuing, use the date the SAR is filed as the ending date.
  - ○ If the SAR is a follow-up on an already filed SAR, the dates in Item #33 should be:
    - ▪ Beginning Date – the date of the original observation of the reported activity
    - ▪ Ending Date – the date of the last suspicious transaction, unless the activity is still ongoing.
      - ● If the activity is still ongoing, then the ending date would be the date of filing of the current SAR.
  - ○ The date range of activity should reflect the activity described in the Narrative section of the SAR. It is important that the written description of suspicious activity and the dates during which it occurred as described in the Narrative match exactly those dates listed in Item #33.
- **Item #34**
  - ○ An aggregated total of all transactions for multiple or related suspicious activities by the same suspect or organization within the same reporting period should be shown in this Item.
  - ○ Enter the amount rounded to the next highest dollar.
  - ○ A break out of this total may be listed in Part V.
- **Item #35**
  - ○ Check all boxes that identify the suspicious activity.
  - ○ More than one box may be checked.
  - ○ If *Other*, enter a brief explanation.

- **Item #36** – In almost all instances this will refer to fraud investigations, e.g., stolen checks, counterfeit checks.
    - If your financial institution has lost funds or assets:
        - Enter the dollar amount prior to recovery.
- **Item #37** – As with Box #36, this will, in most instances pertain to a fraud investigation.
    - If funds have been recovered by the financial institution:
        - Enter the dollar amount of recovered.
    - Use whole dollars rounded up to next dollar.
- **Item #38** – In the vast majority of AML investigations, the answer is likely to be *No*.
    - Check either Box *a* or *b*, as appropriate.
- **Item #39** – In almost all cases, Box b (*No*) will be the appropriate response.
    - Check either Box a or b, as appropriate.
- **Item #40**
    - Check the appropriate box(es).
    - For boxes *g, h,* and *i*, indicate the name of the law enforcement agency and telephone number on the line following box '*j*'.
- **Items #41 - 44**
    - If law enforcement has been contacted:
        - Enter the names and phone numbers of those persons contacted at the law enforcement agencies.
    - If no one at any agency has been contacted:
        - Leave blank.
- **Items #45 - 49**
    - Enter the name, title, and contact phone number of the person at your financial institution who is the contact point for this suspicious activity report.
        - Your bank's procedures may specify that there is a single point of contact for all reports. If so, enter that person's name.
- **Item #50**
    - Enter the date the SAR Form was prepared using the date field guidance as described above.
- **Item #51**
    - This field will generally not apply and may be left blank

Organizing Information in the SAR Narrative

When all applicable information is gathered, analyzed, and documented and a financial institution decides that a SAR is required, the information should be described in the SAR Narrative in a concise and chronological format. Include all elements of the five W's (Who? What? When? Where? and Why?) as discussed in the FFIEC and FinCEN guidance, as well as any other information that can assist law enforcement.

FinCEN suggests that the narrative be divided into three sections:
- o   Introduction
- o   Body
- o   Conclusion

SAR Narrative Introduction

The introductory paragraph can provide:

- The purpose of the SAR and a general description of the known or alleged violation (In some instances, this might warrant mentioning at the outset the type of suspicious activity being observed, such as Informal Value Transfer System (IVTS) operations, smurfing, shell entities, complex layering activities, structuring, check kiting, embezzlement, etc.);

- The date of any SAR(s) filed previously on the suspect or related suspects and the reason why the previous SAR(s) was filed;

- Whether the SAR is associated with the Office of Foreign Assets Control's (OFAC) sanctioned countries or Specially Designated Nationals and Blocked Persons or other government lists for individuals or organizations;

- Any internal investigative numbers used by the financial institution which may be a point of reference for law enforcement should the investigators wish to contact the institution; and,

- A summary of the red flags and suspicious patterns of activity that initiated the SAR. (This information should be provided either in the introduction or conclusion of the narrative.)

SAR Narrative Body

The Body constitutes the next paragraph or paragraphs of the Narrative and should provide all pertinent information supporting why the SAR was filed, and might include:

- Any and all relevant facts about the parties (individuals and businesses) who facilitated the suspicious activity or transactions. Include:
  - any unusual observations such as suspected shell entities;
  - financial activities which are not commensurate with the expected normal business flows and types of transactions;
  - unusual multiple party relationships; customer verbal statements;
  - unusual and/or complex series of transactions indicative of layering;
  - lack of business justification and,
  - descriptions of the documentation supporting the activity, etc.;

- A specific description of the involved accounts and transactions, identifying if known, both the origination and application of funds (usually identified in chronological order by date and amount);

- A breaking out of the larger volumes of financial activity into categories of credits and debits, and by date and amount;

- Transactor and beneficiary information, providing as much detail as possible, including:
  - the name and location of any involved domestic and/or international financial institution(s);
  - names, addresses, account numbers, and any other available identifiers of originator and beneficiary transactor(s) and/or third parties or business entities on whose behalf the conductor was acting; the date(s) of the transaction(s); and amount(s);

- An explanation of any observed relationships among the transactors (e.g., shared accounts, addresses, employment, known or suspected business relationships and/or frequency of transactions occurring amongst them; appearing together at the institution and/or counter);

- Specific details on cash transactions that identify the branch(es) where the transaction(s) occurred, the type of transaction(s), and how the transaction(s) occurred (e.g., night deposit, on-line banking, ATM, etc.); and,

- Any factual observations or incriminating statements made by the suspect.

SAR Narrative Conclusion

The final paragraph of the SAR narrative can summarize the report and might also include:

- Information about any follow-up actions conducted by the financial institution (e.g., intent to close or closure of accounts, ongoing monitoring of activity, etc.);

- Names and telephone numbers of other contacts at the financial institution if different from the point of contact indicated in the SAR;

- A general description of any additional information related to the reported activity that may be made available to law enforcement by the institution; and;

- Names of any law enforcement personnel investigating the complaint who are not already identified in another section of the SAR.

Supporting Documentation & Records Retention

IMPORTANT:

- *Do not* include any supporting documentation with the filed report nor use the term "see attached" in the Narrative Section. Tables, spreadsheets or other attachments are not entered into the SAR System database.

- Keep any supporting documentation in your institution's records for five years.

SAR Narrative Quality Guidance

Since the SAR Narrative serves as the only free text area for summarizing suspicious activity, the care with which the narrative is written may make the difference in whether or not the described conduct and its possible criminal nature are clearly understood by law enforcement. Information provided in SAR Forms allows FinCEN and the federal banking agencies to identify emerging trends and patterns associated with financial crimes. Banks are instructed to file SAR forms that are:

- o   complete,
- o   sufficient, and
- o   timely.

The SAR form should include any information readily available to the filing institution obtained through the account opening process and during due diligence efforts. In general, a SAR narrative should identify the five essential elements of information – who, what, when, where, and why, – of the suspicious activity being reported. The method of operation (or, how) is also important and should be included in the narrative.

The SAR form should include any information readily available to the filing bank obtained through the account opening process and due diligence efforts. In general, a SAR narrative should identify the five essential elements of information, i.e., who, what, when, where, and why) for the suspicious activity being reported. The method of operation (or, how?) is also important and should be included in the narrative.

A bank should not include any supporting documentation with a filed SAR nor use the terms "see attached" in the SAR narrative.
When SAR forms are received at the IRS Detroit Computing Center, only information that is in an explicit, narrative format is keypunched or scanned; thus tables, spreadsheets, or other attachments are not entered into the BSA-reporting database. Banks should keep any supporting documentation in their records for five years so that this information is available to law enforcement upon request.

The Five W's and How:

- • **Who is conducting the suspicious activity?**
  - o   While one section of the SAR form calls for specific suspect information (specific suspect identifying information is provided in Part II of the depository institution Suspicious Activity Report (SAR/TD F 90–22.47)), the narrative should be used to further describe the suspect or suspects, including
    - ▪   Occupation;
    - ▪   Position or title within the business;
    - ▪   Nature of the suspect's business(es);
    - ▪   Date of birth if available;
    - ▪   Social security, alien registration or cedula number.
  - o   If more than one individual or business is involved in the suspicious activity, identify all suspects and any known relationships amongst them in the Narrative Section. While detailed suspect information may not always

be available (e.g., in situations involving non-account holders), such information should be included to the maximum extent possible.

o Addresses for suspects are important; filing institutions should note not only the suspect's primary street addresses, but also, other known addresses, including any post office box numbers and apartment numbers when applicable. Any identification numbers associated with the suspect(s) other than those provided earlier are also beneficial, such as passport, alien registration, and driver's license numbers.

- *What* defines the suspect activity that necessitates an investigation (e.g., structuring) and describes the instruments or mechanisms being used to facilitate the suspect transaction(s)?
  An illustrative list of instruments or mechanisms that may be used in suspicious activity includes, but is not limited to:
  o Wire transfers
  o Letters of credit and other trade instruments,
  o Correspondent accounts,
  o Casinos,
  o Structuring,
  o Shell companies,
  o Bonds/notes, stocks, mutual funds, insurance policies,
  o Travelers checks, bank drafts, money orders, credit/debit cards, stored value cards, and/or digital currency business services.

In addition, a number of different methods may be employed for initiating the negotiation of funds such as:
  o The Internet
  o Phone access
  o Mail
  o Night deposit box
  o Remote dial-up
  o Couriers or others.

In summarizing the flow of funds, always include the source of the funds (origination) that lead to the application for, or recipient use of, the funds (as beneficiary). In documenting the movement of funds, identify:
  o All account numbers at the financial institution affected by the suspicious activity (when the number of accounts exceeds the number of account blocks on the respective SAR form, use the Narrative Section of the SAR to identify the additional accounts and,
  o any other information that cannot be placed in other sections of the SAR form.), and when possible,
  o Any account numbers held at other institutions and,
  o The names/locations of the other financial institutions, including MSBs and foreign institutions involved in the reported activity.

- **When did the suspicious activity take place?**
  When refers to the date or the period of time over which the suspicious activity occurred. Indicate the date when the suspicious activity was *first* noticed and describe the duration of the activity. Filers will often provide a tabular presentation of the suspicious account activities (transactions in and out). While this information is useful and should be retained, *do not* insert objects, tables, or pre-formatted spreadsheets when filing a SAR. Also, in order to better track the flow of funds, individual dates and amounts of transactions should be included in the narrative rather than just the aggregated amount.

- **Where did the suspicious activity take place?**
  Where refers to all the locations involved in the conduct of the suspicious activity. Use the Narrative Section to indicate that multiple branches of a single financial institution were involved in the suspicious activity and provide the addresses of those locations. Specify if the suspected activity or transaction(s) involve a foreign jurisdiction. If so, provide the name of the foreign jurisdiction, financial institution, address and any account numbers involved in, or affiliated with the suspected activity or transaction(s). If the case involves wire transfers, specify the dates, destinations, amounts, accounts, frequency, and beneficiaries of the funds transfers.

- **Why does the filer think the activity is suspicious?**
  FinCEN suggests that institutions first describe briefly their industry or business – depository institution, casino, mortgage broker, securities broker, insurance, real estate, investment services, money remitter, check casher, etc. Then describe, as fully as possible, why the activity or transaction is unusual for the customer; consider the types of products and services offered by your industry, and the nature and normally expected activities of similar customers. Examples of some common patterns of suspicious activity are:
  - A lack of evidence of legitimate business activity, or any business operations at all, undertaken by many of the parties to the transaction(s);
  - Any unusual financial nexus and/or transactions occurring among certain business types (e.g., food importer dealing with an auto parts exporter);
  - Transactions that are not commensurate with the stated business type and/or that are unusual and unexpected in comparison with the volumes of similar businesses operating in the same locale;
  - Unusually large numbers and/or volumes of wire transfers and/or repetitive wire transfer patterns;
  - Unusually complex series of transactions indicative of layering activity involving multiple accounts, banks, parties, jurisdictions;
  - Suspected shell entities;
  - Bulk cash and monetary instrument transactions;
  - Unusual mixed deposits of money orders, third party checks, payroll checks, etc., into a business account;
  - Transactions being conducted in bursts of activities within a short period of time, especially in previously dormant accounts;

- o Transactions and/or volumes of aggregate activity inconsistent with the expected purpose of the account and expected levels and types of account activity conveyed to the financial institution by the account holder at the time of the account opening;
- o Beneficiaries maintaining accounts at foreign banks that have been subjects of previous SAR filings;
- o Parties and businesses that do not meet the standards of routinely initiated due diligence and anti-money laundering oversight programs (e.g., unregistered / unlicensed businesses);
- o Transactions seemingly designed to, or attempting to avoid reporting and record keeping requirements; and
- o Correspondent accounts being utilized as "pass-through" points by foreign jurisdictions with subsequent outgoing funds to another foreign jurisdiction.

For a complete list of red flags, see the sections
- o Money Laundering Red Flags, and
- o Terrorist Financing Red Flags

- **How did the suspicious activity occur?**
  Use the Narrative Section to describe the modus operandi (i.e., the method of operation of the subject conducting the suspicious activity). In a concise, accurate and logical manner, describe how the suspect transaction or pattern of transactions was committed. Provide as completely as possible a full picture of the suspicious activity involved. For example, if what appears to be structuring of currency deposits is matched with outgoing wire transfers from the accounts, the SAR narrative should include information about both the structuring and outbound transfers (including dates, destinations, amounts, accounts, frequency, and beneficiaries of the funds transfers). *How* also refers to *How much,* i.e., the dollar amounts involved in the suspicious activity. This information is vital to law enforcement agencies.

Examples of Complete & Sufficient SAR Narratives

In an effort to provide helpful guidance to financial institutions, FinCEN reviewed the SAR System database to identify previously submitted SARs that contained sufficient and complete narratives. The examples on the following pages are followed by a brief commentary. Investigators' SAR narratives should reflect the content, form and style illustrated in the examples.

SAR Narrative Example #1 (Sufficient)

Sample: COMPLETE and SUFFICIENT SAR NARRATIVE

Investigation case number: A5678910.

The customer, a grocery store and its owner, are suspected of intentionally structuring cash deposits to circumvent federal reporting requirements. The customer is also engaged in activity indicative of an informal value transfer operation: deposits of bulk cash, third party out of state personal checks and money orders, and engaging in aggregate wire transfers to Dubai, UAE. The type and volume of activity observed is non-commensurate with the customer's expected business volume and deviates from the normal volume of similar types of businesses located in the same area as the customer. Investigative activities are continuing. Our bank has elected to directly contact law enforcement concerning this matter along with filing this SAR.

John Doe opened a personal checking account, #12345-6789, in March of 1994. Doe indicated that he was born in Yemen, presented a Virginia driver's license as identification, and claimed he was the self-employed owner of a grocery store identified as Acme, Inc. A business checking account, #23456-7891, was opened in January of 1998 for Acme, Inc.

Between January 17, 2003, and March 21, 2003, John Doe was the originator of nine wires totaling $225,000. The wire transfers were always conducted at the end of each week in the amount of $25,000. All of the wires were remitted to the Bank of Anan in Dubai, UAE, to benefit Kulkutta Building Supply Company, account #3489728.

Reviews covering the period between January 2 and March 17, 2003, revealed that 13 deposits (consisting of cash, checks, money orders) totaling approximately $50,000 posted to the personal account. Individual amounts ranged between $1,500 and $9,500 and occurred on consecutive business days in several instances. A number of third-party out of state checks and money orders were also deposited into the account.

A review of deposit activity on the Acme, Inc. account covering the same period revealed 33 deposits (consisting of cash, checks, money orders) totaling approximately $275,000. Individual amounts ranged between $4,446 and $9,729; however 22 of 33 deposits ranged between $9,150 and $9,980. It was further noted that in nine of 13 instances in which cash deposits were made to both accounts on the same day, the combined deposits of cash exceeded $10,000. The bank filed currency transaction reports to the IRS for all aggregate daily transactions exceeding $10,000.

A search of the world wide web identified a website for Acme, Inc., which identified the company as a grocery store that provides remittance services to countries in the Middle East that includes Iran (an OFAC blocked country). Contact with the Virginia State Department of Banking indicates Acme, Inc. is not a licensed money wire transfer business. The bank will close this account because of the suspect nature of the transactions being conducted by John Doe.

Comments:

This narrative is a well-written summary of all the suspicious activity and supports the stated purpose for filing the SAR. Furthermore, the narrative provides an internal bank reference number for the SAR that can be used by law enforcement should investigators wish to contact the bank to discuss pertinent facts presented in the narrative. Specific information is also provided in the narrative that details the source and application of suspect funds. The SAR also identifies other actions taken by the financial institution as part of its internal due diligence program and its efforts in detecting possible illegal activity being facilitated by the suspect.

SAR Narrative Example #2 (Sufficient)

Sample: COMPLETE and SUFFICIENT SAR NARRATIVE

Doe's Auto Sales, commercial checking account #1234567, is being reported for unusual activity and structured cash deposits. Doe's Auto Sales operates as a small used car lot with an inventory of less than 10 vehicles at any given time. John Doe is the owner of Doe's Auto Sales and a signer on the account. Jane Doe is an additional signer. The account was opened in September 2002 at the Happy Valley branch in Anytown, CA.

Account activity is usually extremely limited and several months involve periods of no account activity. However, many suspicious and structured transactions were conducted in June 2003 at two different bank branches in Anytown. The cash deposits were conducted in a manner possibly to avoid filing a currency transaction report. The structured cash deposits were always conducted for $9,800 each. Immediately following each deposit, a check for $9,800 posted to the account, payable to Doe's Auto Sales. Those checks were deposited to an account at XYZ Bank, also located in Anytown. Structured cash deposits conducted in June 2003 were as follows: 06/03 $9,800; 06/04 $9,800; 06/09 $9,800; 06/10 $9,800; 06/11 $9,800; and 06/12 $9,800. The deposits on 06/03, 06/09, and 06/11 were completed at the Happy Valley branch by John Doe. The remaining deposits, on 06/04, 06/10, and 6/12, were conducted by Jane Doe at the Main Office branch. The source of the cash deposited to the account is unknown.

Checks posting to the account payable to Doe's Auto Sales and deposited at XYZ bank were as follows: 06/04 $9,800; 06/05 $9,800; 06/10 $9,800; 06/11 $9,800, 06/12 $9.800; and 06/13 $9.800. It is unknown what happened to the funds after the deposits to XYZ Bank.

Due to the pattern and manner of recent transactions, it appears that the cash deposits to credit Doe's Auto Sales were structured to evade the reporting requirement of the Bank Secrecy Act. Additionally, the immediate movement of funds out of the bank to another financial institution in amounts slightly below $10,000 seems unusual. A review of prior transactions since the account opened revealed no similar type of activity or in such amounts. Therefore, this suspicious activity report is being submitted.

The bank will continue to monitor the account for further activity and file a supplemental SAR if required. All documentation obtained during this investigation is located in the case file, case #03-501, maintained by the bank's anti-money laundering department. Additional branch location address: Main Office branch –100 West Happy Valley Street, Anytown, CA 12345.

Comments:
Facts presented in this SAR narrative clearly support the purpose of the SAR filing and also provide a disposition on further actions by the financial institution. The location of documentation supporting the SAR is identified. The institution provides information related to previous banking activity and identifies the dates, amounts, and locations of specific transactions to establish the pattern of structured transactions.

SAR Narrative Example #3 (Sufficient)

Sample: COMPLETE and SUFFICIENT SAR NARRATIVE

Bank investigation file number AA67325.

This SAR is being filed to summarize suspicious cash deposits and wire transfer activity conducted by John Doe, account #12345678910. John Doe has been a bank customer since April 2000. Mr. Doe is a college student and employed part-time at Quickie Car Wash.

Cash deposits to Mr. Doe's personal checking account are structured to possibly circumvent federal reporting requirements. The deposits are followed by immediate wire transfers to Aussie Bank in Sydney, Australia to a single beneficiary, Jennifer Doe, account #981012345, with an address located in Australia. Specifically the following activity has been observed: cash deposits (dates followed by amounts): 03/15/02 $9,950.00; 03/17/02 $9,700.00; 03/18/02 $10,000; total: $29,650. Wire transfers out (dates followed by amounts): 03/16/02 $9,900.00, 03/18/02 $9,700.00, 03/19/02 $9,900.00. The volume and frequency of the deposits is not consistent with previous banking transactions conducted by Mr. Doe. The amounts of currency do not appear consistent with the customer's stated employment. Also, the relationship between the customer and Jennifer Doe and the purpose for the wire activity is unknown.

Therefore, due to the structured cash deposits by the customer on almost consecutive days into the account, and the immediate wire transfer of the funds out of the account to Jennifer Doe, Aussie bank, account #891012345, Sydney Australia, this SAR is being filed. Investigation is continuing.

The bank's financial intelligence unit in Big City, FL, maintains all records related to this SAR.

Comments:
The narrative provides a sufficient explanation for the SAR filing in addition to providing an internal bank file number for law enforcement to reference if it wishes to contact the depository institution. Facts presented in the SAR narrative clearly support the purpose of the SAR filing. The narrative includes information on disposition on further actions by the financial institution and identifies the availability and location of documentation supporting the SAR.

SAR Narrative Example #4 (Sufficient)

Sample: COMPLETE and SUFFICIENT SAR NARRATIVE

The Bank of Mainland (BM) filed an initial suspicious activity report (SAR) dated 6/11/01. The SAR was filed due to unusual wire transfer and cash deposit activity involving two BM corporate customers, Sky Corporation and Sea Corporation, both registered in Vermont and having a common Vermont address. BM has also filed numerous CTRs on cash deposits conducted on behalf of the two companies. Our previous and recent reviews of the customers' activities revealed the cash deposits and wire transfers involving the companies might be consistent with money laundering.

Because BM was unable to determine any particulars about the companies in order to establish a business justification for the activity, the following patterns appeared suspicious:

1. A repeating pattern of structured cash deposits into business accounts held by the companies with wire transfers to a particular beneficiary.
2. Individual transactions conducted in large dollar amounts.
3. Individual transactions conducted in even dollar amounts.
4. Individual transactions conducted within a short period of time (i.e., daily basis, 2x's daily, every other day).
5. Periodic incoming wire transfers from a foreign corporation via a correspondent account maintained by a foreign bank at Bank of Mainland.

Specifically, the analysis of the cash deposit and wire activity for the period 2/2/99 through 6/20/01 revealed the following:

1. The Vermont companies are as follows: Sky Corporation and Sea Corporation, both of 1234 North Harvard Street, Suite 81, in Burlington, Vermont.
2. The total number and dollar value of cash deposits into accounts held by the companies are as follows: Sky Corporation, account #54321098, 284 deposits totaling $2,710,000; Sea Corporation, account #12345678, 200 deposits totaling $1,900,000. Reviews of the accounts indicate all the deposits were night deposits conducted through three main branches of BM: North Burlington; South Burlington; and West Burlington. The average amount of deposits negotiated through account #12345678 was from $8,720 to $16,500. Many of the transactions conducted on the same day at multiple branches in amounts under $10,000 may have been conducted to circumvent federal reporting requirements.
3. 15 incoming wire transfers were received from Tolinka Inc. affecting account #12345678. Tolinka Inc. is registered in Utah and is a customer of Bank XYZ in Warsaw, Poland, account #689472. Bank XYZ maintains a correspondent relationship with the Bank of Poland. The Bank of Poland, in turn, maintains a correspondent account at BM. As part of BM's due diligence of foreign wire transactions, we contacted Bank of Poland to have them inquire with Bank XYZ about Tolinka Inc. Bank XYZ could not substantiate the type of business activity or provide any documentation for Tolinka Inc. Bank XYZ's contact with Tolinka Inc.

in response to our query resulted in the business closing its account with Bank XYZ with no explanation provided.

4. The total number and dollar value of outgoing wire transfers from Sky Corporation and Sea Corporation is as follows: Sky Corporation, account #5431098, 274 wire transfer debits totaling $2,697,000; Sea Corporation, account #12345678, 198 wire transfer debits totaling $1,866,000. The day after cash deposits, wire transfers were usually conducted through the use of a remote computer terminal as part of an Internet service for the accounts. The amount of wire transfers usually equaled the aggregate of deposits from the day before. All wire transfers from both accounts were remitted to Paul Lafonte, Artsy Bank, account #456781234, in Paris, France.

At the time the accounts were opened with our financial institution, a registered agent for both companies provided corporate filings filed with the Secretary of State of Vermont indicating the companies are for-profit, engaged in retail shoe sales. As part of our annual review of corporate accounts, we were unable to substantiate if the companies are still active from researching public records, commercial database systems, or the Internet. Attempted telephone contact with the companies identified both numbers as being disconnected. The companies do not appear to maintain operating businesses in Vermont; and there is no indication of legitimate business activity.

Due to these factors and the suspicious demeanor of the account activity, bank management has decided to end our banking relationships with Sky Corporation and Sea Corporation. All records related to this matter are being maintained by the bank's central branch operations officer in Burlington, VT.

Comments:
The narrative is a well-written summary identifying all aspects of the suspicious transactions conducted by the suspect businesses including the apparent structuring of cash deposits on multiple days at multiple branch locations, the use of a foreign account to facilitate wire transfers to the customer's accounts through a correspondent bank, and the use of online transactions to effect outgoing wire transfers. The depository institution documents its due diligence efforts to determine the status and operations of its suspicious customers as well as its efforts to glean information about the originator of the suspicious wire transfers. The financial institution indicates that CTRs (Currency Transaction Reports) and a SAR were filed previously. The institution conveys the disposition of the two accounts and the location where records are stored. (Note: Because of the volume of activity summarized in the narrative, a detailed listing of check numbers, senders, etc. is included in the originally filed SAR but omitted for the purpose of maintaining some brevity within the narrative for this report.)

Examples of Insufficient SAR Narratives

In an effort to provide helpful guidance to financial institutions, FinCEN reviewed the SAR System database to identify previously submitted SARs that contained *insufficient and incomplete* **narratives**. The examples in on the following pages are followed by a brief commentary.

SAR Narrative Example #1 (Insufficient)

Sample: INCOMPLETE and INSUFFICIENT SAR NARRATIVE

John Doe was the originator of nine wires totaling $225,000. All of the wires were remitted to a Dubai based company. During the same period of time John Doe deposited cash, money orders, and checks into his account. See attachment.

Comments:
This SAR fails to provide specific details on the application of the suspect funds (the name, bank, and account number of the beneficiary, if identifiable). The SAR also references an attachment, which is not available to the reader since supporting documents are not entered into the SAR System database. (Please remember that attachments should not be sent with the SAR. Rather, any supporting documentation should be described in the SAR narrative and retained with the financial institution's case file.) The depository institution fails to provide any information concerning the relationship, if any, between the institution and the customer. Also, no specific transaction data is provided that identifies the dates and amounts of each wire transfer.

SAR Narrative Example #2 (Insufficient)

Sample: INCOMPLETE and INSUFFICIENT SAR NARRATIVE

A.) Copy of the questionable activity report (QAR) from Bank Secrecy Act Department outlining the suspected structuring of cash-in activity by our customer, Management Services, a management company for the period of 07/10/02 to 07/22/02. B.) Management Services, financially, via the suspected structuring of cash-in activity to avoid CTR reporting. C.) N.A. D.) See A. above. E.) N.A. F.) Downtown branch, 25 E. Third Street, Anytown, SD 12345. G.) The activity consisted of 4 transactions for the month of July 2002. H.) N.A. I.) N.A. J.) To the best of my knowledge, no information has been excluded from this report. K.) Currency was involved. L.) 224-307711.

Comments:
Although the bank responds to the checklist found in the SAR instructions, it fails to provide a chronological and complete account of the violation of law in order to explain the nature of the suspicious activity. The SAR fails to identify specific examples of the structuring activity, including dates and amounts of the transactions. Additionally, the filing bank does not explain if deposits were consistent with the expected transactions of the business. Finally, the narrative does not identify what happened to the funds after they were deposited into the bank account.

SAR Narrative Example #3 (Insufficient)

Sample: INCOMPLETE and INSUFFICIENT SAR NARRATIVE

We believe this customer is structuring to avoid CTR filing.

Comments:
The bank does not provide any beneficial information in the narrative. It fails to relate the types of transactions (cash-in or cash-out), the amounts and dates, background information on the customer, source or dispersal of funds in customer's account, or other information to support the statement provided in the narrative.

Section VII – Transaction Monitor Alerts and Process Tuning

Introduction

Automated transaction monitoring systems have found their way into bank AML operations with mixed results. The rush to adopt these systems began shortly after passage of the PATRIOT Act. Whether seen as a panacea for compliance purposes or simply a head long rush to appease the regulators is uncertain. While there is no doubt that many of these software systems introduced monitoring capabilities heretofore unavailable, their implementation has also had the unintended consequence of increasing workload –perhaps due little to the fault of the software itself.

Anecdotally, there are few (if any) banks that rely on their transaction monitors to determine whether an alerted activity is reported to FinCEN without first further qualifying the alert and then conducting an investigation. In many cases, the capabilities of the software applications are undermined by the fact that few institutions have dependable customer profiles available to integrate with their transaction monitors. The simplest of monitors can look at transaction thresholds and patterns, but without customer profile information, it is nearly impossible to tell, for example, whether a particular threshold or pattern might in fact be routine for a given customer.

Different vendors' tout different capabilities and technologies for their products, but the old adage about garbage-in, garbage-out still applies. Some high-end technologies, such as neural networks (so called *intelligent machines*) are supposed to actually learn about a customer's behavior over time and thus compensate for the lack of available know-your-customer (KYC) profile information. Success of technologies like neural networks or *link analysis, etc.* are debatable, yet what's not debatable is the cost of owning these systems. They have up until now been cost prohibitive for all but the largest financial institutions, who ironically, have the greatest difficulties providing the data needed by these monitors due to the sheer scale of their operations.

Banks therefore find that their AML regulatory risks are less a function of the fancy transaction capabilities they've purchased but more how the output from their transaction software is dealt with. Tuning (or, adjusting) the output of the software is one way to optimize actionable alerts versus false positives and negatives, but doing so often involves the help of the vendor with large additional costs beyond the originally budgeted acquisition and implementation fees.

With the workload shifted to the investigation and reporting effort, the focus on increasing productivity and reducing regulatory risk should shift as well. Tuning the part of the process that involves human intervention becomes a viable alternative to tuning the transaction monitoring software's output itself.

To achieve measurable results, it is important to understand both how your software generates alerts and how simple statistical modeling can be applied to optimally adjust case assignment to investigators.

Understanding Transaction Monitors

In order to evaluate output of specific systems and conduct fine tuning, or optimization, of output, it is necessary to understand how a specific AML software system implements its core monitoring technology. Typical data-mining and optimization techniques employed by AML transaction monitors generally fall into one or more of the following categories:

- o   Decision trees;
- o   Neural Networks; or,
- o   Statistical profiling.

All three categorizes, as applied to the detection of money laundering, face issues regarding the selection of data to be used as well as other particulars inherent to the statistical methods they employ. The simplest monitors, however, use statistical sampling.

Statistical Sampling

In order to evaluate a transaction, statistical profiling applies a statistical measure of variance to determine the extent to which a transaction departs from the norm. Variance can be measured for many variables. A transaction can be evaluated based on a number of characteristics, such as its absolute amount, its amount compared to the amounts of other transactions within a particular time period (daily, weekly, monthly), transaction frequency during the period the transaction is made, and relationships with counter-parties inside or outside the bank. A transaction can be evaluated against past patterns of behavior for the customer who made the transaction, for the account and its related accounts, and for accounts in the customer's peer group. Statistical profiling software implementations require that the vendor define peer groups based on characteristics that the bank specifies during the setup configuration process. Once the peer groups are specified, their behavior can change dynamically and variance will be measured based on the current behavior of the group.

Statistical profiling can be used in conjunction with list checking and processing rules that flag transactions based on characteristics belonging to known patterns of money laundering. This is important for recognizing known money laundering patters. For example, one pattern might be defined as:

1.   the opening of an individual account; followed by
2.   one or more cash deposits just under the reporting limit; followed by
3.   an international wire transfer out of the account to a single beneficiary.

One major problem associated with statistical sampling is that there is no intrinsic way to flag out-of-pattern transactions as false positives. Some vendors offer facilities to address this. For example, they may allow you to mark an account as a *trusted,* exempting it from further testing. However, doing so relies on sufficient KYC information to make such a decision, which as has been noted previously, may be in short supply. An alternative approach available with some monitors is that a transaction that has been investigated and found to be legitimate can be removed from a customer's account history (e.g., an abnormally large transaction, such as a home purchase) such that it doesn't skew the pattern that the software will compare transactions against in the future.

The major benefits of using statistical sampling based transaction monitors include:

  o   Generally lower acquisition and implementation costs and speedier implementations;
  o   Intuitive methodology that's easy to understand and perhaps as importantly, able to be explained to managers and regulators (in principle, though not at the level of the statistical algorithms);
  o   The potential of the statistical model to recognize new patterns of money laundering, since the software will flag anything that is outside of the norm;
  o   Ease of understanding why a transaction was identified as suspicious

What makes one statistical sampling based monitor different from another? A natural weakness of using this method in transaction monitoring is the inability of the underlying algorithms to consider complex relationships between independent variables. Accommodating these relationships must be somehow incorporated into the algorithms and are routinely done so using proprietary techniques. Such customization leads to a level of sophistication that may render some of the above mentioned benefits moot, but they do allow different vendors to make performance claims that differ from their competitors' products.

Decision Trees and Neural Networks
The higher end transaction monitors use more sophisticated methodologies (not better, necessarily, just more sophisticated) such as decision tree analysis. This is a predictive model of machine learning that maps observations about items to conclusions about their value. Decision tree analysis in AML software is able to discern trends in the underlying data, which is then used to generate alerts based on fitting those trends to known money laundering activity profiles.

Neural networks are based on efforts to model information processing in such a way that mimics the human brain's capacity to learn. This is also referred to as *artificial intelligence.*

Transaction monitors that employ machine learning algorithms are said to *acquire* knowledge and to be *adaptive.* Their claimed advantages include the ability to represent both linear and non-linear relationships as well as the ability to learn these relationships directly from the data being modeled – capabilities not necessarily present with linear, rules based modeling. As such, they are potentially capable of identifying many more new methods of money laundering not originally considered when the system was first implemented.

In BSA investigation environments, a natural weakness of such complex transaction monitoring systems is that sometimes it is difficult to understand how the monitor arrived at its results, which makes explaining the results in a SAR narrative more difficult, as well as defending the decisions based on those results to management and regulators.

Conclusion

How AML transaction monitoring technology is implemented can be more important than what type of technology it employs, especially regarding the hoped for output and efficiency of its use. This includes both how the technology is implemented in the software itself and how it is integrated into the systems and data architecture at a specific financial institution. All AML transaction monitors are heavily dependent on configuration and availability and quality of data. Often, implementation of these monitors is as much art as science. Banks often underestimate the costs of a full implementation and the end result can be the acquisition of burdensome long term staffing costs and higher risks associated with false positives and negatives.

Because vendors are selling technology to non-technical clients (compliance departments), and banks' IT staff often do not understand the business requirements of the compliance software purchaser (i.e., the end user compliance department itself), it is usually a good idea to employ consultants who have expertise in both BSA compliance and technical implementations. Qualified consultants should be able to assist you with choosing the right software, acting as an ombudsman when the sales pitches start flying, and managing the vendor relationship during the implementation phase. (Other services, e.g., negotiating contract provisions such as performance guaranties, maintenance and support, and providing acceptance testing services should be seriously considered.)

Statistical Methods for Process Tuning

Relatively simple statistical methods can be employed to test changes made to transaction monitoring systems or to optimize the assignment of alerts and/or investigations to those most qualified. Familiarity with these concepts is important for managing the statistical modeling/testing, as described in the following sections.

Regression Testing:

This technique focuses on re-testing after changes are made. By re-testing old system states (for example, a threshold within the transaction monitoring alert parameters), you would be looking to see if the changes made had the desired effect. Examination of the new output is meant to validate that the program has not *regressed* to the bad state, i.e., the state which initially precipitated the need for the changes being made. Regression testing is also used to ensure that the changes made did not have any unintended side-effects or consequences that might be unrelated to the changes themselves.

By comparing the historical probabilities observed (i.e., prior to changing a parameter in a rule or other setting) with the resulting probabilities for each outcome –post the change, it is possible to determine the net effect of the change. Continued tuning and regression testing in this manner will allow for optimization of the parameters.

In addition to tuning the transaction monitor to produce an optimal good/bad alert ratio, the *probabilities of the outcomes* raw alert data can be used to measure variance of alert resolutions by individual analysts against independent variables such as alert source and alert type (e.g., structuring, or pouch activity, etc.), for example. Analysis of normally distributed data affords management a simple measure of performance and output deviations from mean or expected values. (See the Alert Outcome Probabilities Section below for more information.)

Correlation:

Correlation is a statistical technique which can show whether and how strongly pairs of variables are related. The main result of a correlation is called the correlation coefficient (or r). r ranges from −1.0 to +1.0. The closer r is to +1 or −1, the more closely the two variables are related.

- o   If r is close to 0, it means there is no relationship between the variables;
- o   If r is positive, it means that as one variable gets larger the other gets larger;
- o   If r is negative it means that as one gets larger, the other gets smaller (often called an "inverse" correlation).

While correlation coefficients are normally reported as r = (a value between −1 and +1), squaring them makes them easier to understand. The square of the coefficient (or r^2) is equal to the percent of the variation in one variable that is related to the variation in the other. (After squaring r, ignore the decimal point). An r of .5 means 25% of the variation is related ($.5^2 = .25$). An r value of .7 means 49% of the variation is related ($.7^2 = .49$). It is important to remember that when working with correlations, never assume a correlation means that a change in one variable *caused* a change in another (i.e., correlation is not to be confused with *causation*).

Correlation results, prior to being used for tuning, should be considered with respect to *statistical significance.*

Statistical Significance:
Statistical Significance is mathematically represented by the Greek symbol α (alpha). A statistically significant result means that the result was unlikely to have been due simply to chance (e.g., a correlation that is 95% statistically significant indicates that the correlation only has a 5% possibility of being due solely to chance).

Standard Deviation, Variance, and Normally Distributed Data:
If data fits a generally *normally distributed* pattern, then the distribution can be specified completely by its mean and standard deviation. For a normal distribution:
- 68% of the data will fall within one standard deviation of the mean (i.e., the highest point of the curve);
- 95% of the data will fall within 2 standard deviations, and;
- 99.7% (or, almost all) of the data will fall within three standard deviations of the mean.

Employee performance is generally considered to be normally distributed. The variance is the measure of how widely dispersed the data is. Mathematically, variance is the square of the standard deviation.

Alert Outcome Probabilities

A model much in use in the banking community is one where transaction monitoring alerts are first reviewed at a high level to determine if the alerts are qualified, i.e., not obvious false positives. At this stage, alerts can be outright dismissed with little or no analysis (such as those coming from the Federal Reserve account, for example) or analyzed to some greater degree and then closed. Alternatively, an alert might be deemed worthy of further investigation and passed onto an investigator (as a suspicious activity case) who will conduct an in-depth investigation. The investigator will subsequently decide if the case has merit. If it does not, it will be closed; if it does, a SAR will be filed. These five outcomes and their probabilities are summarized below:

1. Alert not analyzed and subsequently closed

2. Alert analyzed and subsequently *not referred* to an investigator for further review

3. Alert analyzed and *referred* to an investigator for further review

4. Alert *referred* to an investigator *and closed* (i.e., no SAR filed)

5. Alert *referred* to an investigator and a *SAR is filed* as a result

The probability of any of these (symbolized by P(A), where A is the event) is a number between 0 and 1 (or 0 – 100%), inclusive, that measures the likelihood of the event. For alert/case events, the probability for any of the possible outcomes can be represented as follows:

1.
$$P(Alert\_Not\_Analyzed; closed) = \frac{\#Alerts\_Not\_Analyzed; closed}{Total\#Alerts}$$

2.
$$P(Alert\_Analyzed; closed) = \frac{\#Alerts\_Analyzed; closed}{Total\#Alerts}$$

3.
$$P(Alert\_Analyzed; referred) = \frac{\#Alerts\_Analyzed; referred}{Total\#Alerts}$$

4.
$$P(Alert\_investigated; closed) = \frac{\#Alerts\_Investigated; closed}{Total\#Alerts}$$

5.
$$P(Alert\_investigated; SAR\_Filed) = \frac{\#Alerts\_Investigated; SAR\_Filed}{Total\#Alerts}$$

You can track these probabilities for *each* analyst and investigator. Assuming the distribution of these probabilities across all analysts and investigators is normally distributed, it will become obvious where the production metrics for each analyst and investigator falls relative to the mean for *all* the analysts and investigators within your SAR unit.

The bottom line is that this simple statistical method can be easily programmed into Microsoft Access (or less efficiently, into Excel) to determine what types of alerts are best and most efficiently handled by which staff analyst or investigator. For example, you might find that Mary refers more alerts to investigators that result in a no-SAR decision than the average for the group. You might then be able to make decisions regarding further training for Mary, or perhaps try and determine whether Mary is only looking at specific alert types. By further refining the granularity of the data to adjust for alert types, you can compare performances that may reveal opportunities to further optimize efficiency by assigning certain alert types to certain staff members based on skill set, experience, analytical ability etc. For example, a terrorist financing case is harder to analyze than a structuring case, and therefore, it is better risk management to assign terror financing alerts only to certain experienced analysts.

Types of alerts that can be parsed into the model include those concerning:

- Accounts with previously filed SARs
- Branch Referrals
- EDD Customer Monitoring
- High Risk Wires
- Media Reports
- Monetary Instrument Alerts
- Cash Transactions/Structuring.
- Other Transaction Monitoring System Alerts

Simple Alert Optimization Method

The following method can be easily programmed into Excel and used to calculate the mean, variance, and standard deviation for the data series consisting of the probabilities of a single specific alert outcomes for a single alert type for a group of analysts. The results will allow comparisons to be made regarding referral outcomes by alert type and by individual analysts against the performance of the group of your department's analysts as a whole.

1. Ensure that the key parameters relating to the operational processing of the alert are identified, considered and isolated, as appropriate.

2. Calculate the probability of the unique alert outcome for the alert type for each individual analyst.

3. Sum the data for each outcome by analyst.

4. Determine the mean μ for the probability values for each set of alert data:

$$\mu = \frac{1}{n} \sum_{i=1}^{n} X_i$$

5. Compute the average of the data series of alert probability outcomes.

6. Compute the difference from the mean of each probability in the series.

7. Compute the variance (i.e., the sum of the squared deviations divided by the number of data points in the set):

$$\sigma^2 = \frac{\sum\limits_{i=1}^{n} (x_i - \mu)^2}{n}$$

8. Compute the standard deviation of the outcome for the alert, which is simply the square root of the variance;

$$\sigma = \sqrt{\frac{\sum\limits_{i=1}^{n} (x_i - \mu)^2}{n}}$$

9. Confirm by inspection that the data is normally distributed.

10. Compare each analyst's performance to the distribution parameters for the group as a whole.

(Note: When mean and standard deviation of a normal distribution are known, it is possible to compute the percentile rank associated with any given score. In a normal distribution, about 68% of the scores are within one standard deviation of the mean and about 95% of the scores are within two standard deviations of the mean.

QC Review of Investigation Outcome

Many banks set up their investigation staffs in *teams*, each led by a *Team Leader*. The Team Leader is the ultimate qualifying authority, i.e., she can either have no comment and agree with the investigators SAR/No-SAR decision, disagree with the decision, and/or return the investigation to the investigator asking for additional work on the case.

We can incorporate statistical tuning to optimize results within the investigative staff by programming a simple statistical model that tells us interesting and useful facts regarding each investigators' skills, meticulousness, and efficiency.

QC reviews by the Team Leader have the following possible outcomes:

1. An Investigator's review is found completely lacking by the Team Leader;
2. An Investigator's review is returned with 1 comment by the Team Leader;
3. An Investigator's review is returned with n comments by the Team Leader, where n>1;
4. An Investigator's review results in 0 comments by the Team Leader .

This review outcome can be further parsed by the type of case as well as the final disposition of the case, by investigator:

o Investigator finding on the alert = Not Suspicious;
o Investigator finding on the alert = Suspicious;
o Investigation type (e.g., ATM related, terrorist financing, etc.)

Now, simply set up the same probability equations as was done for the analysts' reviews of alerts.

Assuming the distribution of these probabilities across all investigators approximates a normal distribution, it will become evident, upon computing the associated mean, variance and standard distribution, where the production metrics for each investigator falls relative to the mean for *all* the investigators within your Investigations Department.

Armed with this data, it will become possible for management to more effectively focus time and resources for the QC review process to those investigators whose performance is, to a specified degree, suboptimal to the mean. The derived information will also allow management to more effectively assign specific alert types to specific investigators who appear more proficient at working the associated case, and conversely, identify those in need of additional training or reassignment. QC reviews may also be assigned per investigator more optimally based on the conclusions drawn. For example, a manager may decide that a specific investigator's reviews marked as *not-suspicious, No-SAR required* require more QC than those in the alternative for that investigator.

Section VIII – Conducting Alert Reviews and Investigations

Assigning Alerts and Investigations

Part of the analysis process for alert assignment should include evaluating the severity of the nature of an alert such that it can be referred to the staff member most qualified to conduct the subsequent investigation. For example, reviewing a terrorist financing or fraud alert should take precedence over alerts for plain vanilla structuring. Additionally, prioritizing alerts ensures that your bank is following both regulatory and best practice risk mitigation strategies.

- Priority levels may, for example, be based on the following criteria:
    - Threat to domestic or international security;
    - Violations involving the Bank Secrecy Act, the USA PATRIOT Act or other money laundering or terrorist financing activities;
    - Risk of reputation to the your bank;
    - Intake date.

- Other factors that could elevate a referral's priority level include:
    - Nature of the referral. (i.e., structuring, terror financing, money laundering, etc.)
    - Possible national security implications due to the nature of the identified suspicious activity;
    - On-going activity or one time event;
    - Prior customer history of same type of unusual activity;
    - Case type likely to be of particular interest to law enforcement authorities.

To assign a priority level to an alert, particular attention should be paid to any identifiable factors that could contribute to heightened potential risk.

The three tables in this section provide a non-exhaustive list of factors separated into groupings of either high, medium or low priority levels. No hard and fast rules were used to group these; rather they should serve as a basis and guide for constructing risk based alert assignment prioritization procedures. Keep in mind that an alert that includes a particular risk factor could include other factors that might play a role in elevating the alert's priority level.

Alert Priority Level – High

	ALERT SCENARIO FACTORS – HIGH
H **I** **G** **H**	314(a)
	Casas de cambio
	Companies and individuals involved toxic chemicals
	Companies and individuals involved with nuclear material
	Electronic cash (i.e., stored value cards) (over $2,500)
	Embassy, consulate and other foreign government-related accounts
	Foreign and domestic licensed money service businesses (MSBs)
	Foreign correspondent banks, securities brokers or other foreign financial institutions
	Foreign political parties
	Foreign religious, charitable and non-profit organizations and the heads of such organizations and their immediate family members
	Grand Jury subpoenas
	Informal value transfer systems
	Monetary instruments (over $2,500)
	National Security Letters (NSLs)
	NCCT – Persons, entities and transactions associated with Non-Cooperative Countries or Territories (NCCTs)
	Payable through accounts (PTAs)
	Payable upon proper identification ("PUPID") transactions
	Politically Exposed Persons (PEPs) / Senior Foreign Political Figures (SFPFs)
	Pouch activities (involving cash, monetary instruments or cash letters that aggregate over $2,500)
	Private banking
	Terrorist Financing – Any person or entity alleged to be involved with or connected to terrorist financing
	U.S. religious, charitable and non-profit organizations with foreign activities
	Use of any product or service related to potential terrorist financing

Alert Priority Level – Medium

	ALERT PRIORITY LEVEL – MEDIUM
	314(b) Requests
	Chartering or leasing of aircraft or vessels used for transportation s
	Brokered deposits
	Cash Intensive Businesses (CIBs)
	Casinos, gambling or card clubs (unless owned and operated by Native Americans)
	Concentration accounts
	Customers operating privately-owned ATMs
	Customers operating vending machine businesses
M E D I U M	Dealers (a person who both purchases and sells) in jewels, precious metals, precious stones and/or finished goods including jewelry, numismatic items and antiques
	Foreign business entities
	Independent sales organizations that operate ATMs
	Lending activities
	Manufacturers, distributors or sellers of weapons or military equipment
	Non-deposit investment products
	Non-Governmental Organizations (NGOs)
	Non-Resident Aliens (NRAs) and foreign individuals
	Non-U.S. corporations organized in high risk jurisdictions
	Offshore Entities
	Law enforcement requests other than subpoenas and NSLs
	Private Investment Corporations (PICs)
	Shell entities
	Third-party check cashers not required to register with FinCEN
	Trust and asset management

Alert Priority Level – Low

	ALERT PRIORITY LEVEL – LOW
L**O****W**	Automated Clearing House (ACH)
	Domestic business entities
	Domestic correspondent accounts
	Electronic banking (other than OFAC related activity)
	Professional service provider suspicious activity
	Third-party payment processors
	Trade finance
	U.S. dollar drafts

234 SAR Investigations – The Complete BSA/AML Desktop Reference

Conducting a Basic Investigation

The success of the investigative effort is not just in gathering information, but rather the evaluation of that information by informed and experienced personnel. The investigation process is a culmination of several distinct steps:

o   The collection of raw data;
o   The analysis of that data; and,
o   The accurate reporting of findings in a standard format.

In general, the steps for conducting a timely investigation are:

o   Identifying the nature of the complaint or activity to determine an appropriate course of action;
o   Identifying the suspects, individuals or entities involved in the suspicious activity;
o   Understanding the purpose of the customer's business;
o   Analyzing account activities;
o   Identifying apparent schemes;
o   Identifying possible violations of local state or federal law, for example structuring, wire activity through a non-cooperative country or an unregistered MSB.

A bank should have step-by-step procedures that analysts and investigators can follow. Such procedures not only facilitate standards for detection and reporting purposes, but also flatten the learning curve for new analysts and investigators. In fact, the peripheral benefits of good procedures include reduction of regulatory risk and actual savings from gains in efficiency. Procedures should be clear regarding:

o   Who performs what part;
o   What systems are accessed;
o   What reports are printed;
o   How the case file for the alert/investigation is compiled and maintained;
o   The quality control review steps; and,
o   The final disposition.

Those involved in the process –as well as your regulator– can get a helpful, quick overview of the whole process if your procedures manual contains process flow diagrams. Consider adopting a standard format such that all procedures have a similar look and feel.

The Unified Process is just such a standard. It has found acceptance by regulatory agencies as a framework for documenting complex procedures that are typical of AML alert and investigation resolution. This process is *use case* driven. Simply put, a use case is a procedure conforming to an accepted format, and written in an easy-to-understand structured narrative using the vocabulary of the business owner of the use case.

•   A use case starts with a *Basic Flow* that describes the steps to be completed to reach a final disposition of an investigation or alert. It may also include variants of this sequence, i.e., *Alternative Flows* that may lead to a conclusion but along a different path than usual. (An alternate flow might be used, for example, to document an escalation of an investigation after discovering during the course of the basic flow steps that insider abuse was involved.) An *Extended Flow* would be used to document detailed steps needed to complete any number of specific items contained in the basic or alternate flows.

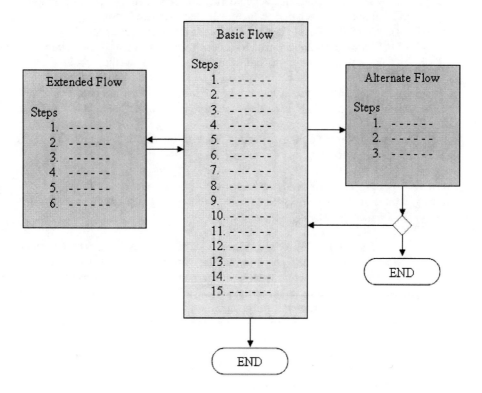

An analyst or investigator may follow a *Basic Flow* straight through to resolution,
–OR–
There may be a need to diverge from the Basic Flow via an Alternate Flow, and then rejoin the Basic Flow at a later step.
–OR–
An *Alternate* Flow may itself lead to resolution.

Extended flows are procedural details required to complete a single step within a Basic or Alternate flow.

Process Flow Diagrams

Inherent to the Unified process are standard flow charts (or, as many regulators often refer to them –*process maps*.). The key features of this standard are:

- They have a consistent look and feel from one procedure to the next, which promotes familiarity and ease of use;
- They contain swim lanes which divide the flow chart into component parts that show what each person (actor) in the procedure is doing;
- They show the system inputs to each relevant step in the procedure;
- They show the outputs (artifacts) at each relevant step of he procedure;
- They show entry points to and from the use case, as well as resolution points;
- Each step and artifact is hyperlinked to the steps in the use case or relevant supporting materials, providing easy reference and QC benefits.

The list of steps below can be used as a starting point or framework to begin writing a formal procedure for structuring investigations.

Steps of an Investigation – Cash Structuring:

Historically, almost half of all SARs filed are for structuring. A structuring investigation may, for example, include the following steps:

1. A background review of the suspect, as well as all the owners of the account would be conducted. Such information, usually available through third party database vendors (e.g., LexisNexis, etc.), may include items related to business operations, litigation, financial strength, employment history, liens, judgments, bankruptcies, professional reputation, etc. All bank systems containing account information should be queried

2. A discovery process to determine all possibly related accounts would be conducted. As above, all available bank systems resources should be considered.

3. Account opening information should be gathered and analyzed.

4. Account activity should be analyzed. This step would typically include pulling:
   i. Customer statements;
   ii. Teller logs;
   iii. Deposit slips;
   iv. Copies of CTRs;
   v. Signature cards.

5. The account manager for the customer should be contacted and interviewed. (The account or relationship manager may be the best source of information regarding the customer's declared purpose for his account.)

6. Transactional analysis would be conducted. The items to consider can be viewed in Section III under Money Laundering Red Flags, Account/Transaction Activity.

7. The gathered raw intelligence would be assessed based on the alert referral information and/or any unusual information gleaned from the data gathering and analysis process. Such analysis would include consideration of:
   i. Financial activities which are not commensurate with the expected normal business flows and types of transactions;
   ii. Unusual multiple party relationships;
   iii. Customer verbal statements;
   iv. Unusual and complex transactions indicative of placement, layering, and/or integration;
   v. Lack of business justification and documentation supporting the activity;
   vi. The specific description of the involved accounts and transactions, identifying if known, both the origination and use of the funds in question listed in chronological order by date and amount;
   vii. Specific details of transactions listing locations of occurrence such as branches, and how the transactions occurred, e.g., ATM, Night Deposit, Mail etc.;
   viii. Transactions listed in detailed tables or Excel sheets (These may be included in this section to support the investigative conclusions. Keep in mind however, that FinCEN does not want excel sheets and tables in the narrative of a SAR. The primary reason is that these forms can not be transformed into the SAR database.);
   ix. Discussions with personnel from other bank departments, branches, tellers, branch managers, loan officers and others who can shed light on events or transactions presented in the findings.

8. LexisNexis, World-Check and/or other internet search tools should be used to analyze individuals or other parties that may be in any way related to the suspect activity and/or transactions.

9. Determine whether unregistered MSB activity is involved;
   i. Check for registration; or,
   ii. Agent status.

10. Ensure that key components of the analysis are checked against federal guidance, SAR tips, and best practices for internet searches, etc. (This is most easily accomplished by using the search capabilities of the electronic version of this book.)

11. The red flags list should be consulted by the investigator as a final check on his analysis. This will ensure that proper consideration and analysis was conducted and that guidance on known schemes and activities related to the suspicious activity was considered in reaching the conclusion.

12. Document all case notes in the case file.

13. Write a proper narrative according to FinCEN guidance. Cite the reportable event accurately by referring to the Definitions & Criminal Statutes section of this book. Examples of complete and sufficient SAR narratives should be referenced as a QC check by the investigator.

14. Complete assembly of the Case File.

15. Submit the investigation for a QC review.

Considerations for Review

Alerts are generated when certain thresholds are violated or an activity is identified by bank employee or automated system that matches a red flag or profile for laundering. Once received by the bank's analysis unit, a review is normally conducted to qualify the alert. The high level review may include the following items to determine if the activity merits further investigation:

- o   Information contained in the alert itself;
- o   Customer profile data; and,
- o   Appropriate bank and third-party systems.

The qualification of the alert may include the items below, but typically, a bank's procedures should specifically assign these items, as appropriate, to either the analysts' tasks or the investigators' tasks, and not both. This will avoid overlap and duplication of effort, and greatly streamline your alert-investigations process.

Specific items for review include the following:

- o   Customer Demographics
- o   General Transaction Activity
- o   Cash Transactions
- o   Charities
- o   Checks
- o   Correspondent Banking
- o   Employee Activity
- o   High Risk Countries
- o   Purchases and Sales of Monetary Instruments
- o   Unregistered Money Service Businesses or NBFI Activity
- o   Network of Accounts
- o   Private Investment Corporations
- o   Politically Exposed Persons
- o   Pouch Activity
- o   Private Banking
- o   Large Currency Transactions
- o   Shell Corporations

Cash Transactions

When analyzing cash transactions, attempt to understand the totality of the customer's activities and the purpose of the account. The following should be items of interest:

- Are there frequent and/or high dollar cash transactions?
    - o   If the business is cash intensive and expected to deposit or withdraw large amounts of cash, look for unusual changes in amounts, timing, and location of activity.

- For reported cash, look for:
    - o   The branches of deposits;
    - o   The timing of deposits; and,
    - o   Attempt to determine if the customer knew his cash activity would result in a CTR. For instance, a CTR may have been filed because the customer made multiple deposits each for less than $10,000, but when they were aggregated over a twenty-four hour period, the amount necessitated a CTR. In this case, the customer may have believed she successfully circumvented the cash reporting requirements.

- Using the deposit/withdrawal tickets, consider these details:
    - o   Time and date of deposit;
    - o   Branch and teller;
    - o   Amount;
    - o   Any teller/customer notes or changes on ticket;
    - o   Was a CTR filed?

- From the CTR, consider the following:
    - o   Conductor;
    - o   Type of cash transaction (currency exchange, foreign currency, monetary instrument);
    - o   Number of deposits/withdrawals;
    - o   Time, date, branch;
    - o   Was a CTR knowingly filed;
    - o   Number of CTRs filed in a month/year.

- Using statements or transaction history reports, consider the following:
    - o   Number of cash deposits/withdrawals in a month;
    - o   Pattern of cash transactions;
    - o   Volume of cash transactions;
    - o   Timing of cash transactions (day of the week, time of the day).

- Look for frequent large cash deposits made by a corporate customer who maintains high balances but does not use the bank's other services. (This limited and/or inconsistent use of services may be suspicious in context with other events. For example, a retail business deposits numerous checks, but rarely makes withdrawals for daily operations.)

- Determine the business or other economic purpose of cash transactions and if the funds are consistent with a business of that size. For instance, a retail business has dramatically different patterns of currency deposits from similar businesses in the same general location.
  - o   Is the amount of cash used appropriate for this type of business?
  - o   Examine other transactions to determine the source and use of the funds. Certain business and industries are more susceptible to dealing with large amounts of cash on a regular basis. Examples of cash intensive business include:
    - Convenience stores;
    - Restaurants;
    - Retail stores;
    - Liquor stores;
    - Cigarette distributors;
    - ATM operators;
    - Vending machine operators;
    - Parking garages

- Even if cash does not appear to be withdrawn or deposited in an unusual manner, the analyst should attempt to determine the source of wealth and possible justification for frequent large cash deposits/withdrawals. For example, a personal account holder who deposits $4,000 cash twenty times in a month for several months, yet lists his occupation as 'student' should raise questions.

Charities and NGOs

Charitable contributions should be examined to determine the legitimacy of the charity and chartered purpose. One example might be when a financial transaction occurs with a nonprofit entity for which there appears to be no link between the stated activity of the organization and the other parties in the transaction. The analyst should try to determine if accounts of non-profit organizations or charities are being used to collect and funnel funds to a small number of foreign beneficiaries.

The US Treasury has published voluntary best practices for US based charities which contains useful information for bank analysts regarding terrorist financing through charities and non-governmental organizations (NGOs). Familiarity with these techniques as well as the safeguards that legitimate charities can adopt can be used in the context of analyzing alerts that are generated on transactions involving charitable institutions or charitable contributions.

Checks

- If there are numerous checks to/from external entities, conduct research to determine how these parties are involved and the reason for the money movement.
  - Are the checks written for normal business activities (inventory, salary, rent) or are they made out to unrelated entities or individuals?
  - Does the volume of deposited checks appear normal?
  - Are there instances where sequential checks are made payable to the same entity?
  - Are there checks made payable to the account holder and deposited at another financial institution?
  - Are there patterns of checks made payable to the same party?

- Using the deposit/withdrawal ticket, consider these details:
  - Time and date of deposit;
  - Branch and teller;
  - Amount;
  - Any teller/customer notes or changes on check;
  - Number of checks deposited;
  - When looking at the image of the check consider the following:
  - Sequence number;
  - Date;
  - Payer;
  - Address of Payer and does the address match the KYC;
  - Payee;
  - Memo notes;
  - Signature (who signed the check, signature card match);
  - If payable to cash, determine if actual currency was paid (as opposed to a monetary instrument purchase, account transfer).

- On the back of the checks or copies of the check, examine the following:
  - Signor on the back;
  - Bank account where the funds were deposited;
  - If deposited in another account at your bank, research that account;
  - How is the signor on the back of the check back and the payer related (e.g. check payable to self and deposited into another financial institution).

- From statements or transaction history reports, consider the following:
  - Number of checks in a month;
  - Sequence number of checks;
  - Pattern of checks;
  - Volume of checks.

Correspondent Banking

Correspondent accounts represent a higher risk for money laundering because the foreign financial institution may not have as stringent regulations as U.S. banks do. Drug traffickers and criminals often use correspondent accounts to move funds through financial institutions because correspondent accounts can offer easy, anonymous access to the U.S. banking system. Because of the large dollar value of funds and the large volume of transactions that flow through a correspondent account on a daily basis, illegal funds can be more easily concealed. Additionally, the structure of correspondent accounts makes it more difficult for U.S. bank's to verify the identity of the foreign financial institution's customers.

- When examining the correspondent account, consider the following:
    - A spike in the volume of activity for a single day above the normal range for the correspondent account;
    - A spike in the value of activity for a single day above the normal range for the correspondent account.
    - A pattern of transactions for a single account to multiple recipients;
    - Multiple transactions from different accounts to a single recipient;
    - The countries involved in the movement of funds.

- When examining the underlying customer utilizing the correspondent account, consider the following:
    - The countries involved in the movement of funds;
    - Prior history of similar transactions from or to the sender or recipient;
    - The nature of the sender or recipient's business;
    - The relationship between the sender and recipient.

Customer Demographics

To the greatest extent possible, utilize the information that the bank has on the customer. Such information is usually spread out among many systems. Banks should ensure that their procedures cover the use of all systems containing customer data.

- Check available KYC information to see if the stated occupation of the customer is commensurate with the type or level of activity. For example:
  - What are the other sources of income (ACH from employment, checks from employers)?
  - Is there a pattern of monthly expenses being paid from the account (rent, utilities, payments made to suppliers)?
  - How long has the customer been an account holder with the bank?

- If there are other accounts, how do those transactions relate to the suspicious activity? For example:
  - Do persons involved in currency transactions share an address or phone number, particularly when the address is also a business location or does not seem to correspond to the stated occupation (e.g., student, unemployed, or self-employed)?

- Ascertain whether there are other accounts located at the same address.

- Does the owner of the business have his/her personal accounts with your bank as well?

- Has the address for the account holder changed often?

- Is the address a Post Office Box?

- For business customers, does the owner of the business have his/her personal accounts with your bank as well?

- Who are the other signors on the account and what is their involvement with the account?

- What is the proximity of the customer's address to the bank?
  - Are the transactions conducted in a foreign country or is the listed address located outside of the bank's footprint of service?

- If the customer is considered a high risk customer, what kind of activity led this customer to be placed on the bank's high risk list?

- How many times and for what reason has the bank filed a SAR on this customer?

- Was this customer's account ever the subject of a subpoena?

- Do the transactions involved in the alert impact how the high risk customer is viewed? For example:
  - A customer might have been placed on the high risk list because a SAR was filed on the account for cash structuring.

- Have there been frequent or otherwise noteworthy changes in the following areas:
  - Account closed?
    - If so, when?
    - Was a new account opened? Look for accounts with the same address or name.
  - Additional accounts opened?
  - Address changes?
  - Additional signors added to account?

- Is this customer a registered money service business (MSB) or non-bank financial institution (NBFI)? Or is an unregistered account holder acting as a money service business (i.e. cashing checks for various individuals, depositing multiple money orders)?

Employee Related

Generally, referrals involving employee related suspicious activity are fraud related. However, money laundering typologies covering private banking activities have established that often there can be a complicit relationship between the customer and the private banker.

- The items below represent criteria related to monitoring of insider complicity risk involving private banking activities and assigned relationship managers. (Generally, EDD compliance managers should meet periodically with managers from your bank's Human Resources Department and the line of business managers to affirm that KYE best practices are reviewed.)

  o Compensation Plans - The bank's Board and senior management should ensure that compensation plans do not create incentives for employees to ignore appropriate due diligence and account opening procedures or possible suspicious activity relating to the account. During alert reviews for insiders, try to assess whether any due diligence process was (or was attempted to be) circumvented by the private banker for himself or for his customer

  o New Hires – Has your bank thoroughly investigated the background of newly hired private banking relationship managers and has there been ongoing monitoring of their personal financial condition to detect any indications of inappropriate activities? If so, review the documentation related to those reviews.

General Transaction Activity

Alerts should be analyzed regarding both the transactions that caused the alert to be generated, as well as other types of transactions that may be related. The analyst should gather current and historic transactions and search for patterns of activity that match red flags for money laundering or terrorist financing, such as funds transfers with high risk countries. Other items and analysis to consider in a transaction review include the following:

o   Review back office journal transactions, where funds move between accounts (e.g., an account holder moves money from his checking account to his Investments account to purchase equities).

o   Determine the source of funds and the purpose of funds received.

o   Review the customer's recent transactions to form a baseline of typical transactional activity. For example:

  ▪ If the customer is an individual, are there regular payments for rent/mortgage, utilities, groceries, etc?
  ▪ If the customer is a business, are there payments to suppliers, employees, etc?

(If some basic expenditures are absent from a customer's transaction history, the customer may have accounts at other financial institutions, may have other sources/uses of funds, or may be conducting unusual activity.)

o   Is the customer receiving payments or receipts with no apparent business or other economic purpose?

  ▪ Does the timing of the transactions cause suspicion?
  ▪ Are the received funds only held in the account temporarily before they are sent to another bank account?
  ▪ Is the account being used as a *pass-through* for monies to be moved from one account/financial institution to another? For example, a customer receives a high dollar incoming wire from the Ukraine and then transfers the funds to an unrelated external account on the same day .

o   Look for accounts with a high volume of activity, which carry low balances or are frequently overdrawn. Such activity may be indicative of money laundering or check kiting.

o   Look for accounts with large deposits and balances, for example, a customer makes large deposits and maintains large balances with little or no apparent justification.

o   Are accounts used as a temporary repository for funds?

- Try to ascertain whether the customer appears to use an account as a temporary repository for funds that ultimately will be transferred out of the bank, perhaps to foreign-based accounts.

o Try to determine why there might be very little account activity.

o Look for significant increases in the number or amount of transactions.

o Look for large increases in the numbers of or amount of transactions involving currency, the purchase of monetary instruments, wire transfers, etc.

o Evaluate the risk arising from the customers who are permitted involvement with concentration accounts (also referred to as *special use*, *suspense*, *settlement*, or *sweep accounts*. (These are internal accounts established to facilitate the processing and settlement of transactions within the bank, usually on the same day).
    - Risks are introduced because identifying information, such as name and account number, can be easily separated from the actual transaction.

o Determine if the customer is a registered money service business (MSB) or non-bank financial institution (NBFI), or is an unregistered MSB account holder acting as a money service business (i.e. cashing checks for various individuals, depositing multiple money orders).

High Risk Countries

If a bank customer is sending funds to a high risk country, search historical transactions to see if the funds were slowly deposited into the customer's account or if they were introduced immediately before the transfer.

If a customer receives funds from an individual/entity in a high risk country
- o   Research historic transactions to determine if a pattern exists;
- o   Examine the wire transmission notes for a purpose; and,
- o   Try to ascertain what activities have occurred after the funds were received.

Although the high risk country may have been the impetus for the alert, look for other high risk transactions conducted by the customer. For instance:
- o   Were there frequent and/or high dollar cash transactions?
- o   Was cash deposited immediately prior to sending a wire?
- o   Was cash withdrawn immediately after receiving a wire?

If there are numerous ACH or wires to or from external high risk entities, conduct research to determine how these parties are involved and the reason for the money movement.

Research senders and beneficiaries of the electronic transmissions in World-Check, LexisNexis, or other public records databases for adverse findings.
- o   Look for international companies/individuals with political ties, criminal convictions/suspicions or other unfavorable news.

Large Single Currency Transactions

Presumably, Currency Transaction Reports (CTRs) are filed by your bank for single transactions in excess of $10,000 in one business day. Cash activity should be aggregated for each customer using a unique identifying number (SSN, TIN) and displayed under the account information where the funds were directed. For example, a customer conducting cash transactions with two different accounts would appear when her aggregate activities exceeded one of the two thresholds even if the separate account's activity would not warrant inclusion on the report. If a customer were to divide $25,000 in cash deposits (all below $10,000) into three different transactions conducted at three different branches in one day, this would also normally be included on a cash report.

The determination of whether an account is conducting suspicious activity with reported cash should start with the transactions, but also include an analysis of account holder demographics.

- Starting with the transactions in question, the analyst should examine the following:
  - Cash deposits or withdrawals made by individuals (non-business accounts) for extremely large amounts. While there is no set threshold for what is an extremely large amount of cash, pay particular attention to those transactions greater than $50,000. For instance, a non-business customer deposits $100,000 in cash.
  - Multiple cash deposits/withdrawals, each under $10,000, conducted by a single customer that, when aggregated, exceed $10,000. Pay particular attention if the customer used multiple branches at various times during the day.
    - For example, an account holder deposits $5,000 at branch X at 12 PM, $6,000 at branch Y at 1 PM, and $7,000 at branch Z at 2 PM. Although this individual may not be aware, the bank has flagged these transactions as reportable and a CTR was sent to the IRS. However, be aware of legitimate business accounts with multiple locations making multiple deposits in one day. For instance, a drug store with ten locations typically makes daily deposits at various branches.

- There are some data quality issues with the reportable cash transactions to be aware of. Customers may appear as conducting cash deposits/withdrawals exceeding $10,000, but in actuality, the teller processing the activity labeled the transaction as cash for ease of processing.
  - Be sure to verify that the transaction was truly cash. For example, a customer transfers $12,000 from his checking to his savings account and the teller labels the shift as cash.

- o Determine:
    - The business purpose of the cash; and,
    - If the funds are consistent with a business of that size. For instance, a retail business has dramatically different patterns of currency deposits from similar businesses in the same general location.
    - The source and use of the funds.

- Determine the type of transaction(s) that generated any CTR.

- Determine whether any part of the transaction history matches a known suspicious profile. For example:
    - o A customer frequently exchanges small dollar denominations for large dollar denominations;
    - o Transactions involving foreign currency exchanges are followed within a short time by funds transfers to high-risk locations.

- Non-cash transactions should be researched to determine the account's purpose and if a combination of products and services are used to move funds. Specifically, search for:
    - o ACH debits to known money transmitters e.g. Western Union, Sigue, RIA;
    - o ACH debits to state lottery commissions. Most state regulations require retailers to have a separate account solely for lottery transactions. The commingling of lottery and retail transactions may be an indicator of suspicious activity or a violation of state law;
    - o Monetary instrument purchases e.g., traveler's checks, cashier's checks (especially payable to cash or the purchaser), stored value cards not consistent with the type of customer or account. For example, a large volume of cashier's checks, money orders, or funds transfers is deposited into, or purchased through, an account when the nature of the account holder's business would not appear to justify such activity;
    - o Wire transactions.

- Establish the timing of other transactions as related to reportable cash withdrawals and deposits. For example, a large cash deposit is made on the first of the month and then, an international wire is sent a week later. Another example may be, a large cash deposit is made and a week later, several checks are written payable to the account holder and deposited in other financial institutions.

- Examine historical activity to determine if there is a pattern of cash deposits/withdrawals or if the alerted transaction is an anomaly.

- Determine other sources of income, expenses, purpose of the account, the primary business activity, and the business structure. For example, the currency transaction patterns of a business show a sudden change inconsistent with normal activities.

- When analyzing cash transactions, attempt to understand the totality of the customer's activities and the purpose of the account.
    - Check available KYC information to see if the stated occupation of the customer is commensurate with the type or level of activity. For example:
        - What are the other sources of income (ACH from employment, checks from employers)?
        - Is there a pattern of monthly expenses being paid from the account (rent, utilities, payments made to suppliers)?

- Some account demographic questions to consider:
    - How long has the customer been an account holder with your bank?
    - If there are other accounts, how do those transactions relate to the suspicious activity? For example, persons involved in currency transactions share an address or phone number, particularly when the address is also a business location or does not seem to correspond to the stated occupation (e.g., student, unemployed, or self-employed).
    - Are there other accounts located at the same address?
    - Does the owner of the business have his/her personal accounts with your bank as well?
    - Who are the other signors on the account and what is their involvement in the account?
    - Who is the conductor of the cash transactions (available from the CTR)?
    - Does it make sense for a 3rd party to be conducting the transactions on behalf on another account holder?
    - Are the transactions being conducting in a geographical proximity close to the account holder address?
    - Is the address changed often?
    - Is the address listed a PO Box?

Examples of cash intensive business include:
- Convenience stores;
- Restaurants;
- Retail stores;
- Liquor stores;
- Cigarette distributors;
- ATM operators;
- Vending machine operators;
- Parking garages.

Monetary Instrument Purchases and Sales

Monetary instruments are products provided by banks and include cashier's checks, traveler's checks, and money orders. Consider the following indicators of potentially suspicious activity:

o   Purchasing monetary instruments just below the $3,000 threshold

o   Sales of sequentially numbered monetary instruments from the same or different purchasers on the same day to the same payee;

o   Sales of monetary instruments to the same purchaser or sales of monetary instruments to different purchasers made payable to the same remitter (For example, customer Smith purchases fifteen $500 money orders all made payable to Jones);

o   Monetary instrument purchases by non-customers;

o   Common:
   - purchasers
   - payees
   - addresses
   - sequentially numbered purchases
   - unusual symbols

o   Depositing multiple money orders (May be a sign the customer is acting as a money service business.)

o   When looking at the image of the monetary instrument consider the following:
   - Sequence number
   - Date and time
   - Branch and teller
   - Amount
   - Purchaser
   - Payee
   - Memo notes
   - Method of purchase (cash, transfer)

o   On the back of the monetary instrument, examine the following:
   - Signor on the back;
   - Bank account where the funds were deposited;
   - If deposited in an account at your bank, research that account;
   - If the signor on back and the payer are related (e.g. payable to self and deposited into another financial institution).

o   From statements or transaction history reports, consider the following:
  - Number of monetary instruments purchased in a month;
  - Sequence number of monetary instruments;
  - Pattern of monetary instruments;
  - Volume of monetary instruments

o   Disbursements of certificates of deposits by multiple bank checks. (A customer may request disbursement of the proceeds of a certificate of deposit or other investments in multiple bank checks, each for or under $10,000. The customer can then negotiate these checks elsewhere for currency. He or she avoids the currency transaction requirements and severs the paper trail.)

MSBs and NBFIs

When examining MSB and NBFI accounts, consider the following:

- o Confirm FinCEN registration, if required;
- o Confirm state licensing, if applicable;
- o Dollar amount of third party checks cashed;
- o Deposits of sequentially numbered monetary instruments;
- o ACH debits to known remitters (e.g. Traveler's Express, Western Union, Money Gram);
- o Frequent deposits of third party checks, yet no cash withdrawals;
- o The names of the payees/recipients to see if there is a pattern of disbursement.

Network of Accounts

Networked accounts refer to the scenario where transactions appearing for the involved accounts may not be unusual in of themselves, but when considered within the totality of the entire network of the relationship they might be considered unusual. Because the nature of the transactions alone may not be the primary impetus for an account's inclusion in this scenario, when conducting a review, analysts need to heavily consider the account demographics and customer background. The determination of whether the alert could be a part of an unusual network should start with an analysis of the focal entity, or the subject of the alert, and should also include an assessment of the transactions and accounts within the network.

The use of an account or accounts solely as a pass-through (i.e., the business or account appears to be setup only to facilitate the transfer of funds from one party to another) may be indicative of a networking of accounts for nefarious purposes. For instance, Customer X, an account holder at your bank, conducts transactions with Customer Y, also an account holder, on a regular basis. Upon receipt of the funds, Customer X wires the funds to an account also labeled Customer X, but at another financial institution.

Look closely for networks involving Private Investment Corporations (PIC), holding companies, or possible shell companies.

The analyst should examine the *timing* of funds transfers to establish a pattern of activity and to understand the possible purpose of funds movement.

- o Is this customer conducting frequent high dollar funds transfers through linked business accounts, and there appears to be no logical business or other economic purpose for the transfers?
- o Is the customer receiving payments or receipts with no apparent business or other economic purpose?
- o Are there many small, incoming transfers of funds received where, almost immediately, all or most of the transfers or deposits are wired to another city or country in a manner inconsistent with the customer's business or history?
- o Are multiple accounts abused to collect and funnel funds to a small number of foreign beneficiaries, both persons and businesses, particularly in high risk locations?

PICs

Look closely for wire transactions involving:

- o Private Investment Corporations (PIC),
- o Holding companies, or
- o Shell companies.

PICs are separate legal entities. PICs offer confidentiality of ownership, hold assets centrally, and may provide intermediaries between private banking customers and the potential beneficiaries of the PIC. A PIC may also be an investment of a trust account. PICs are incorporated frequently in countries that impose low or no taxes on company assets and operations or that are bank secrecy havens.

Money laundering and terrorist financing risks arise because corporate entities can hide the true owner of assets or property derived from or associated with criminal activity. The privacy and confidentiality surrounding some corporate entities may be exploited by criminals, money launderers, and terrorists. Verifying the grantors and beneficial owner(s) of some corporate entities may be extremely difficult, as the characteristics of these entities shield the legal identity of the owner. Few public records will disclose true ownership. Overall, the lack of ownership transparency; minimal or no record keeping requirements, financial disclosures, and supervision; and the range of permissible activities all increase money laundering risk.

While corporate entities can be established in most international jurisdictions, the majority are incorporated in OFCs (off-shore financial centers) that provide ownership privacy and impose few or no tax obligations. To maintain anonymity, many corporate entities are formed with nominee directors, nominee officeholders, and nominee shareholders. In certain jurisdictions, corporate entities can also be established using bearer shares; ownership records are not maintained, rather ownership is based on physical possession of the stock certificates. Revocable trusts are another method used to insulate the grantor and beneficial owner and can be designed to own and manage the corporate entity, presenting significant barriers to law enforcement.

While U.S.-based shell corporations have been used for legitimate purposes, they have also been abused as conduits for money laundering and have hidden overseas transactions or the existence of layered domestic or foreign corporate entity structures. Shell corporations registered in the United States have been identified as conducting suspicious transactions with foreign-based counterparties. These transactions, primarily funds transfers circling in and out of the U.S. banking system, evidenced no apparent business purpose. Domestic corporate entities with bank-like names, but without regulatory authority to conduct banking, should be particularly suspect.

PICs can be identified by looking for vague company names or ending with *holdings* or *limited*, or by address, e.g., a P.O. Box, overseas.

Politically Exposed Persons

While there are many definitions of PEPs, for the purposes of a high level review, a PEP is considered:

- o A senior foreign political figure (SFPF – the term used by US convention in the BSA);
- o A close associate; or
- o An immediate family member.

- When examining SFPF accounts, consider the following:
  - o Country of origin;
  - o Reason for banking with your bank;
  - o Source of funds;
  - o International transactions that do not seem consistent with the account's purpose;
  - o Large transfers of wealth.

Pouch Activity

Pouch activity entails the use of a carrier or courier to transport currency, monetary instruments, and other documents from outside the United States to a bank in the United States. Pouch activity represents a higher risk for money laundering because of the veil of anonymity provided by foreign deposits. If the bank maintains a pouch log which tracks all overseas deposits, the log may need to be referenced when researching an alert for a customer who is being investigated for an alert where pouch activity may play a role.

When examining pouch transactions:
- o   Consider the following about the transactions in the pouch:
    - ▪ Were the instruments purchased on the same or consecutive days at different locations?
    - ▪ Were the instruments numbered consecutively in amounts just under $3,000 or $10,000?
    - ▪ Were the payee lines left blank or made out to the same person (or to only a few people)?
    - ▪ Do the instruments contain little or no purchaser information?
    - ▪ Do the instruments bear the same stamp, symbol, or initials?
    - ▪ Were the instruments purchased in round denominations or repetitive amounts?
    - ▪ Was the depositing of the instruments followed soon thereafter by a funds transfer out in the same dollar amount?
    - ▪ Where and why is this customer conducting activities abroad?

- o   Are the account holder's other transactions (e.g., debit card purchases, deposits, wires) made in a similar geographic area?

- o   Is the account holder in a high risk country or an area dramatically outside of your bank's expected range of activity?

- o   Look for international companies/individual with political ties, criminal convictions/suspicions, or other unfavorable news.

Private Banking

Private banking services are typically offered to individuals of high net worth. Typical private services include:

- Cash management;
- Funds transfer;
- Asset management;
- Mail receipt; and,
- Financial planning.

The PATRIOT Act requires enhanced or increased due diligence on foreign private banking clients (See the Final Rule for Section 312 for information pertaining to the levels of increased due diligence required and the statutory triggers for EDD.) Private banking can be more susceptible to money laundering for the following reasons:

- Powerful clients (often celebrities, PEP/SFPFs);
- Culture of confidentiality;
- Significant profit for the account officers, leading to employee complicity.

As a result of the risk of private banking, the analyst should pay attention to:

- Large movement of funds
- The use of PICs
- Use of shell companies
- Suspicious activity indicators for cash and wires

Structuring

Customers who intentionally structure their cash deposits or withdrawals may be attempting to circumvent government reporting requirements for some of the following reasons:

- o Funds were a result of criminal activity;
- o Under-reporting of revenue to the IRS;
- o Advice from professional services firms (attorney, accountant, insurance);
- o Bank teller advice;
- o Misunderstanding of regulations

- Customers who structure may use some of the following techniques:

- o Deposits/withdrawals of large denominations over several consecutive days;
- o Smaller deposits/withdrawals made several times in one day;
- o Multiple large deposits/withdrawals made at different branches on the same day.

The determination of whether an account is potentially structuring deposits/withdrawals should start with the transactions, but also include an analysis of account holder demographics. Starting with the transactions in question, the analyst should examine the following:

- o Deposits/withdrawals made on consecutive days where the weekly total is greater than $10,000. For example, on Tuesday a deposit of $8,000, on Wednesday a deposit of $8,000, and on Thursday, a deposit of $8,000;
- o Large even dollar amounts made below $10,000. Pay particular attention to transactions between $7,500 and $10,000;
- o Transactions of $9,900 or exactly $10,000;
- o Large withdrawals under $10,000 following receipt of significant funds. For instance, a $50,000 check deposit is withdrawn in cash over a few days;
- o The volume of reported cash deposited or withdrawn. Even if an account holder is depositing some cash above the $10,000 threshold, he may be attempting to underreport deposits by structuring. There are cases where the account holder may have been unaware that CTRs were being filed for their transactions. For example, an account holder who deposits $7,000 in one branch and then $8,000 in another branch on the same day may believe he has avoided detection, but your bank's systems identified the transactions as reportable and filed the necessary CTR;
- o If an account routinely deposits amounts over $10,000 (in an un-suspicious manner) and includes some amounts less than $10,000, they may not be structuring, but instead, depositing whatever cash receipts they had for that day;
- o **CTR Exempt** – Whether the account is exempt from CTR filings;
- o **Weekend deposits** – a potential area of concern because of the way Saturday and Sunday deposits hit Monday's report. For example, this could lead to an apparent deposit of $9,000 on Monday when actually, it was a daily deposit of $3,000 on Saturday, Sunday, and Monday.

- **Type of business involved in the transaction** –Even though a business is known to be cash intensive and routinely conduct large cash transactions because "that's the way they do business," they are still subject to structuring regulations. For instance, a seafood distributor in the Northwest regularly withdraws cash below $10,000 to pay for supplies. Even though the money is used for an apparent legitimate purpose, because the withdrawals could be viewed as a pattern of structuring, the transactions must be referred to investigations.
- **Source of Wealth** – Even if cash does not appear to be withdrawn or deposited in a suspicious manner, the analyst should attempt to determine the source of wealth. For example, a non-business customer deposits $4,000 cash twenty times in a month for several months, yet his source of wealth cannot be determined.
- If the nature of the business does not justify the volume of cash deposited or withdrawn. For instance, if a small grocery store begins to withdraw large amounts of cash for no explainable business purpose.
- Examine the other risk categories exceeded along with the specific structuring thresholds. These risk categories will point the analysis to other transactions the account holder is conducting.
- **MSBs and NBFIs** – Search for money service businesses (e.g. check cashers, money remitters) and non-banking financial institutions (e.g. casinos, broker dealers, loan companies, jewel dealers, pawnbrokers). In particular, look for instances where the owner of both a retail business and a check-cashing service does not withdraw currency when depositing checks, possibly indicating the availability of another source of currency.
- Non-cash transactions should be researched to determine the accounts purpose and if a combination of products and services are used to move funds.
- Examine the timing of transactions to establish a pattern of activity and to understand the possible purpose of the fund movement. Specifically, search for:
    - ACH debits to known money transmitters e.g. Western Union, Sigue, RIA;
    - ACH debits to state lottery commissions. Most state regulations require retailers to have a separate account solely for lottery transactions. The commingling of lottery and retail transactions may be an indicator of suspicious activity or a violation of state law;
    - Monetary instrument purchases below the reporting limit e.g., traveler's checks, cashier's checks (especially payable to cash or the purchaser), stored value cards;
    - ACH debits to online gambling sites;
    - ATM Deposits or withdrawals;
    - Wire transactions.

When analyzing cash transactions, attempt to understand the totality of the customer's activities and the purpose of the account.

- o Check available KYC to see if the stated occupation of the customer is commensurate with the type or level of activity. For example:
    - ▪ What are the other sources of income (ACH from employment, checks from employers)?
    - ▪ Is there a pattern of monthly expenses being paid from the account (rent, utilities, payments made to suppliers)?

Some account demographic questions to consider:

- o How long has the customer been an account holder with your bank?
- o If there are other accounts, how do those transactions relate to the suspicious activity? For example, persons involved in currency transactions share an address or phone number, particularly when the address is also a business location or does not seem to correspond to the stated occupation (e.g., student, unemployed, or self-employed);
- o Are there other accounts located at the same address?
- o Does the owner of the business have his/her personal accounts with Bank as well?
- o Who are the other signors on the account and what is their involvement in the account?
- o Consider the volume of reported cash deposited or withdrawn. Even if an account holder is depositing some cash above the $10,000 CTR filing threshold, in other transactions he may be attempting to underreport deposits by structuring. For example, two $12,000 deposits are made in a month, but the remaining ten deposits are for $9,000. Make sure to consider all the transactions in their entirety.
- o Review past unreported cash activity to identify patterns and total dollar amounts.
- o Examine purchases of monetary instruments just below the $3,000 threshold.
- o Look for sales of monetary instruments to the same purchaser or sales of monetary instruments to different purchasers made payable to the same remitter. For example, customer Smith purchases fifteen $500 money orders all made payable to Jones.
- o Look for sales of sequentially numbered monetary instruments to the same or different purchasers on the same day and made out to the same payee.
- o Look for deposits of consecutively numbered money orders or a large quantity of money orders. For example, a company with ties to a high risk country deposits six sequentially numbered money orders from the same remitter. Depositing multiple money orders may also be a sign the customer is acting as a money service business.
- o Look for deposits/withdrawals made on consecutive days where the weekly total is greater than $10,000. For example, on Tuesday a deposit of $8,000, on Wednesday a deposit of $8,000, and on Thursday, a deposit of $8,000.

o   Look for large cash transactions conducted with multiple banks, branches, customer service representatives, accounts, and/or on consecutive days in an attempt to avoid reporting requirements.

o   Look for large even dollar amounts made at or below $10,000. Pay particular attention to transactions between $7,500 and $10,000.

o   Look for smaller deposits/withdrawals made several times during one day. For example, a customer comes into the branch three times in one day and withdrawals $3,000 in cash each time.

o   Look for transactions of $9,900 or exactly $10,000.

o   Look for large withdrawals under $10,000 following receipt of significant funds. For example, a $50,000 check deposit is subsequently withdrawn in cash over the next few days.

o   Look for instances where the nature of the business does not justify the volume of cash deposited or withdrawn. For instance, if a small grocery store begins to withdraw large amounts of cash for no explainable business or other economic purpose.

o   Look for deposits under the reporting threshold at multiple locations/branches.

o   Consider that if an account routinely deposits amounts over $10,000 (in an unusual manner) and includes some amounts at or less than $10,000, they may not be structuring, but instead, depositing whatever cash receipts they had for that day.

Wire Transfers

The determination of whether an account is conducting suspicious activity with wires should start with the transactions, but also include an analysis of account holder demographics and other transaction activity (i.e., activity not related to the generation of the actual alert). Starting with the transactions in question, the analyst should establish the relationship between the sender and the recipient and attempt to determine how two parties are involved and the reason for the wire transfer. Take note if the other party cannot be identified or if the wire is sent only to an account number. Additionally, inspect the wire and the circumstances as follows:

- Are funds transfers sent or received from the same person to or from different accounts?
  - ○ If the sender and the recipient appear to be the same person, examine the other financial institution(s) involved?

- Use public records databases and the internet to research the identity of the sender/recipient. Pay particular attention to:
  - ○ Funds received from a foreign government or sent to a political official.
  - ○ Activity that occurs to or from a financial secrecy haven, or to or from a high-risk geographic location without an apparent business reason or when the activity is inconsistent with the customer's business or history. For example, funds are generated by a business owned by persons of the same origin or by a business that involves persons of the same origin from high-risk countries.

- Use FinCEN, FATF, and internal high risk country lists as guidance.
  - ○ Determine if/when the country was removed from watch lists.

- Review any transmission notes for details on the purpose of the wire.

- Review timing and volume of wire transmissions. These examples illustrate potentially suspicious activity:
  - ○ Many small, incoming transfers of funds are received, or deposits are made using checks and money orders. Almost immediately, all or most of the transfers or deposits are wired to another city or country in a manner inconsistent with the customer's business or history;
  - ○ Funds activity is unexplained, repetitive, or shows unusual patterns;
  - ○ Funds transfers are ordered in small amounts in an apparent effort to avoid triggering identification or reporting requirements;
  - ○ A large number of incoming or outgoing funds transfers take place through a business account, and there appears to be no logical business or other economic purpose for the transfers, particularly when this activity involves high-risk locations;

- o Multiple accounts are used to collect and funnel funds to a small number of foreign beneficiaries, both persons and businesses, particularly in high-risk locations;
- o Payments or receipts with no apparent links to legitimate contracts, goods, or services are received;
- o The stated occupation of the customer is not commensurate with the type or level of activity.
- o Deposits followed by immediate requests for wire transfers or cash shipments. For instance, a customer makes numerous deposits in an account and almost immediately requests wire transfers or a cash shipment from that account to another account, possibly in another country. Normally, only a token amount remains in the original account. Are these transactions consistent with the customer's apparent business needs?

- Look closely for wire transactions involving Private Investment Corporations (PIC), holding companies, or shell companies. PICs are separate legal entities. PICs offer confidentiality of ownership, hold assets centrally, and may provide intermediaries between private banking customers and the potential beneficiaries of the PICs. A PIC may also be an investment of a trust account. PICs are incorporated frequently in countries that impose low or no taxes on company assets and operations or that are bank secrecy havens.

- Search for funds transfers with higher risk businesses.

- Look for any component of the transaction that involve money transmitters such as Western Union, online gambling sites, or to state lottery commissions (The commingling of lottery and retail transactions may be an indicator of unusual activity or a violation of state law or regulation.) Regulations concerning US financial institutions processing payments to and from online gaming sites was passed in 2007. Make sure your bank's policies and procedures adequately address these.

- Look for incoming/outgoing wire transfers with instructions to pay upon proper identification (also known as PUPID transactions).
  - o If paid for in cash, was the amount just under the $10,000 reporting requirement?
  - o Was the purchase made with numerous official checks or other monetary instruments?
  - o Was the amount of the transfer large, or the funds sent to a foreign country?

- Look for a high volume of wire transfers with low account balances.

- Are there incoming and outgoing wires in similar dollar amounts? Look for instances where there is a pattern of wire transfers of same amount both in and out of the customer's account, or related customers, on the same day or next day.

- Are there international transfers funded by multiple monetary instruments? This involves the receipt of funds in the form of multiple official bank checks, traveler's checks, or personal checks that are drawn on or issued by U.S. financial institutions and made payable to the same individual or business, or related individuals or businesses, typically in U.S. dollar amounts that are below the reporting threshold limit. The funds are then wired to a financial institution outside the U.S.

- Review transmission notes for details on the purpose of the wire. Although transmission notes alone might not excuse a transaction from being unusual, they may offer insight into the relationship between the parties. For example:
  - Transmission notes would explain that a wire was returned to the sender because the recipient's account number was listed incorrectly. As a result, the analyst would realize that the funds were not deliberately being passed back and forth, but instead, were returned due to an error.

- Take note of the countries involved in the movement of funds, especially if the account holder is regularly sending funds to a high risk jurisdiction.
  - If the country is considered high risk, be familiar with the reason why the country is on the high risk list.

- Determine the location of the sending or receiving party and attempt to understand the reason for international activity. For example, an alert generated on a large corporate account that regularly transfers funds to a subsidiary located in a high risk jurisdiction may be normal business activity. However, a corporation may be making bribes or sending gifts to foreign political leaders to win business.
  - If the bank's customer is sending funds to another foreign company, research the receiving company for ties to senior foreign government officials.

- Search for funds transfers with higher risk businesses.
  - Are there ACH transactions to or from known money transmitters (e.g. Western Union, RIA, Sigue), online gambling sites, or to state lottery commissions?
  - If the customer appears to be acting as a money transmitter, a previous bank investigation may have taken place. Search your SAR system to determine if a previous investigation took place.

  - Using the copy of the wire transmission report, consider the following:
    - Name of recipient/sender and possible relationship to other party;
    - Time and date of transaction;
    - Amount;
    - Any wire transmission notes;
    - Address of recipient/sender (PO Box);
    - Country of recipient/sender;
    - Other party's bank;

- Intermediary bank(s) involved;
- If international, is the country on the bank's high risk list?

o From statements or transaction history reports, consider the following for suspicious patterns:
  - Number of wires in a month;
  - Pattern of wire transmissions;
  - Volume of wire transmissions;
  - Recipients/Senders of other wire transmissions;
  - Foreign countries involved in past wires.

Performing Internet Research

Investigators should keep in mind that while much of the data collected by third party sources (e.g., LexisNexis) is accurate, in some instances there may be much that is not. This presents a complication requiring that enough information be considered in order to separate the inaccurate form the accurate and to draw a proper conclusion. Investigators and analysts should acquire secondary verification of information where the initial data set is questionable. For example, FinCEN's list of registered MSBs has been notoriously inaccurate; so, the absence of a customer's name on the FinCEN list would not necessarily mean that said customer is operating as an unregistered MSB.

Many financial institutions' procedures rely on cursory Google searches and a LexisNexis or similar third party database search as being sufficient. Doing so, however, is fraught with peril. Using the advanced Google search techniques described in this chapter will go a long way towards helping you find relevant information among the results returned by Google. Investigators and analysts should become familiar with the internet search sites listed in this section and use them to their advantage.

You should also do a test on your own name using LexisNexis (or other similar database vendor's offering) and see if in fact all the information available about you is accurate. For example, when I search on my name, I find that LexisNexis has listed for me ten of the last *eight* places I've lived through the years! Obviously, I know which two places I've never lived. But if you were conducting a search on me as a customer under investigation, you would have no idea which of the ten addresses were inaccurate. In fact, faulty information may lead you to a faulty conclusions.

Also know that smart terrorists and criminals are well aware of the factors that are used by law enforcement or AML investigators to profile them. They will actively use deceptive practices on the internet and cause information on themselves collected by data mining companies to obfuscate their identity.

Google – Advanced

Most AML investigators use Google to look up information during the course of their investigations. Since Google indexes billions of Web pages containing an enormous amount of information, it is likely that common searches used by investigators, such as those of customer names or businesses, may show up so far down in the search results that they are rendered essentially invisible and useless. However, through the use of several simple techniques, an investigator can greatly increase the chance that the subject or name being searched will return fewer, more relevant search results.

This section of the manual will describe how an investigator can use simple Boolean operators such as NOT, OR, etc., as well as *Special Characters* to improve the efficiency of Google as a tool in suspicious activity investigations. Before discussing these, investigators should understand a few basic Google properties:

- o **Case Sensitivity** – Google queries are not in any way case sensitive, so for the hunt-and-peck typists out there, it is not necessary to waste time worrying about capitalization. The one exception to this rule, as discussed below, is when using Boolean operators (e.g., AND). Google will search for terms with "and" (lower case), but treat AND (all caps) as an operator.
- o **Wildcards** – The Windows operating system interprets the * (asterisk) character to be a symbolic representation of any series of letters or any single letter. In Google, using the * character either at the beginning or end of a word will not provide any more hits than by simply searching on the word by itself.
- o **Ignored Terms** – Google will ignore certain words (called stop words) and characters in searches. Examples of stop words are: *who, what, when, the, an*. If you want to *include* stop words as part of your search, you can either put them in "quote" marks or use a "+" sign in front of the word. For example, a search for *+The Laundrymen* will return only results that include the word "the."
- o **Word Limit** – Google will accept up to 32 words to search on at once.
- o **AND** – Whenever your search contains more than one word, Google searches for all the words. Therefore, the use of the term AND is not necessary.
- o **Phrase Searches** – For searches of exact phrases, insert the whole phrase between quotation marks. This is particularly useful for name searches.
- o **Negative Searches** – If your search term has more than one meaning (*placing*, for example, could refer to a stage in the laundering cycle or horse racing) you can focus your search by putting a minus sign ("-") in front of words related to the meaning you want to avoid. For example, to find pages about placing money, entering *placing –horse* will ensure that your search result does not bring up equine related results.
- o **Alternate Words** – Google usually returns pages that use all of the words you included in your search. Sometimes, however, Google considers other words as substitutes if it will improve the results. For example, if you search for *money launderers*, Google's results might include pages that talk about a *money launderer*.

Using Google *Advanced Search*

By clicking on the *Advanced Search link* from Google's main page (just to the right of the Search button), you will be able to conduct searches that increase the chance of finding what you are looking for. You can conduct searches that:

- o   Contain ALL the search terms you type in
- o   Contain the exact phrase you type in
- o   Contain at least one of the words you type in
- o   Do NOT contain any of the words you type in
- o   Are written in a certain language
- o   are created in a certain file format
- o   Have been updated within a certain period of time
- o   Contain numbers within a certain range
- o   Are within a certain domain, or website

By using your imagination, you can narrow the search return results to a subset that contains more relevant results. Examples for AML investigations using some of these features might include:

- o   Find web pages that have customer's name along with the OR operator, such as joseph corrado OR indicted OR convicted OR arrested OR fraud.

- o   Find web pages that contain customer name but NOT the words actor, hollywood, TV, movie, video (the syntax for this search from the search line would be: customer -actor -hollywood -tv -movie). The NOT operator helps to search on common names especially where a famous person shares the name.

Google Search Operators

Each investigator will use different Google operators in different ways and combinations. Investigators are encouraged to familiarize and experiment with the operators in the table below. While explanations on how to use all of these operators is beyond the scope of this manual, some examples are provided for those operators that have obvious investigatory use. For others, simply do a Google search on the operator to learn more! (Note: some of these are accessible through the Advanced Search interface, explained above.)

Table 8: Google Functionality

Google Functionality	Search Operators
Web Search	allintext: allintitle: allinurl: cache: define: filetype: id: inanchor: info: intext: intitle: inurl: phonebook: related: site: stocks:
Image Search	allintitle: allinurl: filetype: inurl: intitle: site:
News Groups	allintext: allintitle: author: group: insubject: intext: intitle:
Directory	allintext: allintitle: allinurl: ext: filetype: intext: intitle: inurl:
News	allintext: allintitle: allinurl: intext: intitle: inurl: location: source:

phonebook:
If you start your query with [phonebook:] Google shows U.S. residential white page listings for the query terms you specify. For example, [rphonebook: John Doe New York] will show the phonebook listings for John Doe in New York (city or state). Abbreviations like [rphonebook: John Doe NY] generally also work. You can also do reverse phone number lookups, for example [rphonebook:### ### ####] (replace the # characters with the phone number and leave the spaces).

site:
If you include [site:] in your query, Google will restrict your search results to the site or domain you specify. For example, [ochoa site:cia.gov] will show only CIA sites that contain information on persons named Ochoa. This operator is useful for quickly location information on suspicious activity that you are trying to locate from only specific web sites.

filetype:
If you include [filetype:suffix] in your query, Google will restrict the results to pages whose names end in that suffix. For example, ["anti-money laundering" filetype:pdf] will return Adobe Acrobat pdf files that contain the exact term "anti-money laundering". You can restrict the results to pages whose names end with pdf *and* doc by using the OR operator, e.g. ["anti-money laundering:pdf OR filetype:doc]. Without the quotes, the search will return files with any of those words.

location:
If you include *location:* in your query on Google News, only articles from the location you specify will be returned. For example, [yourbank location:canada] will return news articles that match the term Yourbank from sites in Canada. This can be helpful when searching for news about customers whose residence or business is likely covered in more detail in the foreign press than in the US.

related:
The query [related:URL] will list web pages that are in some way similar to the web page you specify. For instance, [related:www.fincen.gov] will list web pages that are related to the FinCEN home page. (Note: Don't include a space between the related: and the web page url).You can also find similar pages from the "Similar pages" link on Google's main results page, and from the similar selector in the Page-Specific Search area of the Advanced Search page.

source:
If you include [source:] in your query, Google News will restrict your search to articles from the news source with the ID you specify.
For example, [source:laundering:wall_street_journal] will return articles with the word "laundering" that appear in the Wall Street Journal.

cache:
Criminals will often use internet sites in conjunction with scams. After they make their money, they will often move on and the site will be taken down. However, Google takes a picture and archives, or *caches*, web pages. Older versions of sites that don't exist

anymore may still be searched using the cache: operator. The operator will search for terms you specify within cached pages only. Additionally, Google may return a search result and when the link is clicked on, a *page not found* error is returned. Clicking on the link *Cached* under the web page link will bring up the old online version of that page. This is very helpful for finding and reading old news articles posted as web pages on the net that have long since been taken down by the publisher or his internet host provider (IHP).

intitle:
Using the operator [intitle:] in your query, Google will restrict the results to documents containing that word in the title. For instance, [intitle:google search] will return documents that mention the word "google" in their *title*, and mention the word "search" *anywhere* in the document (title or no). (Note: there can be no space between the "intitle:" and the following word.)

inurl:
Including the operator [inurl:] in your query, Google will restrict the results to documents containing that word in the url. For instance, [inurl:google search] will return documents that mention the word "google" in their *url*, and mention the word "search" *anywhere* in the document (url or no). (Note there can be no space between the "inurl:" and the following word.)

Google Advanced Search Page
Many of the advanced features described above can be utilized through the interface provided on Google's Advanced Search Page. Simply click on the Advanced Search Link from the Google search page.

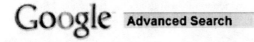

Google is not the only internet resource investigators should be familiar with. Many sites are designed to find specific information and are more surgical in their approach to locating that information. Descriptions of these can be found in the Internet Resources section.

Internet Resources

The internet sites listed here are presented as hyperlinks in the electronic version of this book. However, you can easily locate the urls by using Google.

- **PACER** – Public Access to Court Electronic Records is an electronic public access service that allows users to obtain case and docket information from Federal Appellate, District and Bankruptcy courts, and the U.S. Party/Case Index via the Internet. The PACER System offers electronic access to case dockets to retrieve information such as:
  - A listing of all parties and participants including judges, attorneys, and trustees;
  - A compilation of case related information such as cause of action, nature of suit, and dollar demand;
  - A chronology of dates of case events entered in the case record;
  - A claims registry;
  - A listing of new cases each day;
  - Appellate court opinions;
  - Judgments or case status;
  - Types of documents filed for certain cases.
  - US Party Case Index – The U.S. Party/Case Index is a national index for U.S. district, bankruptcy, and appellate courts. The system serves as a locator index for PACER. Investigators may conduct nationwide searches to determine whether or not a party is involved in federal litigation. The investigator should be aware that not all federal courts participate in the U.S. Party/Case Index. The non-participating courts are listed under the "Courts not on Index" option on the web main menu. These courts do not have data available on the U.S. Party/Case Index. For a complete nationwide search, those courts need to be searched individually. The U.S. Party/Case Index will allow you to search nationwide by name or social security number in the bankruptcy index, name or nature of suit in the civil index, defendant name in the criminal index, and party name in the appellate index. Each hit produced from your searches will give you the party name, the court where the case is filed, the case number, and the filing date. In addition, for bankruptcy searches you will receive the chapter and for civil searches you will receive the nature of suit.
    - To retrieve more information on a particular case found while searching the U.S. Party/Case Index, access the <u>PACER</u> system for the jurisdiction where the case resides. This is indicated by the court abbreviation provided with each hit on the U.S. Party/Case Index. For most hits on U.S. Party/Case Index, the Case Number will be a link to the case summary information at that court's PACER site. All you need to do is click the case number.

- **Social Security Number Verification** – This service, available from the Social Security Online website is available to employers and third-party submitters. It can only be used to verify current or former employees and only for wage reporting (Form W–2) purposes.

- **LexisNexis** – is an on-line research tool that provides background information about individuals and business from sources including:
  - Statewide public records
  - Criminal databases
  - Professional and drivers licenses
  - Selected inmate records
  - Selected marriage/divorce records
  - State professional licenses
  - Voter registrations
  - Possible relatives (also, see Melissadata link below)
  - Asset related information may be located through LexisNexis information or from the internet links provided below:
    - Real estate assets – MelissaData.com
    - Aircraft Ownership / FAA Aircraft Registry (http://registry.faa.gov/aircraftinquiry/NNum_inquiry.asp)
    - Pilot Database (https://amsrvs.registry.faa.gov/airmeninquiry/default.aspx)
    - Boat registrations
    - Driver's record
    - Motor vehicle registrations
  - SmartLinx Business Reports
  - Judgments
  - Jury verdicts and settlements
  - Tax liens
  - UCC liens

- **Business Information Sources:**
  - Hoover's – The Hoover's Online database provides access to in-depth company profiles for more than 40,000 companies, public and private, worldwide, as well as to financial information, news, and industry information. This database is an excellent starting point for company research.
  - D&B – Provides financial and operational information necessary for due diligence and investigations purposes.

- **MTRA** – The Money Transmitter Regulators Association is a non-profit organization whose membership consists of state regulatory authorities in charge of regulating money transmitters and sellers of traveler's checks, money orders, drafts and other money instruments. This MTRA website: www.mtraweb.org/links.shtm provides a list of links to all fifty state's banking and/or securities departments. This resource may be useful to further investigate state licensing requirements for MSBs.

- **Office of Foreign Asset Control** – provides information regarding:
  - Specially Designated Nationals (SDNs)
  - Non-Proliferation Sanctions
  - Narcotics Trafficking Sanctions
  - Cuba Sanctions
  - Other OFAC Sanction Programs
  - OFAC Guidance by Industry

- **Financial Industry Regulatory Authority** – FINRA was created in July 2007 through the consolidation of the NASD and the member regulation, enforcement and arbitration functions of the New York Stock Exchange. Their site provides an excellent tool for OFAC searches (although for regulatory purposes, banks should only use OFAC directly or a vendor providing OFAC scanning tools). The FINRA OFAC url is: http://apps.finra.org/RulesRegulation/OFAC/1/Default.aspx

- **World-Check** – An online tool which is updated on a daily basis provides comprehensive profiles of potential high risk persons and entities and those associated with them in more than 220 countries and territories. Politicians and people of political influence (PEPs), terrorist and organized crime figures, money launderers and fraudsters are all profiled and linked to offer a complex network of public information. World-Check provides:
  - Identification and structured customer identification by first and last name, spelling variations, aliases, dates of birth (in some cases), place of birth, title and position;
  - Relatives, close associates and companies cross-linked;
  - Sanctions & Embargo lists including the U.S. (e.g., OFAC), the European Union, Bank of England, etc.

- **Google** – This search service can be used to find information on available websites as well as on websites that may no longer be online by searching cached web pages. It can also be used to search land line and cellular telephone numbers as well as e-mail addresses. Listed number searches return telephone listings in name and address format. Unlisted numbers (land line or cellular) contained in web pages will also be returned upon searching. The same is generally true for e-mail addresses. Other Google services also can be creatively utilized for investigation purposes. For example, Google Earth images can confirm that the address of a customer's *factory* is not, say, an apartment in a residential neighborhood. See the Google section for more information regarding how to use the advanced search capabilities of Google.

- **Online Newspaper and Library Archives** – Internet-accessible newspapers as well as online library resources can often provide a good collection of searchable information. These databases (sometimes available for free) usually go back in time several years.

- **Property Records** – Usually found at a county's tax assessor or collector websites, these provide information that may prove valuable during an investigation regarding real estate. The use of websites such as Zillow.com can be used to check comparative property values against information provided by a suspect.

- **Criminal Records** – Aside from restricted government systems, there is no publicly available system to conduct nationwide criminal background checks. However, the Federal Bureau of Prisons (BOP) has a database that permits searches as far back as 1982. This searchable database –the Inmate Locator , contains brief records on current and former inmates that were under the control of the BOP.

- **Other Internet Sources** – The following internet sites provide specific information not readily accessed from general purpose websites, such as Google:
    o Search Engine Colossus – Provides links to search engines that are country specific.
    o SearchSystems – A large, up-to-date and reliable directory of public records on the Internet.
    o Archive.org – This Internet archive is a digital library of Internet sites and other cultural artifacts in digital form. Versions of websites that no longer exist on the internet are accessible here using the *WayBack Machine*.
    o Courier Journal – A very comprehensive list of research sites.
    o Melissa Data – is a general purpose lookup site for consumer records.
    o Bankers Online – A reference site for bankers and bank compliance professionals. Especially useful is the Infovault, which is an index of thousands of articles and other information covering a wide range of banking topics.
    o ZabaSearch – Internet website that offers reports on individuals by searching myriad public databases and records. (Fee based service).
    o Dogpile – Combines results for a single search from multiple search engines including: Google, Yahoo, MSN, and Ask.com.
    o Kartoo – Upon launching a search, Kartoo analyses the request, questions the most relevant engines, selects the best sites and places them on the screen. The found sites are represented by icons. When the user mouses-over these icons, relevant keywords are illuminated and a brief description of the site appears on the left side of the screen. Links between sites are also displayed.
    o Vivisimo – Search engine that employs a proprietary mathematical algorithm to find relationships between search terms.
    o Complete Planet – Deep web directory of over 70 thousand searchable databases and specialty search engines, sometimes referred to as the *invisible web*.
    o ThomasGlobal – A global industrial suppliers and product information business search engine.
    o NASS – National Association of Secretaries of State. Provides business registration and filing services for every state.
    o Financial Regulators Gateway – provides online access to financial regulatory agencies around the world and to relevant statutes and rules from numerous jurisdictions.

- o Zipskinny – Provides a wide range of detailed demographic statistics by zip code.
- o The Investigative Project on Terrorism – Provides a list of groups and individuals who may be implicated in some way with terrorism who may not necessarily be on watch lists.

- **High Risk Country Lists** – Various NGOs and US government agencies publish lists of countries designated as being of high risk for money laundering:
    - o OFAC – Countries subject to OFAC sanctions, including state sponsors of terrorism. (Also see OFAC links above)
    - o U.S. State Department – Countries identified as supporting international terrorism under section 6(j) of the Export Administration Act of 1979, as determined by the Secretary of State.
    - o FinCEN USAPA Section 311List – Jurisdictions determined to be of *primary money laundering concern* by the Secretary of the Treasury, and jurisdictions subject to special measures imposed by the Secretary of the Treasury through FinCEN, pursuant to section 311 of the PATRIOT Act.
    - o US State Department's INCSR – Major money laundering countries and jurisdictions identified in the U.S. Department of State's annual International Narcotics Control Strategy Report (INCSR), in particular, countries which are identified as jurisdictions of primary concern.
    - o OFCs – Offshore financial centers (OFCs) as identified by the International Monetary Fund.

Appendix

Source Documents, Websites, Books, etc.

- 2007 National Money Laundering Strategy
- 31 U.S.C. §§ 5311 – 5332 Records and Reports on Monetary Instruments Transactions
- ACAMS Today – Various articles and Association documents
- Administrative Law in the Political System – by Kenneth F. Warren, Westview Press 2004
- Bank for International Settlements (BIS) – Basel Committee on Banking Supervision, Customer Due Diligence for Banks, October 2001
- Bank for International Settlements (BIS) – Basel Committee on Banking Supervision, General Guide to Account Opening and Customer Identification (Attachment to Basel Committee publication No. 85 "Customer Due Diligence for Banks"), February 2003
- Bankers Online – Various resources
- Chasing Dirty Money: The Fight Against Money Laundering – Reuter and Truman
- CIA World Fact Book
- Confronting Terrorist Financing – American Foreign Policy Council, 2005
- Council on Foundations, Treasury Guidelines Working Group of Charitable Sector Organizations and Advisors – Principles of International Charity, March 2005
- Countering Terrorist Financing; Lessons From Europe – Michael Jonsson & Svante Cornell – Georgetown Journal of International Affairs
- Critical Reflections on Transnational Organized Crime, Money Laundering and Corruption – Margaret Beare
- FDIC FIL–121–2004 Computer Software Due Diligence – Guidance on Developing an Effective Computer Software Evaluation Program to Assure Quality and Regulatory Compliance
- Federal Financial Institutions Examination Council (FFIEC), Bank Secrecy Act Anti-Money Laundering Examination Manual, June 2005
- Federal Financial Institutions Examination Council, Bank Secrecy Act / Anti-Money Laundering Examination Manual, July 2007
- Federal Financial Institutions Examination Council, Bank Secrecy Act Ant-Money Laundering Examination Manual, June 2005
- Federal Money Laundering Regulation: Banking, Corporate, and Securities Compliance, by Steven Mark Levy, Aspen Publishers, June 2003
- FIN–2006–G006, Registration and De-Registration of Money Services Businesses, February, 2006
- FIN–2007–G002 Guidance to Financial Institutions: Request by Law Enforcement to Maintain Accounts, June 2007
- Financial Action Task Force (FATF) – Guidance on Terrorist Financing, SR VIII: Combating the Abuse of Non-Profit Organizations – International Best Practices, October 2006

- Financial Action Task Force (FATF) – Guidance on Terrorist Financing, SR VIII: Non-Profit Organizations – Interpretive Note, February 2005
- Financial Crimes Enforcement Network, Anti-Money Laundering Programs; Special Due Diligence Programs for Certain Foreign Accounts – Final rule, January 2006Financial Crimes Enforcement Network, FACT SHEET Section 312 of the USA PATRIOT Act Final Regulation and Notice of Proposed Rulemaking, December 2005
- Financial Crimes Enforcement Network, Anti-Money Laundering Programs; Special Due Diligence Programs for Certain Foreign Accounts - Notice of proposed rulemaking, January 2006
- Financial Crimes Enforcement Network, SAR Narrative Guidance Package, Part I: Guidance on Preparing A Complete & Sufficient Suspicious Activity Report Narrative, November 2003
- Financial Crimes Enforcement Network, SAR Narrative Guidance Package, Part II: The Suspicious Activity Report (SAR) Form, November 2003
- Financial Crimes Enforcement Network, SAR Narrative Guidance Package: Part III: Keys to Writing a Complete & Sufficient SAR Narrative, November 2003
- Financial Crimes Enforcement Network, The SAR Activity Review By the Numbers, Issues 1–7 Inter–agency Advisory, Federal Court Reaffirms Protections for Financial Institutions Filing Suspicious Activity Reports, May 24, 2004
- Financial Crimes Enforcement Network, The SAR Activity Review Trends, Tips & Issues, Issues 1 through 12 (2008)
- Financial Crimes Enforcement Network, Treasury Department Form 90–22.47 Suspicious Activity Report (for Depository Institutions), July 2003
- Financial Investigation and Forensic Accounting – George Manning
- FinCEN Ruling 2005–6 Suspicious Activity Reporting (Structuring)
- FinCEN website – Regulations and Rulings. Various
- Getting it Right" Questions and Answers – OTS Interpretive Guidance, July 2006
- Google Guide, Nancy Blachman, www.googleguide.com
- Google Hacking, by Johnny Long, Syngress Publishing, 2005
- Guidance to Financial Institutions on the Repatriation of Currency Smuggled into Mexico from the United States – FIN–2006–A003, April 2006
- Internal Revenue Service Manual
- Money Laundering – A New International Law Enforcement Model – Guy Stessens
- Money Laundering in the Commercial Real Estate Industry; An Assessment Based Upon Suspicious Activity Report Filings Analysis – FinCEN Regulatory Policy and Programs Division, July 2006
- Money Laundering.com and Money Laundering Alert – Various
- Money Laundering: A Guide for Criminal Investigators – John Madinger
- MoneyLaundering.com – Various resources
- Mortgage Loan Fraud: An Industry Assessment Based on SAR Analysis – FinCEN 2006

- National Strategy for Combating Terrorism – National Defense University Library, 2006
- Office of the Comptroller of the Currency, Advisory Letter 2000-3, Subject: Bank Secrecy Act Compliance Programs – Suspicious Activity Reporting Requirements, Description: Common BSA Compliance Deficiencies, April 2000
- Office of the Comptroller of the Currency, Bank Secrecy Act / Anti-Money Laundering: Comptroller's Handbook, Revised for Web Publication, December 2000
- Office of the Comptroller of the Currency, Bulletin 2004-50, Subject: Bank Secrecy Act/Anti-Money Laundering, Description: Enforcement Guidance for BSA/AML Program Deficiencies, November 2004
- Office of the Comptroller of the Currency, Compliance Management System: Comptroller's Handbook, August 1996
- Office of the Comptroller of the Currency, Money Laundering: A Banker's Guide to Avoiding Problems, December 2002
- Potential Money Laundering Risks Related to Shell Companies – FIN–2006–G014, November 2006
- Requests by Law Enforcement for Financial Institutions to Maintain Accounts – FIN–2007–G002, June 2007
- Sharing Suspicious Activity Reports with Head Offices and Controlling Companies – Interagency Guidance, January, 2006
- Suggestions for Addressing Common Errors Noted in Suspicious Activity Filings – FinCEN Oct. 10, 2007
- Suspicious Activity Report Supporting Documentation – FIN2007–G003, 2007
- The Art and Science of Money Laundering – Inside the Commerce of the International Narcotics Traffickers – Brett Woods
- Transaction Monitors Under the Hood, by Ed Levy
- Transnational Criminal Organizations, Cybercrime, and Money Laundering – James Richards
- U.S. Government, Interagency Guidance On Enhanced Scrutiny For Transactions That May Involve The Proceeds Of Foreign Official Corruption, January 2001
- U.S. Government, Interagency Interpretive Guidance on Providing Banking Services to Money Services Businesses Operating in the United States, April 2005
- Unitary Filing of Suspicious Activity and Blocking Reports (Final Rule) – Guidance (Interpretive Release No. 2004-02) December, 2004
- Univ. of Toledo College of Law – Online
- US Department of the Treasury – Anti-Terrorist Financing Guidelines: Voluntary Best Practices for U.S.-Based Charities, January 2003
- US Money Laundering Threat Assessment, December 2005

Index

—D—

—E—

—F—

—G—

—H—

—I—

—N—

—O—

—P—

—T—

End Notes

[1] Rules issued by FinCEN that are published in the Federal Register are generally referred to as "legislative" rules that impose a distinct obligation on the public and are binding. Agencies may issue such rules to the extent authorized by statute. Under the Administrative Procedure Act, such rules must generally be published in the Federal Register according to a three-step process as outlined in its section 553: (1) issuance of a notice of proposed rule making (issuance of an additional advance notice of proposed rule making is also acceptable); (2) receipt and consideration of comments on the proposed rule; and (3) issuance of a final rule incorporating a statement of its basis and purpose. Section 553(b)(B) of the APA contains an exception for "good cause". The good cause exception authorizes departures from the APA's requirements only when compliance would interfere from an Agency's ability to carry out its mission. (hence, the existence of interim final rules, which are binding). "Interpretive" rules (i.e., rules that provide interpretive guidance, but create no distinct substantive obligation) and "procedural" rules (i.e., rules that only provide for processes related to a substantive obligation) do not need to be published according to the preceding three-step procedure; however, in order for a rule to be binding, it must be developed and published according to the three-step procedure or fall within the good cause exception.

[2] Some Suspicious Activity Reports may list multiple suspicious activities.

[3] The characterizations of the suspicious activity Identity Theft and Terrorist Financing were added to form TD F 90-22.47 in July 2003. Statistics date from this period.

[4] The characterization of suspicious activity Computer Intrusion was added to form TD F 90-22.47 in June 2000. Statistics date from this period.

[5] 18 USC 1956(c)(4)(A)(iii) defines the term "financial transaction" as "involving the transfer of title to any real property, vehicle, vessel, or aircraft, etc...."

[6] Pursuant to Section 6(j) of the Export Administration Act of 1979, the Departments of State and Commerce have designated the countries noted in the table above as state sponsors of terrorism Further information about these designations is available at online at the US State Department's website's Country Reports on Terrorism.

[7] The Terrorist Exclusion List is published on the US State Department's Fact Sheet web page.

[8] The FTO list as well as additional background information on FTOs can be found on the US State Department's Fact Sheet web page.

[9] See question 4 from the "Anti-Money Laundering Program and Suspicious Activity Reporting Requirements For Insurance Companies Frequently Asked Questions" found at http://www.fincen.gov/nrfaq10312005.htm.

[10] Variable annuity contracts typically have a "free look" period of ten or more days during which a purchaser may terminate his contract and receive a refund without paying surrender charges. The amount of the refund may be the account value when the contract is terminated or the purchase price, depending on the terms of the contract and applicable state law

[11] In the "Advance Fee Fraud" or 4-1-9 schemes, victims may receive emails and letters from groups of con artists, often located in Nigeria, who claim to have access to a very large sum of money and want to use the victim's bank account to transfer the funds. In exchange for the victim's services, they claim they will give the recipient of the email/letter a large percentage of the funds. These schemes have a common denominator - eventually the target of the scheme will be required to pay up-front (advance) fees (licensing fees, taxes, attorney fees, transaction fees, bribes, etc.) to receive the percentage of funds promised. The con artists usually request that they be furnished with blank company letterhead and/or bank account information

[12] When a sole proprietorship incorporates, the customer's Taxpayer Identification Number may appear to have changed, but technically has not. Most likely, the customer will retain his or her Social Security Number, and the now incorporated business will be a separate person as defined by 31 C.F.R. § 103.11(z), with a separate Employer Identification Number.

[13] An ITIN is a nine-digit number issued by the U.S. Internal Revenue Service (IRS) to individuals who are required for U.S. tax purposes to have a U.S. taxpayer identification number but who do not have, and are not eligible to obtain, a social security number (SSN). See IRS Discussion of ITINs at http://www.irs.gov/individuals/article/0,,id=96287,00.html.

[14] A "person" is an individual, a corporation, a partnership, a trust or estate, a joint stock company, an association, a syndicate, joint venture, or other unincorporated organization or group, an Indian Tribe (as that term is defined in the Indian Gaming Regulatory Act), and all entities cognizable as legal personalities.
31 C.F.R. 103.11 (z)

[15] http://www.fincen.gov/guidance04262005.pdf and
http://www.fincen.gov/fincenadv04262005.pdf.

[16] In addition to violating the FinCEN registration regulation, which can result in both civil and criminal penalties, failure to register with FinCEN is a violation of 18 U.S.C. 1960. See U.S. v. Uddin, No. 04- CR-80192 (E.D.Mich. April 11, 2005). Under certain circumstances, failure to obtain a required state license to operate an MSB can also result in a violation of 18 U.S.C. 1960. See U.S. v. Velastegui, 199 F.3d 590 (2nd Cir. 1999). Currently, the regulation requiring registration of MSBs does not apply to the U.S. Postal Service, to agencies of the United States, of any State, or of any political subdivision of a State, or to a person to the extent that the person is an issuer, seller, or redeemer of stored value. (See 31 C.F.R. § 103.41(a)).

[17] On February 3, 2006, FinCEN issued guidance entitled, "Registration and De-Registration of Money Services Businesses." That guidance can be located at http://www.fincen.gov/msbregistration_de_registration.pdf.

[18] See 31 C.F.R § 103.18(a)(2)(iii) and the other SAR rules

[19] Financial institutions may not disclose to the person involved in a transaction that the transaction has been, or will be, reported. See 31 C.F.R § 103.18(e).

[20] See 31 C.F.R § 103.18(a)(2)(ii) and other SAR rules.

[21] The BSA provides protection from civil liability for all reports of suspicious transactions made to appropriate authorities, including supporting documentation, regardless of whether such reports are mandatory. Specifically, the BSA provides that a financial institution, or a director, officer, employee, or agent of a financial institution, that makes a "voluntary disclosure of any possible violation of law or regulation to a government agency" shall not be liable to any person under "any law or regulation of the United States, any constitution, law, or regulation of any State or political subdivision of any State, or under any contract or other legally enforceable agreement (including any arbitration agreement), for such disclosure or for any failure to provide notice of such disclosure to the person who is the subject of such disclosure or any other person identified in the disclosure." 31 U.S.C. § 5318(g)(3).

[22] A controlling company is defined as:
a) a bank holding company, as defined in Section 2 of the Bank Holding Company Act;
b) a savings and loan holding company, as defined in Section 10(a) of the Home Owners' Loan Act. For purposes of this guidance, a controlling company also includes a company having the power directly or indirectly, to direct the management or policies of an industrial loan company or a parent company or to vote 25% or more of any class of voting shares of an industrial loan company or a parent company.

[23] Under the Right to Financial Privacy Act of 1978 ("RFPA"), "financial records" are defined as "an original of, a copy of, or information known to have been derived from, any record held by a financial institution pertaining to a customer's relationship with the financial institution." 12 USC 3401(2).

[24] Section 374 of the Intelligence Authorization Act for Fiscal Year 2004 (Pub. Law 108-177 (Dec. 13, 2003) amended the definition of "financial institution" for purposes of the Right to Financial Privacy Act of 1978 (12 USC 3414) to incorporate the definition of "financial institution" in the Bank Secrecy Act, 31 USC 5312(a)(2) and (c)(1).

[25] The USA PATRIOT Act changed the standard predicate for FBI RFPA National Security Letters to one requiring that the information being sought through the National Security Letter is "for foreign counter intelligence purposes to protect against international terrorism or clandestine intelligence activities, provided that such an investigation of a United States person is not conducted solely on the basis of activities protected by the first amendment of the Constitution of the United States." The USA PATRIOT Act also provided authority for the Director of the FBI to delegate signature authority for National Security Letters to Special Agents in Charge serving in designated field divisions.

[26] Foreign counter (or positive) intelligence activities could include, for example, the audit of customer records of a financial institution related to the clandestine activities of an intelligence agency, pursuant to the RFPA, 12 U.S.C. §314(a)(1)(A). See, e.g., Duncan v. Belcher, 813 F.2d 1335, 1339 and 1339 n. 1 (4th Cir. 1987).

[27] The RFPA, 12 U.S.C. §3414(a)(1)(B), permits certain disclosures of financial records to the United States Secret Service for the purposes of conducting its protective functions.

[28] The RFPA, 12 U.S.C. § 3414(a)(1)(C), permits certain disclosure of financial records pursuant to a request from a federal government agency authorized to conduct investigations or intelligence or counter-intelligence analyses related to international terrorism.

[29] In Doe v. Ashcroft, 334 F. Supp.2d 471 (S.D.N.Y. 2004), a federal district court held that 18 U.S.C. 2709, which authorizes the issuance of national security letters to Internet service providers, is unconstitutional on account of its nondisclosure provisions and lack of judicial review. The Federal Bureau of Investigation appealed the decision and obtained a stay pending appeal, so it is continuing to issue national security letters under that statute. That decision did not adjudicate the constitutionality of the statute authorizing the issuance of national security letters to financial institutions, 12 U.S.C. 3414.

[30] Pursuant to 12 U.S.C. § 3414(a)(3) and (5)(D), no financial institution, or officer, employee or agent of the institution, can disclose to any person that a government authority or the FBI has sought or obtained access to records through an RFPA National Security Letter.

[31] See Office of the Comptroller of the Currency Interpretive Letter #1003, "Suspicious Activity Reports" (Aug. 2004).

[32] Each Federal bank regulatory agency has adopted suspicious activity reporting requirements that contain additional factors and triggers, including (1) involvement of an insider (no dollar threshold); (2) over $5,000 is involved and the institution can identify a suspect; (3) over $25,000 is involved but the institution cannot identify a suspect; or (4) the transaction involves $5,000 or more and involves potential money laundering or violations of the Bank Secrecy Act. See, e.q., 12 CFR 21.11(c). Furthermore, under FinCEN's suspicious activity reporting requirements, the dollar thresholds vary (e.g., for casinos and broker-dealers in securities, the dollar threshold is at least $5,000; for money services businesses, the dollar threshold is at least $2,000 or $5,000 if the identification of transactions is derived from a review of clearance records.)

[33] Investigators should also be aware that the section 314(a) lists cannot be shared with any foreign office, branch or affiliate (unless the request specifically states otherwise), and the lists cannot be shared with affiliates, or subsidiaries of bank holding companies, if the affiliates or subsidiaries are not financial institutions as described in 31 USC 5312(a)(2). Each financial institution must maintain adequate procedures to protect the security and confidentiality of requests from FinCEN. The responsibility to maintain confidentiality of the 314a list extends to investigators, who should not disclose to those involved in their investigation that the reason for the investigation extends from a 314(a) inquiry.

[34] For TD F 90-22.47 (Suspicious Activity Report), Box 9;